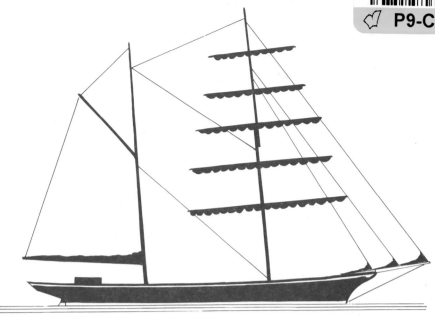

— BRIGANTINE —
Two masts, the foremast being fully square-rigged and the main mast being
fore-and-aft rigged.

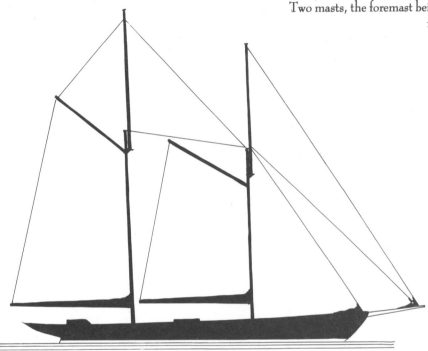

— SCHOONER —
Two or more masts, fore-and-aft rigged. The foremast may have square
topsails. A two-masted schooner's masts are of equal height or with the
foremast the shorter.

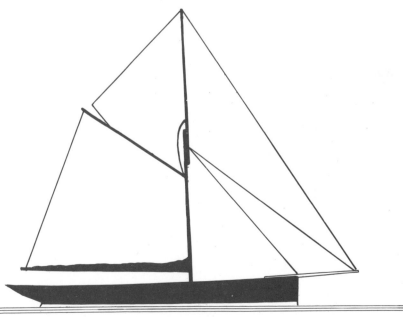

— CUTTER —
Single mast, either gaff- of bermudan-rigged, with two or more foresails.

BY APPOINTMENT TO
H.R.H. THE DUKE OF EDINBURGH
MARINE PHOTOGRAPHERS

BEKEN OF COWES
SAILING SHIPS
OF THE WORLD

BEKEN OF COWES

SAILING SHIPS
OF THE WORLD

with a foreword by
HRH The Prince of Wales

TEXT BY
Erik C. Abranson

WITH PHOTOGRAPHS BY
Frank William Beken
Alfred Keith Beken
Kenneth John Beken

Reed's Nautical Books

London   Hamburg   Boston

First Published
in Great Britain 1992 by
Thomas Reed Publications Ltd
Hazelbury Manor
Wadswick
Box
Corsham
Wiltshire
SN14 9HX
UK

Photographs © Beken of
Cowes 1992

Text © Thomas Reed
Publications Ltd. 1992

Some material in this book,
including the foreword by HRH
The Prince of Wales, appeared
in *A Century of Tall Ships*
published by Harrap Limited,
London 1985

ISBN 0 947637 47 8

Design and production
consultancy by
PAPERWEIGHT
379 Lewisham High Street,
London

Typeset in Bernhard Modern by
Falcon Graphic Art Ltd
Wallington, Surrey

Printed by Vincenzo Bona,
Turin, Italy

CONTENTS

KENSINGTON PALACE

There is something irresistibly romantic about large sailing ships which appeals to the vast majority of mankind. I remember reading about a recent gathering of tall ships - it may have been in Canada - where the organisers were overwhelmed by nearly a million people who wanted to come and see these beautiful maritime works of art. The paradox of our contemporary existence, with its constant emphasis on even more sophisticated technology and modes of transport, is that so many people develop an acute awareness of the value of our past and of such miracles of human ingenuity as these great ships, which have been so superbly illustrated in this book.

The Beken family of Cowes, on the Isle of Wight, have been marine photographers for several generations and have been photographing successive generations of my family as we tacked up and down the Solent during Cowes Week. I feel sure that this book, so skilfully produced, will strike a seafaring chord in the hearts of many a true Briton and will remind us of the unique value these training ships can have as a kind of floating "initiation test" for today's young people. If only there were more of these elegant vessels......

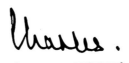

BEKEN OF COWES
A HISTORY

In the late 1880s, the family of Beken moved from Canterbury to Cowes, a small port on the north of the Isle of Wight. Frank Beken was then barely ten years old and, under the guidance of his father, a chemist, he started to experiment with photography. He was soon afloat in a dinghy, photographing the magnificent ships and yachts that graced the Solent area, with their beauteous and classical lines.

With his keen eye for composition, he made many a fine study of the early liners, steamers, square-riggers and schooners and later the 'J' class that attended and raced off Cowes, usually manned by visiting Royalty, nobility and other wealthy gentlemen. The art of Frank was repeated by his son Keith. Together they experimented with existing cameras, adapting them to their own special needs.

They could find no better cameras than the ones constructed by themselves to their own design — a wooden box with a ground glass viewfinder and a lens, the whole apparatus refined to their own special needs. These cameras used 8″ × 6″ glass plates and, over the past 100 years, a collection of over 50,000 fine negatives has been carefully stored and filed — a unique library. In 1970 Kenneth Beken joined his father and grandfather in the family company and for a short time, until the death of Frank, there were three generations making up 'Beken of Cowes'.

Each one of them, in turn, attained perhaps the highest honour in photography — a 'Fellowship of the Royal Photographic Society'. Beken of Cowes have the distinction of being 'by appointment to HRH The Duke of Edinburgh, marine photographers'.

In his early days, Frank Beken used only a dinghy, rowed by a competent oarsman, to negotiate his way through the biggest of the 300- and 400-ton schooners of 1890 vintage. Many years later he graduated to a steam launch, and then a petrol launch which had a maximum speed of eight knots, thus recording for posterity the passage of these great ships.

Keith Beken, his son, returning from his war years at sea, picked up his camera again and, with a somewhat faster launch, continued to build up their collection of

FRANK WILLIAM BEKEN   ALFRED KEITH BEKEN   KENNETH JOHN BEKEN

photographs of ships of the era. With an eye for colour photography, he then built his own camera to a 5″ × 4″ format. It was designed to stand up against rough seas and weather in general, factors which quickly destroy so many cameras.

It was not long before Kenneth Beken showed a flair for his family's work and found himself following in his father's footsteps. With the current world demand today for colour, in sport and action photographs, Kenneth now uses the modern medium-format cameras, such as the Hasselblad. With the help of a fast (35-knot) 'Boston Whaler' launch, and a helicopter for aerial work at sea, a further 150,000 2¼″-square colour transparencies have been added to this valuable collection of maritime history.

The Bekens depend upon the elements for their results — a critical factor. Rough weather and seas give fine pictures, but are enemies to the photographer who needs a stable platform for his camera. Light and shade are also all-important, but are not always available.

Each 'Beken' works alone — in his own launch — so that he can concentrate on his subject without any distraction, for photographs often have to be taken in awkward and even dangerous circumstances; it is hardly necessary to add that each photographer has to be a 'man of the sea'.

This volume represents pictures of one hundred of the best 'Tall Ships', taken in locations which include Hawaii, Canada, the USA, the Caribbean, The Mediterranean and Europe, and Russia.

Included are the *Sedov*, the largest; to perhaps one of the smallest, *Black Pearl*. From the famous *Victory* to the tragic *Marques* — each has her own story to tell.

Photograph by Colin Rogers Photomaster, Weymouth

INTRODUCTION

BY KENNETH J. BEKEN

Her great sails bellied stiff, her great masts leaned.
They watched how the seas struck and burst, and greened.

The very name 'Tall Ships' creates in the imagination a vision of grace and beauty;
yet, at the same time, an image of majesty and power as we remember the 'Cape
Horners' battling their way around the great oceans of the world. Cresting these
seas were the 'greyhounds', the clippers, such as *Cutty Sark* and *Thermopylae*,
vying with each other to be the first home to Britain with the new tea crop. In
those early days they flew over the seas as a bird goes − chartless; their crews
revealed as passionate men at battle with the sea.

Gone now are such ships as the *Archibald Russell*, the *Pamir* and the *Lawhill*:
ships of 5,000 tons and more, with a waterline length of over 300 feet, able to

GEORG STAGE 1956

11

HMS MARTIN

carry 4,000 tons of grain across thousands of miles of desolate ocean. Above those solid decks awash with green seas would stand four giant masts up to 200 feet above the keel, carrying a multitude of sails, adding up to 50,000 square feet of canvas with names to conjure with — Royals, topgallants, and the old clippers' skysails and moonrakers. These were set on yards up to two feet thick, ninety feet in length and weighing up to five tons.

In the face of a sudden squall or approaching storm, the entire crew, down to the cook, would be sent aloft to gather in the thrashing canvas. The ships would roll thirty degrees to port, thirty degrees to starboard; and, in extreme latitudes, ice would fill the rigging, which meant that the crew had to chip it away to avoid a top-heavy ship capsizing onto her beam ends.

Their savage eyes, salt-reddened at the rims
And icicles on their sou'wester brims.

Round trips for these ships took months and even years. Ships would wait for cargoes to be negotiated; there would then be weeks of back-breaking loading and a lull before the trade winds arrived to spirit them homewards. Harsh discipline prevailed and creature comforts were few. Clothing and bedding would be at best damp, and at worst frozen solid.

Opposite page
PASSAT

It is a wonder today why men still dream of running away to sea. But then life afloat has changed to accommodate today's standards. The Tall Ships we see now would be regarded as luxury cruise ships by the men of yester-year.

The very term 'Tall Ships' has now been extended to encompass not only the square-rigged vessels of the last century, but cadet-training ships, luxury charter yachts and big schooners.

It is gratifying that navies, corporate groups, and even private individuals still regard Tall Ships as being worth the considerable expense required to keep them afloat.

After the introduction of steam power in the nineteenth century, the bulk-carrying square-riggers continued to hold their own for a number of years. Early steam power was understandably unreliable, but the first successful crossing of the Atlantic under auxiliary steam power was accomplished by the *Sirius* in 1838. Although the days of sail power then began to wane, it was not until some thirty-one years later, with the opening of the Suez Canal, that commercial sailing ships realized they could no longer compete with steam.

To ease costs, crews were often made up with trainee cadets. Up to the Second World War, those sailing bulk carriers that still remained would often train cadets who were ultimately destined for merchant and military naval careers. Even today, many navies still insist that a 'spell before the mast' is essential as basic training and character building for their cadets. Since the Second World War most of

MERCATOR

these training ships have been purpose built for their roles. Some are converted bulk carriers, such as *Kruzenshtern* and *Sedov*; others, such as *Dar Mlodziezy* and *Simon Bolivar*, were especially commissioned, to designs inspired by early working vessels, with no cargo hold for training purposes only.

With each country showing great pride in owning its own Tall Ship it was a natural progression for them to meet, with a view to friendly competition and international exchange. Thus it was in 1956 that the Sail Training Association of Great Britain held their first Tall Ships Race from Torbay in England to Lisbon in Portugal, some 760 miles.

The race was an immediate success and since then every year sail training events have taken place all over the world. Interest in sail training is still very strong, with new ships being commissioned and launched, adding to or replacing those which have been lost. These ships are rarely allowed to fade away; they are loved and cherished and in their retiring years are often preserved as museum ships or commercial exhibits.

Thus, not only are we presented with a ship in mid-ocean, under full sail with a 'bone between her teeth', but we may also wander to our heart's content over such ships that have been preserved and opened to the public. We have seen the young people of today, of both sexes and sixteen or seventeen years old, strung out on the yards — 'the flying topsails thundering like a drum, battling the gale that makes men dumb'. So to them we say:

Adventure on, and if you suffer, swear,
That the next adventure shall have less to bear:
Your way will be retrodden — make it fair.

The American bald eagle figurehead of the US barque EAGLE

This figurehead replaced the original German eagle which had been the figurehead of the barque when she was built as a schoolship for the German Navy. The ship was transferred to the United States in 1946 and her original figurehead is preserved at the Mystic Seaport Museum in Connecticut. A full description of the *Eagle* appears on page 80 of this book.

ADIX

The *Adix* is one of the biggest private sailing yachts built since the second World War. She cost more than £5 million to build and was launched under the name of *Jessica* in 1983. She was completed the following year at Cowes and was rigged as a three-masted double topsail schooner by Spencer. Her owner was Mr Carlos Perdomo, an Argentine businessman who had previously owned the schooner-yacht *America* (p.24). She had accommodation for 8 persons in the owner's party and a crew of 14. She was British registered. She made her debut in the public eye at the 1984 Cowes Week.

Under Mr Perdomo's ownership the *Jessica* cruised extensively in Western Europe and the Mediterranean, and made a voyage to the East Coast of the United States and to the West Indies. She sailed back to southern Europe from the Caribbean in early 1987.

The following year she was sold to Alan Bond's XXXX Brewery and was renamed *Schooner XXXX*. She sailed to Fremantle, Western Australia, for use as Alan Bond's headquarters afloat for his defence of the *America's* Cup. Bond failed to retain the Cup and he soon was to lose his business empire. The *Schooner XXXX* was one of the first assets to be put up for sale.

The yacht was bought in 1990 by a Spanish gentleman for private use (no chartering). He renamed the schooner *Adix*, a more suitable name than *Schooner XXXX* for such an elegant schooner-yacht although it derives from it ('Add X'!). The schooner was re-registered in the UK (in London). To fit the requirements of the new owner the schooner was virtually rebuilt. The design consultancy was made by Gerard Dijkstra, naval architect in Amsterdam, and the work was carried out at the Pendennis shipyard in Falmouth, under the supervision of the new skipper Paul Goss. The schooner's aspect was changed from that of a square topsail schooner to that of a vintage fore-and-aft gaff yacht such as the *Atlantic*. The interior accommodation was also extensively rebuilt. The owner's suite has two connecting cabins with a bed each and there are three other cabins for up to five guests.

The stern was lengthened by 9.8 ft (3m). The original keel, full length with a long cutaway forefoot, was replaced by a fin keel that increases the draught by 3 ft (90 cm); a new balanced rudder was fitted to a skeg. The bowsprit was lengthened by 6.6ft (2m); the main and mizzen masts were respectively lengthened by 4.9 and 9.8 ft (1.5 and 3 m); the mizzen boom and gaff were lengthened; the yards on the foremast were removed and new aluminium masts were fitted. The aluminium deck gear was upgraded to bronze and many other alterations were made. The engine room, including fuel tanks, was completely renewed; a 540 hp MAN replaces the original 550 hp GM.

The conversion was sufficiently complete to allow the *Adix* to sail to St Tropez to take part in the Nioulargue vintage yacht race in September 1991, after which she returned to Falmouth for completion by the end of the year. In 1992 she will be sailing to Scotland and Scandinavia, then to Sardinia, Italy, and St Tropez for the '92 Nioulargue, then to the Caribbean. After the West Indies she will be cruising to the US East Coast and on her return to Europe she will attempt to break the *Atlantic's* record Atlantic passage.

Name of vessel	Adix, ex-Schooner XXXX, ex-Jessica
Year built	1984
Designer	Arthur Holgate, South Africa
Builder	Astilleros de Mallorca SA, Mallorca, Spain
Current Owner	Ocean Sailing Adventures Ltd., Guernsey
Current flag	Great Britain
Rig	Three-masted gaff schooner
Construction	Steel; teak-clad deck
Length extreme	211.6 feet (64.50 m)
Length of hull	183.7 feet (56.00 m)
Length waterline	139.1 feet (42.40 m)
Beam	28.2 feet (8.60 m)
Draught	15.7 feet (4.80 m)
Tonnage	370 td
Sail area	18,514 sq. feet (1,720 m^2) (28,000 sq. feet/2,600 m^2 total)
Engine	540 hp MAN
Complement	14 crew + 7 in Owner's party
Photograph date	1991
Photograph location	St Tropez, France

ALEXANDER VON HUMBOLDT

The Sail Training Association Germany (STAG) was set up in the early 1980s to act as an umbrella body for the country's many sail training organizations and vessels, and also in view of acquiring a square-rigged youth training ship of national importance.

In 1986 a trust closely linked to STAG, the Deutsche Stiftung Sail Training, was created for the latter purpose. It brought the lightvessel *Kiel* just taken out of service from her station in the German Bight, for conversion to a sailing barque. Her hull was ideal for such a conversion: it had sailing ship lines, it was in excellent condition and it already had a large number of watertight bulkheads meeting modern safety requirements. The conversion plans were drawn by Zygmunt Choreń, the Polish naval architect who had designed the *Dar Mlodziezy* class of full-riggers (p.76) and the *Pogoria* class of barquentines (p. 156), and by Captain Manfred Hövener, her future master and director of the DSST.

Under the interim name of *Confidentia*, the lightvessel went from Willhelmshaven to the Motorenwerk GmbH yard in Bremerhaven for conversion work. The project, which cost 2.2 million Deutsch Mark, had three main sponsors: the Beck Breweries, MBB (Messerschmidt) and an anonymous donor with Bremerhaven interests. The barque was named after the German explorer and earth-scientist Alexander von Humboldt (1769–1859).

She is one of the easiest square riggers to recognize on account of her bottle-green sails, the 'trademark' colour of Beck beer, on account of her green hull which is the same colour as the livery of the ships of Rickmers Rederei, a Bremerhaven company that used to own many Cape Horners, and on account of her very long superstructure which extends almost to the fore mast.

The masting and rigging are modern 'Polish' style, with masts in one piece (without doublings) and with standing yards that are not lowered when the sails are furled. The double spanker, with two gaffs, is a typical German feature.

The superstructure is actually built in the 'three island' style, with a poop, a midship Liverpool house (extending to the ship's sides) and a raised fo'c's'le. The accommodation under the poop and the Liverpool house are linked by a wide companionway, leaving on either side two sheltered boarding bays at main deck level. The main deck is open to the sky only along a short distance on either side of the fore mast, between the Liverpool house and the raised fo'c's'le.

The poop accommodation comprises the captain's quarters and the officers' saloon; the crew and trainee messes, washrooms and the galley are in the Liverpool house. The 'tween deck is entirely occupied by cabins for the crew and trainees. The latter are housed in 2- to 4-berth cabins.

The *Alexander von Humboldt* is homeported in Bremerhaven and carries a permanent crew of 15. Her trainee complement of 45 consists of young men and women aged between 16 and 24.

The barque made her inaugural cruise in March 1988. In summer she operates 7- to 14-day cruises in the Baltic and North Sea and she regularly takes part in the Tall Ships Races. She is not laid up in winter but continues her training cruises in the warmer climes of the Canaries.

Name of vessel	Alexander von Humboldt, *ex* Confidentia, *ex* Kiel, *ex*-Reserve Holtenau, *ex*-Reserve Sonderburg
Year built	1906 – Converted in 1987–8
Builder	Werft AG Weser, Bremen, Germany
Current Owner	Deutsche Stiftung Sail Training
Current flag	Germany
Rig	Barque
Construction	Steel; wood-clad deck
Length extreme	206.7 feet (63.0 m)
Length of hull	173.9 feet (53.0 m)
Length waterline	141.1 feet (43.0 m)
Beam	26.3 feet (8.02 m)
Draught	16.0 feet (4.88 m)
Tonnage	450 grt, 800 td
Sail area	10,872 sq. feet (1,010 m^2)
Engine	510 hp MAN
Complement	15 crew + 45 trainees
Photograph date	1989
Photograph location	Cowes, England

ALEXANDRIA

The *Alexandria* was built as a three-masted fore-and-aft schooner of about 160 tons deadweight (cargo capacity). Fitted with a 55 hp auxiliary engine she was launched as the *Yngve* owned by the Swedish captain Karls Anders Ögård of Graverne. In 1937 she was re-rigged as a galease (two-mast schooner). She was mostly used in the fish trade between Iceland and Scandinavia. She was sold to another Swedish owner in 1939 who re-named her *Lindö* and re-fitted her with a 100 hp engine. During the war years she traded in the Baltic, relying on her name painted in big letters on her hull and on a big flag likewise painted on her side, proclaiming her neutral status in the hope that she would not be taken as target by any of the belligerents.

She changed hands several times between 1940 and 1955, but always remained Swedish. In 1955 her rig was reduced to auxiliary status but she carried on working as a fish carrier and trader, under the Swedish flag, until 1969 when she was laid up.

In 1970 she was sold to the Baltic Schooner Association of Denmark for conversion to a holiday charter vessel. The new owners were Peter Wood, an Englishman, and Klaus Jacobi, a German. They already owned the topsail schooner *Gefion* which was registered in the Cayman Islands. The *Lindö* was likewise registered but her nameboard was written the Danish way, *Lindø*. The rebuild and conversion work of the *Lindø* began at Gunnar Brink Christensen's yard at Hobro, Denmark, but in 1974 the vessel was bought by the Canadian Brian Watson of the Flying Turtle Charter & Trading Co. Work was completed, and the *Lindø* was rigged as a three-masted topsail schooner at the J. Ring Andersen yard at Svendborg, Denmark. The *Lindø*

remained registered at Georgetown, Grand Cayman.

In 1976 she took part in the Plymouth-Tenerife-Bermuda-Newport-New York-Boston Tall Ships Race. The following year she was sold to the American captain Greg Birra of the Atlantic Schooner Association of New Jersey, and she was registered at Wilmington, Delaware. She chartered in the West Indies and in 1978 she was used for the making of Peter Benchley's movie *The Island*. Later she was chartering out of Antigua where the picture opposite was taken in 1980. Later that year she sailed to Boston and took part in the Boston to Kristiansand Tall Ships Race and then went back to Denmark for an overhaul at J. Ring Andersen's, prior to sailing back to the Caribbean and the eastern United States.

In 1983 the *Lindø* was acquired by the Alexandria Seaport Foundation of Alexandria, Virginia, for the purpose of engaging in social work and sail training after refit. She is however mostly used for promotional work, being an itinerant ambassador and goodwill messenger of Alexandria, with youngsters as part of her crew, not as trainees. The *Lindø*'s first foreign charter under her new ownership was by Armada '84, to take part in the tall ships gathering at Quebec in June—August 1984. It was while she was in Quebec that she was officially renamed *Alexandria*.

She has had an uneven career since then, with periods of sailing separated by long periods tied up to Alexandria's waterfront. She was one of the ships that escorted the *Danmark* (p. 74) into Washington DC in 1985; she took part in the New York OpSail '86 and in the American Sail Training Association's Tall Ships Rally in Chesapeake Bay in 1991.

Name of vessel	Alexandria, ex-Lindø, ex-Lindö, ex-Yngve
Year built	1929
Builder	Albert Svensson, Björkenås, Sweden
Current Owner	Alexandria Seaport Foundation, Alexandria, Virginia, USA
Current flag	United States of America
Rig	Three-masted topsail schooner
Construction	Wood
Length extreme	125.0 feet (38.10 m)
Length of hull	90.2 feet (27.50 m)
Length between perpendiculars	84.1 feet (25.60 m)
Beam	22.0 feet (6.70 m)
Draught	9.2 feet (2.80 m)
Tonnage	102 grt, 65 nrt, 176 t TM
Sail area	7,000 sq. feet (650 m^2) (total)
Engine	230 hp
Complement	about 15
Photograph date	1980
Photograph location	Antigua

AMERICA

When John Cox Stevens, Commodore of the newly-founded New York Yacht Club, and some of his friends decided to order the construction of a schooner-yacht to enter the hundred guinea cup race marking the opening of London's Great Exhibition in 1851, they could not have imagined they were setting in motion yachting's most prestigious and enduring event. The lines of the yacht were inspired by the New York's pilot schooners and the keel of the proudly named *America* was laid in the winter of 1850 at the William Brown yard in New York City.

The race, a 58-mile circuit around the Isle of Wight, was held on 22 August 1851. The *America* was a lone American entry competing against the cream of British yachting, 17 of the fastest schooners and cutters of the Royal Yacht Squadron. The starting gun was fired at 10 am. Ten and a half hours later the *America* crossed the finishing line, her nearest rival lagging out of sight eighteen minutes astern. Queen Victoria, who was watching from the Royal Yacht *Victoria and Albert*, asked who was second — 'Ma'am, there is no second . . .' Britain was not amused.

The hundred guinea cup, a silver beaker, was taken back to the New York Yacht Club. It became known as the *America's* Cup when the NYYC decided to stake it in 1857 as prize for an international challenge. The gauntlet was first picked up in 1870, by the British. The rest is part of yachting legend. Countless millions were spent in trying to wrench the Cup away from the NYYC where it lay for 132 years, until 1983, when *Australia II* won that coveted prize. After the burlesque

show in San Diego in 1988, the establishment of the new *America's* Cup Class rating in 1989 laid the ground for the continuation of the challenge into the 21st century . . .

In 1966 Rudolf J. Schaefer commemorated the 125th anniversary of the founding of his company, Schaefer Breweries, by building a replica of the legendary yacht. Referring to plans held by the British Admiralty, that had them drawn when the original yacht passed under British ownership, Sparkman & Stevens, the American yacht designers, drew the lines for the new schooner. She was traditionally built of pine using period tools and, although up-to-date below deck and with an auxiliary engine, she was identical to the original in all other respects. Even the sails were made by Ratsey & Lapthorn, who had supplied the original yacht with a jib some 116 years previously. The new *America* attended the 1967 Cup challenge at Newport and was as much a star of the show as *Intrepid* and *Dame Pattie*, that year's defender and challenger.

Ownership subsequently passed to the Schooner *America* Corp. of Wilmington, Delaware, a charter company, and then, in 1979, to Mr Carlos Perdomo, a shipping broker from Spain and Argentina. He lived aboard much of the time, running his business through the schooner's very 'unperiod' telecommunications systems. When he decided to have the much larger *Jessica* built (see *Adix*, p. 18), he sold the *America* to Mr Ramon Mendoza of Spain, in 1981. Although now painted white, she is shown in this picture in her period and original livery of high gloss black.

Name of vessel	America
Year built	1967
Designer	George Steers, William Brown and Sparkman & Stevens
Builder	Goudy & Steven, East Boothbay, Maine, USA
Current Owner	Ramon Mendoza
Current flag	Spain
Rig	Gaff schooner
Construction	Wood
Length extreme	130 feet (39.6 m)
Length of hull	104.8 feet (31.9 m)
Length waterline	90.7 feet (27.6 m)
Beam	22.8 feet (7.0 m)
Draught	11.5 feet (3.5 m)
Tonnage	92.24 grt, 66 nrt, 190t TM, 165.5 td
Sail area	5,387 sq. feet (500.5 m²)
Engine	320 hp GM SV-71
Complement	7
Photograph date	1968
Photograph location	Cowes, England

AMERIGO VESPUCCI

The *Amerigo Vespucci*, one of the largest sailing ships in the world today, is the training ship for the cadet officers of the Leghorn Naval Academy of the Italian Navy. She is the only three-decked square rigger currently in existence and her appearance is very reminiscent of the sail and steam ships-of-line of the 1850s and 60s — complete with a stern walk, a steeply steeved bowsprit and long jibboom, and an elaborate gilded figurehead and trailboards.

The ship is named after the Florentine traveller and cartographer (1454–1512) who put his first name on his maps of the new continent discovered by the Genoese navigator Cristoforo Colombo.

The *Amerigo Vespucci* was built under Mussolini who had a liking for monumental projects. Her keel was laid on 12 May 1930 and she was launched the following year. She was the second of a pair of sisterships, the first one was the *Cristoforo Colombo* launched in 1928. This earlier vessel was seized in 1949 as war prize by the Soviet Union and renamed *Dunay*. She carried on sailing as a Soviet training ship in the Black Sea until laid up in 1963; she was broken up in Odessa in 1971.

The *Amerigo Vespucci* was retained by the Italian Navy which has kept her in commission and which maintains her in immaculate condition. All the belaying pins and cleats are labelled with sparkling brass plaques, and halyard falls are neatly coiled inside varnished tubs. The cadets cut a dashing figure when, in harbour, they race up the rigging to man the yards in their well-tailored navy-blue uniforms, white caps and white gloves. Like the ponderous ships-of-the-line of old that sacrificed speed and weatherliness to firepower, the *Amerigo Vespucci* takes a gale of wind to get moving and her windward performance is debatable. As a result she does tend to rely rather a lot on her twin electro-diesel engines which can push her at 10.5 knots. But she does sail every year on extended voyages and the seamanship of her crew and cadets was well demonstrated in 1991 when they had to strike the topgallant masts in order to pass under some overhead power cables while crossing the Kiel Canal, and then had to set them up again.

Normally the ship, which is based at La Spezia, commissions in June for a short Mediterranean cruise with only her permanent crew onboard, and then undertakes a three-month voyage (July to September) with cadets to North Western Europe and sometimes the Baltic. She often has a few exchange foreign cadets, mostly from Latin America and the Third World. She also makes frequent appearances at tall ship festivals such as Sail Amsterdam (held every five years on years ending with 0 and 5) and the American OpSails, and she is scheduled to take part in the Columbus Quincentenary New York OpSail in July 1992 — but because of her poor sailing abilities she never actually races with the Tall Ships, although she sometimes accompanies them with her 'iron topsail'.

Name of vessel	Amerigo Vespucci
Year built	1931
Designer	Lt. Col. Francesco Rotundi
Builder	Castellamare di Stabia shipyard, Naples, Italy
Current Owner	Italian Navy (attached to the Leghorn Naval Academy)
Current flag	Italy
Rig	Full-rigged ship
Construction	Steel; wood-clad deck
Length extreme	330.1 feet (100.60 m)
Length of hull	270.0 feet (82.30 m)
Length between perpendiculars	229.7 feet (70.00 m)
Beam	50.9 feet (15.50 m)
Draught	23.6 feet (7.20 m)
Tonnage	2,686 TM; 3,543 td (standard), 4,146 td (load)
Sail area	27,771 sq. feet. (2,580 m^2)
Engines	2 × 950 hp Fiat — Marelli electro diesels; 1 propeller
Complement	303 permanent crew + 105 cadets
Photograph date	1977
Photograph location	Cowes, England

AMPHITRITE

The *Amphitrite* is the oldest Camper & Nicholson's yacht still sailing today, a true survivor of the age of clipper bows and aristocratic yachtsmen. She was launched under the name of *Hinemoa* for Colonel MacGregor, the Viceroy of India. She had a two-masted schooner rig with a huge main boom overhanging the stern and a main gaff club topsail with a jackyard. She had a sail area of 6,458 square feet (600 m²) and, of course, she did not have the present-day clutter of deckhouses. Although she did some racing in the Solent, she was built primarily for cruising. Her hull planking, frames and deck are entirely made of teak, and she is copper sheathed below the waterline.

In 1892 the *Hinemoa* was sold to the Earl of Harewood who renamed her *Amphitrite* (the wife of Poseidon in Greek mythology). The schooner was sold again in 1930, to the Earl of Arran. He had her converted to a barquentine with a sail area of 8,234 square feet (765 m²), and setting four square sails on the fore mast. The barquentine was bought in 1965 by a Swedish millionaire, Mr Hans Ostermann.

In 1969 she was bought by Mr François Spoerry, the French property developer who was building Port Grimaud near St Tropez. The *Amphitrite* was used for Port Grimaud's 'Club de la Mer' as an adventure sail training vessel for 21 trainees with a minimum age of 16 and no upper limit. The professional crew numbered 7. By that time the *Amphitrite's* hull was painted white and the sail area was 5,600 square feet (520 m²).

She made a number of such adventure cruises but she was back on the market by late 1970 and she was bought later that year by Horst Film GmbH of Berlin and was re-registered at Kiel. In 1971 ownership was transferred to Amphitrite Schiffahrts KG of Berlin, which used the ship for film charters after a major overhaul at Toulon, France. She featured in a film on the *Mary Celeste* and she appeared as the *Niobe* in a dramatised documentary about Count Luckner.

The *Amphitrite* was sold in September 1974 to the Clipper Deutsches Jugendwerk zur See e.V., a youth sail training organization now based in Hamburg, and which also owns the three-masted schooner *Albatros*, the schooner *Johann Smidt* and the large wooden gaff ketch *Seute Deern II*. The *Amphitrite* was extensively overhauled at the Hapag Lloyd yard in Bremerhaven in 1975 and her rig was changed to that of a three-masted fore-yard schooner. The large fore-course, that is set when running, brails against the mast. The hull colour was changed to brown in the early 1980s.

The Clipper association is volunteer-run and its ships sail under the command of a rota of volunteer masters many of whom are former captains of the barque *Gorch Fock* (p. 106) and some of whom are Cape Horners. The trainees, boys and girls, are aged from 16 to 25.

The *Amphitrite* is registered in Bremen but she usually sails out of the Baltic port of Travemünde. She usually takes part in the Tall Ships Races when they are held in the Baltic. She winters in the port of Bremerhaven.

Name of vessel	Amphitrite, ex-Hinemoa
Year built	1887
Designer	Camper & Nicholson's
Builder	Camper & Nicholson's, Gosport, England
Current Owner	Clipper Deutsches Jugendwerk zur See e.V., Hamburg, Germany
Current flag	Germany
Rig	Three-masted fore-yard gaff schooner
Construction	Wood
Length extreme	139.1 feet (42.40 m)
Length of hull	125.5 feet (38.30 m)
Length waterline	93.8 feet (28.60 m)
Beam	18.8 feet (5.72 m)
Draught	12.1 feet (3.70 m)
Tonnage	110.84 grt, 61.60 nrt, 170 TM
Sail area	5,877 sq. feet (546 m²)
Engines	2 × 220 hp Mercedes; twin propellers
Complement	5−6 crew + 23 trainees
Photograph date	1967
Photograph location	Marseilles, France

ANNA KRISTINA

The *Anna Kristina* is a beautifully restored Hardanger *jakt* or yacht — a yacht in the original meaning of the Dutch root word *jacht* that was applied to fast boats that were used to bring ashore the catch of the herring fleets out in the North Sea. The Hardanger yachts were so called because they were fast and handy. They were used to bring fish from the Lofoten to Bergen and southern Norway, to ferry goods and passengers along the coasts of Norway and even to carry Norwegian emigrants to America. Many were used as sealers which hunted as far afield as the Barents Sea and the White Sea. They were built in their thousands, from the 1840s until after the First World War. Most of those that have survived to our days did so by remaining in trade by becoming motorized, by losing their masts and by acquiring a wheelhouse on the stern.

The *Anna Kristina* was bought in such a condition by Hans Van de Vooren, a Dutchman established in Norway. He restored her in 1978–81 to a sailing *jakt* for use as a charter *yacht*. She cruised in Norway's magnificent Fjordland with up to 14 guests or as many as 40 day trippers, often in company with her owner's other Hardanger yacht, the *Anna Rosa*.

In 1986 both yachts were chartered by the Landmark School of Pride's Crossing, Massachusetts to sail European waters as seagoing classrooms.

In 1987 the *Anna Kristina* was chartered with three weeks' notice to take part in the First Fleet Reenactment sailing from Portsmouth to Sydney for the Australian Bicentenary. She was made ready however for the grand departure on 13 May and she is seen here

at the start of that voyage, astern of the *Bounty*.

Tragedy struck on the passage from Rio to Capetown. The first mate, who was working at night out on the bowsprit, lost his footing and fell into the sea, as the *Anna Kristina* was making six or more knots. Two shipmates jumped overboard to his rescue and were very lucky to be picked up, but he was never seen again.

After the Parade of Sail at Sydney on 26 January 1988 (Bicentennial Day) the *Anna Kristina*, along with the other ships of the 'First' Fleet, cruised along the eastern seaboard of Australia. When that charter ended, in June 1988, she operated head-berth cruises to New Zealand, Tahiti, the Cook Islands, Samoa, Tonga, Fiji., etc., on her own or in company with the *Søren Larsen* (p. 182), the *R. Tucker Thompson* (p. 166) and the topsail schooner *Tradewind*. In early 1989 the *Anna Rosa* sailed to join the *Anna Kristina* in Tahiti. They were chartered for a film in Samoa; they did whale-watching trips and were chartered by Auckland's museum as quayside attractions and for day, weekend and week trips.

They left New Zealand on 7 April 1991 and the *Anna Kristina* arrived in Tenerife on 15 September; the *Anna Rosa* was delivered to France, to the Boat Museum in Douarnenez which had bought her. The *Anna Kristina* is running winter charter cruises in the Canaries. In the summer of 1992 she will be taking part in the Columbus Regatta and will then return to the Canaries for the winter 1992–93 before sailing home to Norway in the summer after an absence of six years.

Name of vessel	Anna Kristina
Year built	1889–90 Rebuilt 1978–81
Builder	at Stangvik, Norway
Current Owner	Hardanger Yacht Sailing (Hans Van de Vooren), Tysnes, Norway
Current flag	Norway
Rig	Ketch
Construction	Wood
Length extreme	105.9 feet (32.00 m)
Length of hull	75.0 feet (22.90 m)
Length waterline	65.6 feet (20.00 m)
Beam	21.0 feet (6.40 m)
Draught	9.0 feet (2.80 m)
Tonnage	83.6 grt
Sail area	4,327 sq. feet (402 m^2)
Engine	275 hp Volvo Penta
Complement	6 crew + 14 passengers
Photograph date	1987
Photograph location	Solent, England

ARTEMIS

The keel of this trading schooner was laid down in 1902 at the yard of Zacharias T. Jacobsen in Troense, Denmark. She was launched in January 1903 under the name of *Noah*. For many years and like many other similar three masted topsail schooners, she traded across the Baltic, the North Sea, to England, France and Germany, Iceland, Italy, Africa, Newfoundland and all the places where large trading schooners could still find cargoes. She mainly carried salt (for the Newfoundland fisheries), salted cod (from Newfoundland to Spain, Italy and Africa), timber from the Baltic or Canada, bricks, coal, china, clay and sundry commodities.

The *Noah* was fitted with her first engine in 1930, a 110 bhp diesel. Fifteen years later she passed into the hands of new owners who renamed her *Peder Most* and registered her in Svendborg, Denmark. She was very soon re-sold to become the *Anna Thora* of Aalborg. Resold again in 1946 her name was shortened to *Thora*. Since the beginning of the War she had been restricted to coastal sailing and her rig had been reduced to an auxiliary configuration. In 1947 she was sold to H. Jeppesen and became the *Artemis* of Copenhagen.

From 1954 to 1965 she was operated as a motor coaster by a Marstal joint ownership. Then she was bought by Captain Nicholas Dekker who registered her in Rotterdam. He restored her to a three-masted schooner with a single deep topsail fitted with a roller-furling gear handed down from the French naval schooner *Belle Poule* (p. 50). His idea was to transport antiques in her hold to offer them for sale at various ports, but red tape and customs bureaucracy made things difficult. He lived aboard with his Parisian wife and daughter and a piano installed in the hold. In 1976 Nicholas Dekker entered the *Artemis* in the trans-Atlantic Tall Ships Race with the intention of selling her in the USA. In December 1976 she was bought by Rick and Sharron Harrington of Texas who made her into an itinerant maritime museum mostly based in Galveston, Texas, and Mobile, Alabama. This venture was not a financial success and the Artemis was sold once more, in 1979, to Chris Guiry, an Englishman established in St John, New Brunswick.

On 5 May 1980 the *Artemis* left Mobile bound for St John with eight crew and a cargo of wood-burning stoves. In the early hours of 9 May she was struck by a storm with vicious squalls that twice knocked the schooner on her beam ends. Although she righted herself both times, the second knock-down had sprung a plank near the keel and she began to make water at a rate that could not be coped with by the pumps. For twelve hours the crew battled at the pumps but by nightfall, as the schooner was very low in the water, she suddenly rolled over. In doing so one of her masts broke and Chris Guiry, her master, was caught in the rigging and started going under with his ship. He managed to break free and to join the rest of the crew in a liferaft. The *Artemis* sank in 1,500 feet (450 m) of water but all her crew were saved.

Name of vessel	Artemis, *ex*-Thora, *ex*-Anna Thora, *ex*-Peder Most, *ex*-Noah
Year built	1903
Designer	Z.T. Jacobsen
Builder	Z.T. Jacobsen, Troense, Denmark
Last Owner	Schooner Ventures, Canada
Last flag	Canada
Rig	Three-masted topsail schooner
Construction	Wood
Length extreme	147.7 feet (45.0 m)
Length of hull	120 feet (36.6 m)
Length waterline	106 feet (32.3 m)
Beam	25.9 feet (7.9 m)
Draught	10.2 feet (3.1 m)
Tonnage	240 grt, 284 TM, 380 td
Sail area	6,027 sq. feet (560 m^2)
Engine	120 bhp Burmeister & Wain Alpha
Complement	Variable − min. 7 for passage-making.
Photograph date	1976
Photograph location	Plymouth, England

ASGARD II

This fine emerald-green brigantine is the national youth training ship of Ireland. Her construction was paid for by the Department of Defence and she is consequently owned by the Irish Navy but she is strictly used for civilian youth training. Her running costs are subsidized by a direct grant from the Department of Finance. She is managed and operated by the Coiste an Asgard, a government-appointed committee.

The first *Asgard*, named after the home of the Norse gods, was a 45 ft Colin Archer ketch built in 1905 and originally owned by Erskine Childers, an Englishman. Espousing the cause of the Irish nationalists he used the *Asgard* to run guns to Ireland from Hamburg in 1914. The *Asgard* was bought in 1961 by the Irish government on account of her historical associations. In 1968 the government formed the Coiste an Asgard to operate her as a youth training vessel. She had to be retired in 1975 on account of her age and condition and she is now preserved as a national monument. She was replaced, from 1975 to 1980, by a small wooden Bermudan ketch, the *Creidne*, while plans were being made for the design and construction of a brigantine, the *Asgard II*.

The *Asgard II* is built of iroko on oak. She was commissioned in Arklow on 7 March 1981 by Charles Haughey, the Prime Minister. The first master of *Asgard II*, until his retirement in 1988, was Capt. Erick Healy, the former skipper of the old *Asgard* and of *Creidne*.

The trainee accommodation is in an open plan mess-deck forward of the waist. There are double-tiered bunks along the sides and two mess tables along the centreline. The floor of the aft accommodation, under the quarter deck, is raised, allowing the 'infernal' combustion engine to be tucked under, thus saving some prime accommodation space. This area comprises the galley, three permanent-crew cabins and a congenial 'great cabin' in the stern. The chartroom is in a deckhouse on the poop deck.

The *Asgard II* has a permanent crew of 5 and a complement of 20 passage crew. The latter normally consists of two experienced but paying adults (navigator and purser) and 18 trainees aged from 16 to 24, three of whom, among the oldest with previous experience, are made watch leaders. Some early and late season cruises will accept ordinary adult trainees. Most cruises are of 6 days' duration, with a few longer ones in summer, notably when the ship sails further afield in the Tall Ships Races in which she regularly takes part.

In 1985 the brigantine sailed to the East Coast of the United States on a courtesy visit. She also took part in the 1988 Hobart to Sydney Tall Ships Race and in the celebrations of the Australian Bicentennial — but she went to and came back from Australia as deck cargo on a freighter! She was perfectly able to make such a voyage under her own sails but that would have removed her too long from her normal programme and would have entailed prohibitively expensive crew changeovers along the way. In the summer of 1992 the *Asgard II* will be making a call at Seville's World Expo.

Name of vessel	Asgard II
Year built	1981
Designer	John Tyrell
Builder	Tyrell & Sons, Arklow, Co. Wicklow, Ireland
Operator	Coiste an Asgard, Dublin, Ireland
Current flag	Eire
Rig	Brigantine
Construction	Wood
Length extreme	104 feet (31.70 m)
Length of hull	94 feet (28.65 m)
Length waterline	70 feet (21.34 m)
Beam	21 feet (6.40 m)
Draught	9.5 feet (2.20 m)
Tonnage	92.67 grt, 50.06 nrt; 120 td
Sail area	4,000 sq. feet (372 m²)
Engine	160 bhp Kelvin Marine
Complement	5 permanent crew + 20 trainees and passage officers
Photograph date	1982
Photograph location	Cowes, England

ASTRID

Laid down at the very end of the Great War this vessel was caught in the shipping slump that followed and was only sold in 1921, still on the stocks, to Nicholas Muller who completed her in 1924 as an auxiliary trading schooner, the *Wuta* of Dordrecht, Holland. Ten years later he reduced her rig to that of a *vracht logger*, a freight logger with an auxiliary ketch rig without topmasts. He sold her in 1937 to the Jeppsson family who renamed her *Astrid* and re-registered her in Skillinge, Sweden. Under that ownership she engaged in the Baltic trade (timber, grain and coal) for the next 38 years — as an unrigged motor logger from 1957 onwards. One year after the death in 1975 of Capt. Edmund Frohm, her sole master during that period, she was sold to Karim Ahmed & Shafsack Mohammed Bassam who re-registered her in Tripoli, Lebanon, without changing her name. She traded between the Middle East and northern Europe. Suspected of drug running, she was ordered by British Customs to heave-to on 15 July 1977, while on passage off Dungeness. The crew set fire to the ship and jumped overboard — two were drowned and three were not accounted for. The burnt out hulk was towed to Newhaven and later virtually abandoned on a mud berth in the Hamble. Five years later it was acquired by John Amos who intended to restore it.

Meanwhile, Commander Graham Neilson had retired from the Navy in 1982 with the intention of setting up a youth training scheme with a square rigger. He bought the *Astrid*, still as a hulk, from John Amos in 1984. The superstructures were razed down to and including the deck and a new deck of mild steel was laid (later to be clad in soroya timber). The non-profit charitable Astrid Trust was constituted in the spring of 1985 and carried on the project under the direction of Cmdr. Neilson. The rigging and sail plans were made by Capt. Michael Willoughby and Bob Casson; Douglas firs were cut down in the New Forest and shaped into masts and spars by Jack Barnes.

After more than four years of incredibly hard work, tenacity and constant financial wrestling, the *Astrid* undertook her sea trials at the end of 1988. She performed even better then expected under sail. The following months were spent putting the finishing touches and on 24 May 1989 the brig was dedicated to the service of youth by HRH the Princess Royal.

The *Astrid* normally runs two three-month training cruises a year with young people aged 17 to 25 inclusive, leaving England in September, operating a crew changeover over Christmas in the Caribbean, and returning to England in the spring (in 1992 she is staying an extra 2 months in the Caribbean, for a 'Columbus commemorative cruise'). During the summer she runs a series of shorter cruises where over-25s are also welcome, mostly in the Channel, and she also takes part in Tall Ships Races and events. On these short cruises the crew is reduced to 7 (minus the diving instructor); the freed berth is made available for an extra trainee.

The *Astrid* was converted to the latest Board of Trade safety regulations. She is the most recently commissioned British youth training tall ship and despite being the oldest in age, her iron construction is so superior to modern shipbuilding practices that, barring ill-fortune, she should outlive most of the recently built windjammers.

Name of vessel	Astrid *ex-*Wuta
Year built	1924; converted 1988
Designer	Greg. van Leeuwen
Builder	Greg. van Leeuwen, Scheveningen, The Netherlands
Current Owner	Astrid Trust, Weymouth, Dorset
Current flag	UK
Rig	Brig
Construction	Iron; Soraya-clad steel deck
Length extreme	138 feet (42.06 m)
Length of hull	108 feet (39.92 m)
Length waterline	101 feet (30.78 m)
Beam	22 feet (6.71 m)
Draught	8.5 feet (2.59 m)
Tonnage	170 grt, 120 nrt, 270 td (load)
Sail area	5,250 square feet (488 m^2)
Engine	290 hp 6-cylinder Scania
Complement	8 crew + 26 trainees
Photograph date	1988
Photograph location	Solent, England

ATLANTIS

The *Atlantis* was launched in 1905 as the *Bürgermeister Bartels*, a light vessel which served for nearly eighty years at the Elbe II station off the mouth of the Elbe river. Now that lightships are being replaced by automated buoys, decommissioned lightships are frequently converted to sailing vessels as they have good sailing lines. Other examples in this book are the *Alexander von Humboldt* (p. 20) and the *Belle Blonde* (p. 48).

It was Captain Hartmuth Paschburg, former master and part-owner of the three-masted schooner *Ariadne* (p. 108) and of the four-masted barque *Sea Cloud* (p. 170) who promoted the conversion of the *Atlantis*. The rebuilding and conversion work was done in 1984–85 at the yard of Scheel & Joehnk in Hamburg and mostly in Szczecin, Poland. The original sail plan was that of a conventional barquentine, with a gaff mainsail and setting a fore-royal. With this rig she made her sailing trials in the early summer of 1985, flying the Fijian ensign and with the homeport of Suva painted on her stern. She was indeed intended to be operated in the Pacific by Tallship Cruises Ltd of Fiji, but plans were changed and the *Atlantis* began operating in the Western hemisphere under Panamanian registry.

In 1986 her sail plan was reduced as it was found to be excessive in respect to the stability. The fore-royal was removed and the gaff main sail was replaced by two mizzen staysails – but the main gaff was still left standing and setting the main gaff topsail, an unusual arrangement. However this gaff and its topsail were subsequently dispensed with also.

Since 1988 the barquentine has been operating only in European waters, no longer going to the West Indies, and around 1989 her registry was transferred to Valetta, Malta. She operates both scheduled 'head berth' cruises (individual bookings) and charters.

The *Atlantis* is in Germanische Lloyds Class ✠ 100 A4 Passenger Sailing Ship. She can carry up to 34 passengers in double cabins and up to 70 day passengers. She normally has a crew of 15 consisting of 10 officers and seamen, 3 stewards, a purser and a chef.

The general arrangement is purpose-designed for passenger work. There is a very long poop, extending to just forward of the main-mast, which contains a large dining room saloon with bar and, aft, two passenger cabins and the officers' quarters for the master, chief mate and chief engineer. A midship deckhouse prolongs the poop to the fore-mast, leaving two external gangways on the main deck, along the sides. This houses the galley and crew mess. The upper deck, along the poop and over the midship deckhouse, has a charthouse and is used as a sundeck by the passengers.

The 'tween deck is divided into six watertight compartments: forepeak, crew quarters, three compartments with passenger cabins, and the engine room aft. The propulsion system is unusual: the ship has two Schottel-driven propellers mounted on lateral struts.

The passenger cabins are like small hotel rooms: all have twin beds (no upper bunks), a television, a small refrigerator for drinks, and an en-suite washroom with shower and toilet. The ship is air conditioned throughout and has worldwide direct-dialling telephone and telex links via satellite. The *Atlantis* is German-owned and her clientele is mostly German.

Name of vessel	Atlantis, *ex*-Bürgermeister Bartels
Year built	1905. Converted 1985
Builder	J.N.H. Wichhorst, Hamburg, Germany
Current Owner	Partenrederei SY Atlantis, Lübeck, Germany
Current flag	Malta
Rig	Barquentine
Construction	Steel; teak-clad deck
Length extreme	186.2 feet (56.75 m)
Length on deck	150 feet (47.25 m)
Length waterline	131.2 (40.00 m)
Beam	24.6 feet (7.50 m)
Draught	16.4 feet (5.00 m)
Tonnage	369 grt; 138 nrt
Sail area	7,981 sq. feet (741.5 m^2)
Engines	2 × 135 hp Mercedes; 2 Schottel propellers
Complement	15 crew + 34 passengers
Photograph date	1989
Photograph location	Cowes, England

BALCLUTHA

The *Balclutha* was built in Glasgow for Robert McMillan of Dumbarton on the Clyde — hence her name, the Gaelic for Dumbarton (*Bal*: town; *Clutha*: Clyde). She was a typical British Cape Horner representing the last flowering of centuries of deep sea trade under sail and of square rigger design, solidly built and seaworthy, with a good cargo capacity and yet a reasonable speed. Her maiden voyage was around Cape Horn to San Francisco. She was to round the Horn no less than 17 times during her prime. She carried coal and manufactured goods from Britain, grain from California, nitrates from Chile, guano from Peru, rice from Rangoon, wool from New Zealand.

British shipowners were fast converting to steam. Still almost new, the *Balclutha* was sold in 1899 to the Colonial Shipping Co. of San Francisco (J.J. Moore and associates) which operated her under the Hawaiian flag. She carried timber from the northwestern United States to Australia and coal from Newcastle, NSW, back to the West Coast.

In 1901 she was acquired by Pope & Talbot of San Francisco (the Puget Sound Commercial Co.) and registered under the American flag for use in the Alaska salmon fisheries. This was a seasonal trade operated from San Francisco. Each year in spring large numbers of fishermen and canners were shipped out to Alaska on old sailing ships (most of them big square riggers) which were used on site as factory ships for the salmon netted in the mouths of the rivers. At the end of the season, in autumn, they would sail back to San Francisco with the personnel and 'packed' salmon.

In 1903–04 the *Balclutha* was chartered by the Alaska Packers Association of San Francisco. In May 1904 she ran aground on Sitkinak Island; she was holed and flooded. The barque was purchased in that condition by the Alaska Packers Association which managed to refloat her and to bring her back to San Francisco in the spring of 1905. There she was repaired and at the same time her poop was extended forward to increase her accommodation space. Renamed *Star of Alaska* — all Alaska Packers ships had names beginning with *Star of* — she sailed each year to Alaska from 1906 until 1930 when the fisheries were at an end. The barque was sold the following year to Frank Kissinger, a movie man from Los Angeles. He renamed her *Pacific Queen* and used her in several movies and sailed her to various ports, dressed up as a pirate ship, as a public exhibition. This circus act came to an end with the Second World War. The old Cape Horner was laid to rest on a mud berth near Sausalito.

And there she laid in a state of utter neglect until she was bought for restoration in 1954 through the intervention of Karl Kortum, the director of the San Francisco Maritime Museum (since then renamed the National Maritime Museum in San Francisco). Those were the days when people began to realize that the ships from the age of sail had almost disappeared and that the survivors deserved to be preserved for posterity. Karl Kortum was at the forefront of this maritime heritage movement and the *Balclutha* was the first of many ships he helped to save.

The *Balclutha* was given back her original name and was restored to her original appearance (albeit keeping her long Alaska Packers poop), and she has been open to the public as a historic ship since 1954, in San Francisco.

Name of vessel	Balclutha, *ex*-Pacific Queen, *ex*-Star of Alaska, *ex*-Balclutha
Year built	1886
Designer	Charles Connell & Co.
Builder	Charles Connell & Co., Glasgow, Scotland
Current Owner	National Maritime Museum in San Francisco
Current flag	USA
Rig	Barque
Construction	Steel; wooden deck
Length extreme	300.2 feet (91.50 m)
Registered Length	256.3 feet (78.12 m)
Beam	38.5 feet (11.73 m)
Draught	22.7 feet (6.92 m)
Tonnage	1,862 grt; 1,590 nrt; 2,660 tdw
Sail area	20,500 sq. feet (1,900 m^2) (approx.)
Engine	None
Complement	26 (in her deep-sea trading days)
Photograph date	1990
Photograph location	San Francisco, California, USA

BARBA NEGRA

The *Barba Negra* was built as a galease, a Scandinavian type of schooner rig where both masts are about the same height but where the mainsail is often of a somewhat lesser area than the foresail if the main boom is shorter than the fore boom. The *Barba Negra* is said to have been built for Arctic whaling and to have engaged in that trade for the first four years of her existence, fitted with a harpoon gun in the bows.

In 1900 the vessel went into the fish-carrying trade, hauling fish from the Lofoten and Northern Norway to the towns in the south. She only became motorized in 1956 and she remained in trade, as a motor coaster, until 1970 when she was bought by her current owners, Mr Albert Seidl, a German master shipwright, and his partner, also from Germany, Mr Gerhard Schwisow. They renamed the vessel Barba Negra and registered her under the Canadian flag. They converted her into a picturesque barquentine equipped for whale watching, whale research and charter work in the West Indies. She was used in a number of film productions and played host to the French diver Jacques Cousteau on one of his research voyages.

The *Barba Negra* visited England in 1974 and took part in the Royal Review past HMS *Britannia* in the Solent off Cowes, at which time the picture opposite was taken.

In 1976 the *Barba Negra* joined the American Bicentennial Tall Ships Race in Bermuda. She carried a harpoon gun in her bows and a crow's nest was fixed to the main topmast above which flew a Jolly Roger. Bearded Captain Seidl looked the part, complete with a live parrot on the shoulder. Captain Seidl, as well as being a shipwright, is also a marine artist and uses the *Barba Negra* as a floating studio.

A few years later the *Barba Negra* was based in Savannah, Georgia, flying the American flag as an unregistered yacht, although still registered at Halifax, Canada. She was used as a marine environment awareness centre and as an art studio. She was scheduled to take part in the 1986 New York OpSail but needed a refit which was postponed as Captain Seidl was suddenly contracted as a shipwright for the building of minesweepers urgently wanted by the US Navy for use in the Persian Gulf which had been mined in the Iran-Iraq conflict. So the *Barba Negra* stayed in Savannah and did not attend the New York event.

At present, early 1992, the *Barba Negra* is still in Savannah, in the process of getting a new mast as part of a wider rebuilding programme. Her ownership has not changed and Captain Seidl and his parrot, the same as in 1976, are still aboard. The *Barba Negra* should once more be actively sailing by 1993.

Name of vessel	Barba Negra
Year built	1896
Designer	John Lekve
Builder	John Lekve, Hemne, Norway
Current Owner	Mr Gerhard Schwisow and Mr Albert Seidl, Savannah, Georgia, USA
Current flag	Canada
Rig	Barquentine
Construction	Wood
Length extreme	110.0 feet (33.53 m)
Length of hull	82.0 feet (24.99 m)
Length waterline	79.0 feet (24.08 m)
Beam	21.0/23.0 feet (6.40/7.01 m) (hull/hull + external channels)
Draught	12.0 feet (3.66 m)
Tonnage	55.64 grt; 123 t TM
Sail area	6,500 sq. feet (604 m²)
Engine	230 bhp Scania
Complement	8 crew + 10 participants (when sailing)
Photograph date	1974
Photograph location	Solent, England

BELEM

The *Belem* was built for the South Atlantic trade between France and Europe and the East Coast of South America and the West Indies. Her first owners were Denis Crouan Fils & de Lagotellerie, of Nantes. In 1907 they sold her to Demanges Frères, also of Nantes. In 1914, just before the outbreak of war, she was bought by the Duke of Westminster for conversion to a luxury yacht. She spent the war years in the yard of Camper & Nicholsons at Gosport, where she was given her first engine and fitted out as a yacht. From 1919 to 1921 she cruised in the Mediterranean and then was sold to Lord A.E. Guinness, the brewer, who renamed her *Fantome II*. He used her well and kept her until his death after World War II. In the early Twenties the *Fantome II* sailed around the world westabouts, via Panama, Japan, Hong Kong and Suez. Later she made several cruises to Spitzberg and the Arctic, and she sailed to Montreal in 1937.

She was laid up at Cowes during World War II. In 1951 she was sold to the Italian Count of Cini who gave her to the Cini Foundation of Venice for use as a training ship. The *Fantome II*, renamed *Giorgio Cini*, was re-rigged as a barquentine. By 1972 the Foundation had become unable to keep up with running and maintenance costs and the *Giorgio Cini* was sold to the Carabinieri, the Italian constabulary. They gave her to a yard in Venice for an overhaul including new engines and re-rigging as a barque — but they failed to pay the yard(!) which put the ship up for sale in 1974, to recover its costs.

She was bought back under French ownership in 1979, by the Fédération Nationale des Caisses d'Epargne, the French State Savings Bank. The idea was that the Caisses d'Epargne would lend the barque to the French Navy for use as a sail training ship, in exchange of her manning and upkeep and a couple of months a year of availability for promotional use by the owner. The Navy towed the *Belem* (which was given back her original name) from Venice to Brest where the Navy laid her up and ignored her.

In 1980 the Caisses d'Epargne established the Fondation Belem to own and manage the vessel and late that year took the decision to transfer her to Paris for preservation as a museum ship. Fortunately that decision was reversed in favour of active recommissioning. In late 1981, after some replating work in a yard at Lorient, the *Belem* was nonetheless towed to Paris for public exhibition while some refitting work was progressed. Eight 4-berth and eight 2-berth cabins were built in the 'tween deck around the trainees' mess, etc. The barque left Paris in 1985 and completed her fitting out at Le Havre and Caen and made her sea trials that summer. In 1986 she sailed to New York for the Statue of Liberty Centennial and re-dedication and the attending OpSail. Her first full normal year was 1987.

The *Belem* sails from March or April to October or November, doing short cruises (3 to 6 days) along the coasts of France (mainly in the Atlantic and Channel but also in the Mediterranean) interspersed with harbour functions and day trips for the Caisses d'Epargne. She winters in her home port of Nantes.

Name of vessel	Belem, ex-Giorgio Cini, ex-Fantome II, ex-Belem
Year built	1896
Designer	Chantiers Dubigeon
Builder	Chantiers Dubigeon, Nantes, France
Current Owner	Fondation Belem, Paris, France
Current flag	France
Rig	Barque
Construction	Steel; wood-clad deck
Length extreme	190.3 feet (58.00 m)
Length of hull	167.3 feet (51.00 m)
Length waterline	157.5 feet (48.00 m)
Beam	28.9 feet (8.80 m)
Draught	11.5 feet (3.50 m)
Tonnage	537 grt; 750 td (load)
Sail area	12,900 sq. feet (1,200 m^2)
Engines	2 × 300 hp Fiat Iveco; twin propellers
Complement	16 crew + 48 trainees
Photograph date	1987
Photograph location	Cowes, England

BEL ESPOIR II

This vessel was designed and built in 1944 by the reputed yard J. Ring Andersen in Svendborg, Denmark. Her first name was *Nette S.* of Svendborg, a three-masted fore-yard schooner with a 116 hp Alpha diesel auxiliary, and she was owned by A.E. Sørensen. She was intended for the Baltic and Newfoundland trades but was at first restricted to local trade by the war. In 1946 she was renamed *Annette S.*, and then *Peder Most* when she was transferred by A.E. Sørensen to his son M.H. Sørensen. In 1950 she was engaged in the Greenland fisheries.

In 1954 the *Peder Most* was employed in livestock transport between Copenhagen and Hamburg, carrying 200 head of cattle a trip. This did not last long, however, as the vessel was bought the following year by the British Outward Bound Trust and re-named *Prince Louis II*, registered at Glasgow. She was operated by the Moray Sea School as a youth training ship with a 24-trainee complement — in which work she had been dedicated by HRH the Duke of Edinburgh.

In 1968 the *Prince Louis II* was sold to the Paris-based association 'Les Amis de Jeudi-Dimanche', a youth social work charity run by the indefatigable Jesuit priest Fr. Michel Jaouen. She was renamed *Bel Espoir II* and registered at Le Havre. The same association also operates, since 1972, a three-masted centreboard steel schooner, the *Rara Avis*, but the two schooners do not usually sail together in tandem.

The *Bel Espoir II* was fitted out for 30 trainees and was fitted with a square topsail with a roller furling gear which, like that of the *Artemis* (p. 32), was handed down from the French naval schooners *Belle Poule* and *Etoile* (p. 50).

The *Bel Espoir* and *Rara Avis* are in principle operated for the rehabilitation of juvenile delinquents and drug addicts but, with a shortage of funds for this purpose, they are in fact predominantly and more and more operated as adventure training vessels for people of all ages who can afford to pay their own way. The schooners are frequently chartered by 'Comités d'Entreprise'. These are workers' councils established by law, in France, in all firms employing 50 or more people, and employers finance them with 1% of their wage bills. These funds can be used by the councils to subsidize leisure activities (such as sailing) for their members by as much as 50%.

The *Bel Espoir II* is sailed hard — she sails around the year, with little time for yard or in-harbour maintenance. Most years she spends the winter season in the West Indies — there are cheap flights from Paris to Martinique and Guadeloupe which make chartering out of those islands an affordable proposition. In summer the *Bel Espoir II* sails mostly along the western coasts of France. She frequently turns up at tall ships gatherings and festivals, on both sides of the Atlantic such as Sail Amsterdam '85 and the New York OpSail '86, but she seldom enters the Cutty Sark Tall Ships Races on account of temperament clashes between her very Gallic and Latin management and the oh-so-British Sail Training Association that runs the Races and lays down the Rules.

Name of vessel	Bel Espoir II, *ex-*Prince Louis II, *ex-*Peder Most, *ex-*Annette S., *ex-*Nette S.
Year built	1944
Designer	J. Ring Andersen
Builder	J. Ring Andersen, Svendborg, Denmark
Current Owner	Les Amis de Jeudi-Dimanche, Paris, France
Current flag	France
Rig	Three-masted topsail schooner
Construction	Wood
Length extreme	122 feet (37.20 m)
Length of hull	96 feet (29.26 m)
Length waterline	90 feet (27.43 m)
Beam	23.3 feet (7.10 m)
Draught	8.5 feet (2.60 m)
Tonnage	99 grt; 71 nrt; 183 t TM; 190 td
Sail area	5,870 sq. feet (545 m²)
Engine	288 hp Baudouin
Complement	6−8 crew + 30 trainees
Photograph date	1975
Photograph location	River Thames, London, England

This vessel was built as the United States Coastguard lightvessel *LV 88*. She was built of riveted black iron with bottom plates half an inch thick, and she had two wooden decks. She was built near New York but her intended station was off the mouth of the Columbia River in Oregon. The steam engine she had was only intended to allow her to move on and off station without tug assistance and her bunkers were not big enough for the long haul around South America (the Panama Canal was not yet opened in those days), so the ship was fitted with an auxiliary staysail schooner rig for the delivery passage round Cape Horn. That rig was removed before she was anchored on her station.

She remained on that station, apart from periodic maintenance dockings, until 1960 when she was replaced by a newer lightvessel built in 1954. *LV 88* was acquired for preservation in 1962 by the Columbia River Maritime Museum in Astoria, Oregon. Around 1980 the USCG decommissioned in turn the newer lightvessel, replacing it by an automated lightbuoy. This 1954 vessel was the last in service on the US West Coast; the Columbia River Maritime Museum acquired it as a more interesting exhibit and sold *LV 88* to a private individual in 1981.

The following year *LV 88* was bought by Mr Claude Lacerte, a Canadian, to replace the three-masted topsail schooner *Belle Blonde* he had just lost. In 1983 he converted the lightvessel to a brigantine which he also called *Belle Blonde*. He added an extra deck, a spar deck linking the raised poop deck to the raised fo'c's'le deck, and he built up the sides of the hull to enclose the former waist. The master's cabin is in a deckhouse built around the foot of the mainmast. There is a deck saloon in a deckhouse curiously placed forward of the foremast which is stepped unusually far aft. All the remaining accommodation is on the main deck below or on the lower deck. The latter consists of a huge storeroom with built-in coldroom and crews' quarters on the port side. Abaft this storeroom there is a large engine room with a diesel engine that had replaced the steam plant in the 1930s. Abaft the engine room there is a large workshop. The ship was licensed by the Canadian authorities for only 15 passengers plus crew, so there is a lot of spare space. The crew was normally 12 strong on charter work.

The *Belle Blonde* sailed from Victoria, British Columbia, in February 1984, for the Caribbean where she joined the Tall Ships Race to Bermuda, Halifax and Quebec. She returned to the Caribbean in the autumn and operated charters out of St Martin. She was chartered for sail training purposes, for a period, by the Canadian Armed Forces (in replacement to the *Our Svanen*, p. 148).

In March 1988 the *Belle Blonde* was sold to a Japanese company the main shareholder and President of which is Mr Tomoyuki Nishida. That company is engaged in property developments including flats, sports grounds and marinas, on the island of Kyushu, the southern-most main island of Japan. The company bought the *Belle Blonde* along with four other tall ships for an itinerant promotion in Japan of its developments.

The *Belle Blonde* was given a refit in Santo Domingo and was delivered to Japan by Claude Lacerte, via Panama and the Marquesas. She arrived in Kyushu in mid-July 1988 and Claude Lacerte stayed on until the end of August to train the new owner's crew. The *Belle Blonde*'s registry was changed to Japan but she has retained her French name.

Name of vessel	Belle Blonde, *ex* LV 88 (Columbian Lightvessel)
Year built	1907. Converted 1983
Builder	New York Shipbuilding Co., Camden, New Jersey, USA
Current Owner	Hokoku Kosan Kabushiki Kaisha, Tokyo
Current flag	Japan
Rig	Brigantine
Construction	Iron and steel; wooden decks
Length extreme	165 feet (50.29 m)
Length on deck	130 feet (39.62 m)
Length waterline	113 feet (34.44 m)
Beam	30 feet (9.14 m)
Draught	13 feet (3.96 m)
Tonnage	479 grt; 273 nrt; 650 td (light)
Sail area	15,000 sq. feet (1,394 m^2)
Engine	350 hp Washington
Complement	12 crew (+ 15 passengers under Canadian flag)
Photograph date	1984
Photograph location:	Bermuda

BELLE POULE

The sisterships *Belle Poule* and *Etoile* are training vessels of the French Navy attached to the Naval College (*école Navale*) of Lanvéoc-Poulmic near Brest.

They were built in 1931–32 (the *Belle Poule* was launched in January 1932; the *Etoile* in July) at the Chantier Naval de Normandie at Fécamp. Although purpose-built for the Navy these two schooners are identical to the famous 'Paimpol' or 'Iceland' fishing schooners of the late 19th and early 20th centuries, many dozens of which used to set sail every spring from Paimpol and other Breton harbours to fish for cod off Iceland and Greenland. One distinguishing feature of most of these schooners was their roller-furling topsail that could be entirely set, reefed or furled from deck — a system invented in 1875 by Mr Dowman, an Englishman.

The *Belle Poule* (literally 'Pretty Chick') is an old name in the French Navy list, going back to the 18th century. The first three *Belle Poules* were sailing frigates; the present schooner is the fourth. The *Etoile* ('Star'), likewise, is the eighth of her name since 1622.

The galley and crew toilets are located in the fore deckhouse. The entrance to the captain's quarters, his bathroom, the access to the engine room, and the chartroom are located in the aft deckhouse. Below deck, the permanent deckhands are berthed in a very traditional fo'c's'le forward of the trainees' half-deck abaft which are the NCOs' quarters, the engine room and, in the stern, the captain's quarters consisting of his cabin, a small saloon and a spare cabin for a supplementary guest but usually used as a pantry.

The training cruises vary in length but are nearly always short, 5 to 14 days, with new trainees on every cruise. The schooners nearly always sail together, which provides good competitive training for the crews. The schooners sail mostly in French western waters but occasionally make courtesy calls abroad such as New York in July 1976. They occasionally take part in the Cutty Sark Tall Ships Races.

The trainees number 20 on ordinary cruises and 15 on long ones as their half-deck is very cramped with framed bunks, settee bunks and, mostly, hammocks. The trainees are midshipmen from the Naval College or reserve officers undergoing a refresher course. The *Belle Poule* is the senior ship of the two and her commanding officer, a Lieutenant Commander, is Commodore of the pair. Since 1989 the *Etoile* has been commanded by a Lieutenant; prior to that her commanding officer was a Chief Petty Officer. In addition to the commanding officer each schooner has a permanent crew of 15 comprising both career NCOs and lower ratings, and national servicemen who in civilian life are fishermen or merchant seamen.

The schooners are today the oldest ships in the French Navy's list. They are the only remaining ones that were in commission during World War II, which they spent in England with the Free French Forces. Today, when in harbour, they still proudly fly from the tip of their bowsprit, the FFF Jack which is a Tricolour bearing a Cross of Lorraine.

Name of vessel	Belle Poule
Year built	1932
Builder	Chantier Naval de Normandie, Fécamp, France
Current Owner	French Navy
Current flag	France
Rig	Topsail schooner
Construction	Wood
Length extreme	123.0 feet (37.50 m)
Length of hull	106.5 feet (32.45 m)
Length waterline	83.0 feet (25.30 m)
Beam	23.6 feet (7.20 m)
Draught	11.8 feet (3.60 m)
Tonnage	227 td (standard)
Sail area	7,728 sq. feet. (718 m^2)
Engine	300 bhp Sulzer
Complement	16 crew + 15–20 cadets
Photograph date	1982
Photograph location	Cowes, England

BLACK PEARL

This very small but beautifully proportioned brigantine was built by C. Lincoln Vaughn as his private yacht and he used her for cruising along the American East Coast. She was purchased in 1959 by Barclay H. Warburton III who was to found the American Sail Training Association (ASTA) and become its first President. For the first six years of his ownership, until 1966, Barclay Warburton used the *Black Pearl* for cruising in the Bahamas and between the West Indies and Nova Scotia. In 1964 she was the only private vessel in that year's New York OpSail (the first), with five trainees aboard.

In 1972 Barclay Warburton entered the *Black Pearl* in the Cutty Sark Tall Ships Race from Cowes to the Baltic, the first American vessel ever to take part in those races, along with the US Coast Guard barque *Eagle* (p. 80). It was the success of that voyage that inspired Barclay Warburton to set up the American Sail Training Association along the lines of the British Sail Training Association. In the 1976 trans-Atlantic American Bicentennial Tall Ships Race it was the ASTA that organized the event from Bermuda to Boston via Newport and New York. The *Black Pearl* participated in it under the command of Warburton's son Barclay Warburton IV. The *Black Pearl* has accommodation for up to ten persons with a four berth fo'c's'le, two double cabins and a double master cabin. Barclay Warburton III died prematurely in 1983 and bequeathed the brigantine to the ASTA. However the ASTA had to clear a $15,000 lien against the *Black Pearl* and borrow more money to get her back into shape, and she would not pass US Coast Guard

requirements for sail training with more than six trainees at a time. With such a small payload the bills could never get paid, so the ASTA reluctantly put her up for sale, proceeds to go to its Sail Training Fund.

Fortunately she stayed in the sail training/maritime heritage 'family': she was purchased by the Ship Trust of New York, an organization closely linked to the American National Maritime Historical Society, and put into a holding company, 'Brigantine Black Pearl Inc.' The purpose was to create a sail training programme for the volunteers working on the restoration of the *Wavertree*, a Cape Horn full-rigged ship built in Southampton, England, in 1885 and now preserved at the South Street Seaport museum in New York City. Those volunteers are recruited through advertisements offering 'hard work, long hours, no pay', so they well deserve the opportunity of getting some sailing experience in a smaller but sea-going square rigger. The ASTA was still able to use the *Black Pearl* for sail training for one month a year for a charter fee of $1.

In 1985 the *Black Pearl* was given a thorough overhaul. She took part in the 1986 New York OpSail. A one-hour documentary film called *The brigantine Black Pearl*, a Schumann-O'Brian production supported by the National Maritime Historical Society, was started in 1990; the second part of this production will record the *Black Pearl*'s participation in the trans-Atlantic Columbus Regatta, the 1992 Tall Ships Race from Cadiz to New York via the Canaries and Puerto Rico, one of the festivals marking the 500th anniversary of Columbus' first voyage to the New World.

Name of vessel	Black Pearl
Year built	1951
Designer	Edson Shock
Builder	C. Lincoln Vaughn, Wickford, Rhode Island, USA
Current Owner	Brigantine Black Pearl Inc., New York, USA
Current flag	United States of America
Rig	Brigantine
Construction	Wood
Length extreme	69.5 feet (21.18 m)
Length of hull	59 feet (17.98 m)
Length waterline	41.5 feet (12.65 m)
Beam	15.5 feet (4.72 m)
Draught	8.2 feet (2.50 m)
Tonnage	27 grt; 41 t TM; 36 td
Sail area	1,991 sq. feet (185 m²)
Engine	165 bhp Hercules
Complement	2 volunteer officers + 4 trainees
Photograph date	1972
Photograph location	Kiel, Germany

BLUE CLIPPER

The *Blue Clipper* is a new charter schooner launched in 1990, completed in May 1991 and registered in Karlskrona. She is purpose-built for luxury charters, corporate events and adventure cruises, and is built and fitted out to SOLAS requirements. In October 1991 she took part in the Nioulargue vintage yacht racing off St Tropez, where she was photographed and where she obtained the Third Prize. Later in the same year she set sail for Malaysia and the Far East on a six-month time-charter for a promotion for the French cognac Hennessy. She may remain in Far Eastern waters for a couple of years before sailing back to Europe.

The hull design is semi traditional, with a false clipper bow, a long ballast keel with a cutaway forefoot, and a counter stern with a half-transom. The deck is steel clad in teak and the poop deck is raised.

The rig is traditional; the masts have a slight rake aft and have fidded topmasts. The main mast is taller than the fore and mizzen masts. The mizzen mast is stepped further aft than usual, at the vertical of the propeller, and the mizzen boom overhangs the stern by about two-fifths of its length. This amount of sail area aft is balanced by a substantial fore-triangle supported by a long spike bowsprit.

The fore deckhouse, built around the fore mast, follows the old custom of being the galley; it also shelters the companionway to the fo'c's'le. The midship deckhouse is abaft the main mast and extends slightly beyond the break of the poop. It is a deck saloon and contains stairs leading down to the passenger cabins. A companionway on the poop abaft the midship deckhouse provides access to the officers' quarters and the engine room. The stern deckhouse is the chartroom, with navigational electronics. It also has an 'indoor' steering wheel which is appreciated in bad weather, but the main steering wheel is 'outdoors' on the poop deck, just in front of the chartroom.

The crew accommodation forward consist of 2 two-bunk cabins, port and starboard, just abaft the collision bulkhead, a mess with two tables and two settees that convert at need into two bunks each, and a toilet and shower room. A watertight bulkhead separates this fo'c's'le from the midship accommodation which is fitted out with 6 two-bunk cabins (three to port and three to starboard, with a centreline companion) and, at its after end, a full-beam cabin with a double bed. These are the passenger cabins and all have an en-suite toilet and shower. The aft accommodation is 'officer country', with four single cabins and a shared toilet and shower room.

The engine room is right in the stern. As there is no space to install the engine in the conventional way in direct line with the propeller, the engine is placed facing forward, above the propeller shaft to which it is linked by a belt drive. The propeller is three-bladed and is fully feathering. The speed under power is 8 knots.

The *Blue Clipper*'s equipment is up-to-date. It includes air conditioning, heating, forced ducted ventilation, a freshwater maker (5 tons/day), an IN-MARSAT C telex, SSB and VHF radiotelephones, a Satellite navigator, a Decca navigator, a Brookes & Gatehouse integrated navigation computer, an auto-pilot, a radar, a sonar, automatic fire sprinklers, two Emergency Position Indicating Radio Beacons, and much more.

Name of vessel	Blue Clipper
Year built	1990
Designer	Per Fagerlund
Builder	Mastrandsverken FEAB, Marstrand, Sweden
Current Owner	Svenska Skonarkompaniet, Torslanda, Sweden
Current flag	Sweden
Rig	Three-masted schooner
Construction	Steel; teak-clad deck
Length extreme	144.4 feet (44.00 m)
Length of hull	105.0 feet (32.00 m)
Length waterline	88.6 feet (27.00 m)
Beam	24.3 feet (7.40 m)
Draught	13.1 feet (4.00 m)
Tonnage	137 grt; 210 td
Sail area	7,266 sq. feet (675 m^2)
Engine	315 bhp Caterpillar
Complement	8 crew + 14 passengers
Photograph date	1991
Photograph location	St Tropez, France

BLUENOSE II

The *Bluenose II* is the exact replica of the legendary Grand Banks racing fishing-schooner *Bluenose*. The fishermen from Nova Scotia, Newfoundland and New England had evolved superb schooners to fish the far-from-sedate banks off their coasts. Their crews of true salts watched with amazement the vast fortunes sunk into the *America's* Cup challenges and with amusement the expensive, delicate toys built for those races. When in 1920 an *America's* Cup race was postponed because of a mere 23 knots of wind, the editor of a Halifax newspaper put up the International Fishermen's Trophy and substantial prize money for a race between *real* sail carriers — between genuine American and Canadian fishing schooners. After eliminatory trials as in *America's* Cup racing, the *Esperanto* of Gloucester, Massachusetts, won the first Trophy on 1 November 1920 over the *Delawana* of Lunenburg.

With national pride at stake significant money moved in (but nothing like the megabucks of the *America's* Cup) but the crews remained fishermen and the schooners had to fish commercially before being eligible for the competition. The *Bluenose*, named after the Nova Scotians' nickname (because of the cold damp climate), was designed by William Roue, and was skippered by the redoutable Angus Walters until she was sold abroad. She was every bit a Lunenburg fishing schooner although her masts were a bit taller and her keel a bit deeper. Three weeks after her launch in March 1921 she sailed on her maiden voyage, a fishing trip — and she brought back the biggest catch of the fleet. On 21 October she raced against the American *Elsie* and won the Trophy. Despite many challenges she was never to let go of it. Even the magnificent *Gertrude*

L. Thebaud was unable to wrest the Trophy from her in the last IFT race in 1938. Then the war and changing times put an end to the fishing schooners, those Queens of all fore-and-afters, and hence to the Trophy. The *Bluenose* was sold in 1942 to a West Indian company for freighting in southern waters. Sadly she was wrecked on a reef off Haiti on 29 January 1946.

The *Bluenose II* was ordered built as an exact replica by the Halifax brewery Oland & Son Ltd. She was built at the very same yard that had built the original and even some of the men employed for the building of the replica had worked on the original! Launched on 23 July 1963 she only required a crew of 14 instead of the original's 29, as there are a few modern aids aboard such as hydraulics to raise the anchor and sails and, almost inevitably, two 'infernal' combustion machines.

After eight years in the charter trade the *Bluenose II* was sold in 1971 to the Government of Nova Scotia for $1 and she now fulfils the dual role of Nova Scotia's ambassador at large and as a tourist attraction at home. As ambassador she sails to other Canadian Provinces and to the USA to promote Nova Scotia, and she takes part in tall ships gatherings such as the Canadian Windjammer Rally of 1974, the New York OpSails of '76 and '86 and at Quebec in '84. In 1992 she will be celebrating the 125th anniversary of the Canadian Confederation by sailing to Toronto. She will be calling on the way at Montreal which will be celebrating its 350th anniversary. As a tourist attraction, when in Halifax, she runs three two-hour trips a day out of the harbour, with up to 80 deck passengers. Her crew consists of 6 afterguard (her master Don Barr, an engineer, 3 mates and a cook) and 12 young deckhands signed on for the season.

Name of vessel	Bluenose II
Year built	1963
Designer	William Roue
Builder	Smith & Rhuland Ltd., Lunenburg, Nova Scotia, Canada
Current Owner	Government of the Province of Nova Scotia
Current flag	Canada
Rig	Gaff schooner
Construction	Wood
Length extreme	160.5 feet (48.92 m)
Length of hull	143 feet (43.58 m)
Length waterline	112 feet (34.14 m)
Beam	27 feet (8.23 m)
Draught	15.8 feet (4.82 m)
Tonnage	191 grt; 96 nrt; 285 td
Sail area	12,594 sq. feet (1,170 m^2)
Engines	2 × 250 hp Caterpillar; twin propellers
Complement	18 crew + 80 deck passengers
Photograph date	1982
Photograph location	Philadelphia, Pennsylvania, USA

BOUNTY

The original *Bounty* was a former merchant ship, the *Bethia* of Hull, built in 1784. She had been bought and renamed by the Admiralty for a voyage to the South Seas under the command of Lt. William Bligh. The mutiny led by her mate Fletcher Christian, on 28 April 1789, has inspired countless books and three feature films. The *Bounty* featured here is the one built for the third film and the only movie *Bounty* to be an externally accurate replica of the original.

The rig is entirely authentic and the ship has to be handled under sail exactly the same way as in the 18th century. Instrument dials and engine controls are hidden in the replica binnacle. The engine exhausts are disguised as kevels. The hull is actually built of steel, clad in wood above waterline.

Below deck there was no attempt to follow period style. There were lateral ballast trim tanks to give the ship photogenic angles of heel and even to sink and raise her; there were powerful generators for filming floodlights, dressing rooms, a make-up room, a lab in which to develop the rushes, etc. And twin engines.

The *Bounty* was built for a David Lean project, but by the time of her launch in December 1978 the project was in deep trouble. The building costs had vastly exceeded estimates and the ship was in the eye of a legal and financial hurricane. Except for the sea trials in March 1979 and a few local goodwill tours for charity, the *Bounty* remained in Whangarei. Eventually she was acquired by the Dino De Laurentiis Corporation and filming of *The Bounty* went ahead in 1983, in Tahiti and New Zealand, under the direction of Bernard William, with Mel Gibson as Fletcher Christian and Anthony Hopkins as Lt. Bligh.

The *Bounty* sailed to Los Angeles for the launch of the film and was laid up there for sale. She was sold in 1986 to Bounty Voyages Ltd, of Sydney, and registered in England. She sailed to Vancouver for Expo 86 and was converted there for adventure cruises with fee-paying guests. However her next charter was for another film, a TV dramatised documentary serial about Captain Cook, for which she returned to Tahiti.

She then sailed to Australia and on to England for the First Fleet Re-enactment. She had been chartered to be part of that fleet commemorating Australia's Bicentenary. The Fleet left from the Solent on 13 May 1987. After calls in Tenerife, at Rio and Capetown, in Mauritius and at Fremantle, the Fleet sailed into Sydney harbour on Australia Day, 26 January 1988. With other 'First Fleet' ships the *Bounty* then engaged in a series of cruises along the coasts of Australia until June 1988.

The *Bounty* then made a number of cruises in the South Pacific, New Zealand and Queensland. On 3 April 1989 she set sail from Tahiti under the command of Captain Ron Bligh-Ware, a descendant of Lt. Bligh. On 28 April the *Bounty* was off Tofua, Tonga, two hundred years to the day and on the very spot where the mutiny had occurred — and Capt. Bligh-Ware ceded command to his mate, Lt. Cdr. Gerry Christian, a descendent of Fletcher Christian!

Shortly after that voyage the *Bounty* was stationed in Sydney to run short harbour trips. On 20 June 1991 she was sold by auction to an American syndicate, but those buyers defaulted and on 6 July the ship was bought by Bruce Reid, a Sydney property and shipping businessman. The *Bounty* is still in Sydney operating harbour trips.

Name of vessel	Bounty
Year built	1978–9
Builder	Whangarei Engineering Co., Whangarei, New Zealand
Current Owner	Pitcairn Shipping Co. Ltd, Hong Kong (subsidiary of Minnamarras Enterprises Pty Ltd, Sydney)
Current flag	UK
Rig	Full-rigged ship
Construction	Steel (wood-clad); wood-clad deck
Length extreme	137.8 feet (42.00 m)
Length of hull	105.0 feet (32.00 m)
Length waterline	86.8 feet (24.47 m)
Beam	24.8 feet (7.57 m)
Draught	12.5 feet (3.81 m)
Tonnage	247.40 grt; 168.23 nrt; 205 t TM; 387 td
Sail area	7,500 sq. feet (697 m²)
Engines	2 × 415 hp Kelvin; twin propellers
Complement	13 crew + 25 cruise participants or 75 day passengers
Photograph date	1987
Photograph location	Solent, England

CENTURION

The *Centurion* was built as a luxury yacht for the private use of her owner, a British gentleman, and she flies the white ensign of the Royal Yacht Squadron. She was designed for long distance cruising in maximum comfort and with minimum crew. She is obviously no traditional, old-fashioned brigantine.

All the sails are roller furling and can be rolled manually or electrically from the deck. The aluminium yards are all standing and their sails, bent to a rotating jackstay under the yard, roll up like window blinds. The staysails and headsails roll on their stays and the fore and main sails roll on a jackstay abaft the mast. One person can set and trim the sails from either wheel position. The *Centurion* probably has the most advanced automatic sail handling system built on a yacht to date.

The hull and superstructures are built in aluminium; the clipper bow is adorned by trailboards and a figurehead (representing a Tahitian princess) carved by Norman Gaches, the Isle of Wight ship-carver.

The deck is teak-clad and flush. The aft deck is an uncluttered open space with two aft-facing settees, a deck dining table and the 'outdoor' steering wheel. The large deckhouse (over 350 sq. ft. – 33 m^2) is at deck level and serves as deck saloon, chartroom and wheelhouse.

A companion leads down forward from the deckhouse to the main saloon which features a large gimballed dining table, a cosy corner with a coffee table, and a wet bar. A door in the saloon's fore bulkhead leads down to the galley. Four steps lead down through the aft bulkhead to a library. In addition to book shelves, a table and an Apple computer, it has its own shower and WC for day guests and whoever might sleep on the library's sofa which converts into a bed. The guest cabin, opposite the library, to port, is fitted with twin beds and an en-suite bathroom. The owner's suite is aft – a very large cabin with two beds (one double and one single), and with an en-suite bathroom featuring a full size bath tub and a bidet.

The crew quarters, forward, consist of two cabins with upper and lower bunks (the uppers can be extended to form double berths), a shared washroom and a mess opposite the galley.

The engine room, which has full standing headroom, is located beneath the saloon; it is accessed through a door in the crew's quarters, by the galley.

Sadly, all was not plain sailing. When completed the *Centurion* floated 12 inches below her marks *and* was tender. The rig was one ton overweight and a number of construction defects were noted. The *Centurion* was sailed 'down' to Fort Lauderdale, Florida, where she was made fit for sea, and then sailed over to Cowes for a proper rebuild. After lengthy legal wrangles the yacht was made good at Cowes, including new, lighter masts, proper through-hull fittings, and a new keel with a lower centre of gravity was installed.

Then, whilst en route for the Canaries in early 1985, the *Centurion* ran aground on the Portuguese coast. After some on-the-spot repairs she sailed back to Coles yard in Cowes where, in addition to making good the damage caused by the grounding, the yacht was given another extensive overhaul, with some changes to the accommodation and a complete updating of her equipment. That refit was completed in 1989 and the *Centurion* is now happily cruising in the Mediterranean.

Name of vessel	Centurion
Year built	1983
Designer	MacLear & Harris, New York
Builder	Palmer Johnson, Wisconsin, USA
Current Owner	Mr J.H. Millar
Current flag	British registered in Bermuda
Rig	Brigantine
Construction	Aluminium; teak-clad deck
Length extreme	110 feet (33.53 m)
Length on deck	90 feet (27.43 m)
Length waterline	77 feet (23.47 m)
Beam	21 feet (6.40 m)
Draught	11.5 feet (3.50 m)
Tonnage	109 td
Engine	215 hp Caterpillar
Complement	4 crew + 4 in owner's party (max: 6+6)
Photograph date	1989
Photograph location	Off the Isle of Wight, England

CHARLES W. MORGAN

The *Charles W. Morgan* was built in the heyday of Yankee whaling, when more than 700 New England whaling ships plied the Pacific, Indian and Atlantic Oceans and earned fortunes for their owners.

Named after her first principal owner, she was built as a full-rigged ship; it was only in 1867 that her rig was changed to a barque, to economize on manpower. The deep single main topsail was replaced by a double topsail in 1881; the fore topsail was likewise split in 1883. The double topsail arrangement is a labour-saving device, obviating the need to reef, which first appeared in the mid-1850s.

From 1841 to 1886 the *Charles W. Morgan* made ten voyages from New Bedford to the Pacific and one each to the South Atlantic and Indian Ocean. The whaling grounds near New England had already been depleted by the end of the 18th century and the distances to the Pacific and Indian Ocean grounds called for big ships that remained on station for years on end, until their holds were full, to minimize passage costs. By 1886 the New England whaling industry was in decline; many of its ships had been sunk by Confederate raiders during the Civil War (1861–65); whale products were less in demand (notably lamp oil, replaced by paraffin) and the sort of whales it caught were becoming harder to find.

In 1886 the *Charles W. Morgan* left New Bedford for new but seasonal whaling grounds in the Behring, Beaufort and Okhotsk Seas. Like many other New England whalers, she was then based at San Francisco, a more convenient wintering and refit harbour. She returned to New Bedford in 1904 and made a further three voyages, to the South Atlantic and Indian Ocean, before being laid up at Fairhaven in 1913. She was recommissioned in 1916 and made another four voyages. Her last, her 37th all told, ended on 28 May 1921.

The *Charles W. Morgan* was re-rigged as a ship in 1922 for a couple of film productions. In 1924 she was bought by Colonel E.H.R. Green, a wealthy grandson of one of her principal owners in the 1850s, and he berthed her near New Bedford as a museum ship. She was eventually given to the Mystic Seaport Museum in 1941. She was preserved at Mystic, with some maintenance, in a sand berth until 1973 when she was refloated after repairs to her bottom. The following year she was rerigged once more as a barque. Her detailed appearance in the period 1883–85 is very well documented by photographs and other records, whereas there are no surviving pictures of her from her early days; so rather than restore her to a supposed 1841 appearance, she has been accurately restored to the very well documented period of 1883–85, as a barque with double topsails, with a galley house forward and with a 'hurricane house' built on her stern. The hurricane house is a typical New England whaling ship feature that appeared in the 1860s — two small deckhouses at the aft corners of the deck and linked by an awning deck which sheltered the helmsman. The helm is typical of New England whaling ships: the wheel and its drum are mounted on the tiller itself, the ends of the tiller rope being made fast to the sides of the deck. Other typical features are the heavy wooden davits for the whaleboats, the tryworks on deck where the blubber was tried (rendered), the cutting stage along the starboard side of the hull and the lookout hoops above the crosstrees.

The *Charles W. Morgan* underwent a long term extensive rebuild from 1980 to 1984 and her future is well assured for the foreseeable future.

Name of vessel	Charles W. Morgan
Year built	1841
Designer	J. & Z. Hillman
Builder	Jethro & Zachariah Hillman, Fairhaven, Massachusetts, USA
Current Owner	Mystic Seaport Museum Inc., Mystic, Connecticut
Current flag	USA
Rig	Barque
Construction	Wood
Length extreme	169 feet (51.51 m)
Length of hull	118.8 feet (36.20 m)
Registered length	105.6 feet (32.19 m)
Beam	27.7 feet (8.44 m)
Draught	17.5 feet (5.33 m)
Tonnage	313 grt; 296 nrt
Sail area	8,590 sq. feet (798 m^2)
Engine	None
Complement	30 to 38 men (in the past)
Photograph date	1990
Photograph location	Mystic Seaport, Mystic, Connecticut, USA

CHARLOTTE RHODES

The *Charlotte Rhodes* is a ship known to millions thanks to her star role in the BBC TV 'The Onedin Line' serial — a nautical soap opera which was produced throughout most of the 1970s.

This vessel was launched under the name of *Christian* for the Danish shipowner Christian Mortensen. It is claimed that she was the first Danish three-masted schooner to have been built as an auxiliary schooner — with an engine from the outset — and she had a baldheaded rig (without topmasts or topsails). She was originally employed carrying dried fish on the North Atlantic run.

In the mid and late Sixties she was still trading under the Dannebrog (the Danish flag) under the name of *Meta Jan*. She had been recently laid up for sale when purchased in 1968 by Captain Jim 'Mac' Mackreth, a retired British airline captain. He renamed her *Charlotte Rhodes* and transferred her to the British registry. With his wife Monty he spent thousands of hours and of pounds refitting the vessel and rigging her up as a fine-looking three-masted topsail schooner.

Below decks she was left as she had always been — a traditional crew fo'c's'le with four bunks and little else; the master's quarters aft under the slightly raised poop deck and monkey poop; and, between the two accommodation areas, two cargo holds with cargo hatches and the engine room. The holds used to be loaded with up to 160 tons of cargo. Thirty tons of ballast were put in the bilges and tongue-and-groove oak floors were installed in the holds which were otherwise unconverted until 1974 when some rough bunks were put in around the sides.

The *Charlotte Rhodes*, which was based at Dartmouth, was chartered part time by the BBC for the filming of the series *The Onedin Line* until 1975. The schooner was also chartered out for advertising promotions and by parties of traditional sail enthusiasts. The owner's resources plus the revenue from film and other charters were not, however, on a scale commensurate with the problems of the ageing schooner.

In 1975, after some *Onedin Line* shooting off Devon and some Channel cruises with sailing enthusiasts, the *Charlotte Rhodes* was chartered for a round-Britain voyage by an office-computer company, as an itinerant showroom. On that voyage the *Charlotte Rhodes* called in the Pool of London in August for a tall ships gathering and then sailed up the East Coast to the Caledonian Canal which she transited. While on a passage to Swansea she was caught in a gale and a garboard strake worked loose and the holds were flooded. The schooner was towed into Belfast in a near-sinking condition. The Board of Trade declared her unseaworthy.

She was laid up for sale and some months later she was sold for £45,000 to Mr Tido Gedeonse, a Dutch businessman. He took her to near Amsterdam where, in 1977, he spent nearly as much again in redecorating the schooner, not on a rebuild. She was chartered out for cruises on Dutch inland waters until stopped from doing so by the Dutch authorities. She was put up for sale again, with an asking price of £90,000. While waiting to find a buyer she was arrested for some harbour 'parking' offence and taken to the Entrepot Dock in Amsterdam. There, in the very early hours of 12 October 1979, someone poured petrol in her bilges and set her alight. She burned down to the waterline in a couple of hours. Although the police believed they knew who the arsonist was, no charge was made, through lack of proof.

Name of vessel	Charlotte Rhodes, *ex-*Meta Jan, *ex-*Christian
Year built	1904
Builder	F. Hoffman, Fjelleborn, Fyn, Denmark
Last owner	Stichting Charlotte Rhodes, The Netherlands
Last flag	The Netherlands
Rig	Three-masted topsail schooner
Construction	Wood
Length extreme	125 feet (38.10 m)
Length of hull	88.4 feet (26.94 m)
Beam	21.8 feet (6.64 m)
Draught	7.6 feet (2.32 m)
Tonnage	102 grt; 5 nrt; 160 tdw
Sail area	3,700 sq. feet (344 m^2)
Engine	210 hp Rolls Royce
Complement	5 crew + 18 cruise participants
Photograph date	1971
Photograph location	Cowes, England

CHRISTIAN RADICH

The Norwegians have always been a strong seafaring nation and when it became necessary to replace the Oslo Schoolship Association's brig *Statsraad Erichsen*, they commissioned a new 676-ton full-rigged ship. With money donated by a benefactor, Mr Christian Radich, the ship was built in Sandefjord and launched in 1937. The following year she sailed to New York for the World Fair.

The *Christian Radich* sailed back to Norway late in 1939, and was placed under the control of the Norwegian Navy. She was seized by the Germans at Horten, near Oslo, and was used by them as a submarine depot ship. She was taken to Germany in 1943, and in 1945 she was found by the Allies at Flensburg in a capsized condition and without her masts or equipment. She was towed back to Norway to the yard that had built her, for rebuilding.

She resumed her schoolship operations in 1947. In 1956–57 she went on a long trans-Atlantic cruise during which the wide-screen Cinerama film *Windjammer* was shot aboard. The shanty-singing bo'sun in that production was 34-year old actor Lasse Kolstad and he caught 'ship fever' on that voyage — that is, he fell in love with the ship. He was to spearhead the campaign to save her from being laid up and possibly scrapped in the early Seventies and became a member of her Board of Trustees, of which he is today the Chairman.

In the 1970s the *Christian Radich* also played a leading role in *The Onedin Line* TV series, like the *Charlotte Rhodes* on the preceding page. In 1976 she took part in the American Bicentennial trans-Atlantic Tall Ships Race and her master, Captain Kjell Thoresen, was married aboard during the call at New York. In 1978 she set out on a long voyage to the West Indies and the US West and East Coast, returning to Norway in 1980.

She then underwent a major refit and accommodation modernization (with bunks replacing hammocks) from which she emerged in 1983. She took part in the Quebec Tall Ships Parade in 1984. In 1986 she sailed to the New York OpSail marking the Centennial and re-dedication of the Statue of Liberty, and Captain Thoresen and his wife, who had sailed with him, were able to celebrate the 10th anniversary of their wedding aboard and in the same place where they had been married.

With the reduction of the demand by the Norwegian merchant navy for new officers, funding of the *Christian Radich* had become somewhat erratic and unpredictable. In an attempt to earn some of her own keep she operated a series of one-week passenger cruises in the Canaries over the Christmas 1987 period, with a limited number of passengers aboard. Likewise, during the winters 88–89 and 89–90, she operated three-month 'residential' sea-semesters with 70 Norwegian school students, in the Mediterranean.

Her normal schoolship programme involves 88 young men and women envisaging a career at sea and the course normally runs from August through to June, with adaptations as necessary to fit in other activities. In 1992 the *Christian Radich* will be taking part in the Columbus Regatta, the Tall Ships trans-Atlantic Race marking the 500th anniversary of the discovery of America.

Name of vessel	Christian Radich
Year built	1937
Designer	Captain Christian Blom
Builder	Framnæs Mek. Verksted A/S, Sandefjord, Norway
Current Owner	Ostlandets Skoleskib, Oslo, Norway
Current flag	Norway
Rig	Full-rigged ship
Construction	Steel. Teak-clad deck
Length extreme	241.1 feet (73.50 m)
Length of hull	205.1 feet (62.50 m)
Length between perpendiculars	175.0 feet (53.35 m)
Beam	32.0 feet (9.76 m)
Draught	15.5 feet (4.72 m)
Tonnage	676 grt; 208 nrt; 773t TM
Sail area	13,283 sq. feet (1,234 m^2)
Engine	450 hp General Motors
Complement	16 crew + 88 cadets
Photograph date	1976
Photograph location	Plymouth, England

USS CONSTITUTION

Because American shipping was being preyed upon by North African corsairs the US Congress passed a bill in 1794 creating the Federal Navy of the United States of America and authorizing the construction of six frigates. Three of these were to be 44-gun frigates, the other three, 36-gun frigates.

The *Constitution* was the first forty-four to be laid down. Like her sisters and the thirty-sixes, she was designed to outclass any similarly rated European frigate and to outsail the more powerful ships-of-the-line.

The American forty-fours were the biggest frigates of their time. Whereas the gun deck of European frigates was open to the sky in the waist, the American frigates had an upper deck connecting the poop deck to the fo'c's'le deck. This spar deck, as it was called, was light and un-armed but it facilitated sail handling and boarding action.

Construction of the frigates was suspended in 1795 when the Dey of Algiers sued for peace, but was resumed in 1797 on account of troublesome French privateers in the West Indies. The *Constitution* captured a few French privateers and their prizes and that quasi war with France was over in 1801. In 1803 the Barbary Corsairs, notably the Tripolitans, were again causing trouble and the *Constitution* was sent out to the Mediterranean as flagship of a squadron consisting of another frigate, two brigs and three schooners. She sailed home in 1807.

Meanwhile relations with England were fast de-

teriorating owing to Royal Navy ships boarding American vessels on the high seas to press any British seamen found aboard and even some American citizens. There was an outcry in the States for 'Free trade and sailors' rights' and Congress declared war on 18 June 1812. The *Constitution* distinguished herself in that war with the captures of the 38-gun frigates HMS *Guerriere* and HMS *Java*, and of the 32-gun frigate HMS *Cyane* and the 20-gun sloop-o'-war HMS *Levant* which had engaged her simultaneously from different quarters. The *Constitution* acquired her nickname of 'Old Ironsides' during her action against the *Guerriere*, when round shot was seen bouncing off her hull.

In 1830 there was talk of scrapping the *Constitution* but she was saved by the emotive poem *Old Ironsides* by Oliver Wendell Holmes. She remained on active duty until 1855, after which she became a naval training ship. She last sailed in 1881.

She was restored as an historic ship in 1907 and was rebuilt in the late Twenties. She made, under tow, a grand tour of 90 US ports on the East, Gulf and West Coasts in 1931–34, where she was visited by 4,614,792 people. Since then she has been berthed at Boston as a museum ship — but also, since 1941, in commission as the flagship of the First Naval District.

She underwent a major rebuild in 1973–76. Her condition these days is so sound that she could be fitted out to sail again if the money and will were available. An oak grove was planted in 1976 to provide the timber for her next major refit in 2018.

Name of vessel	Constitution
Year built	1797
Designer	Joshua Humphreys, Josiah Fox and William Doughty
Builder	Edmund Hart Yard, Boston, Massachusetts
Current Owner	United States Navy
Current flag	United States of America
Rig	Full-rigged ship
Construction	Wood
Length extreme	305 feet (92.96 m)
Length of hull	204 feet (62.18 m)
Length between perpendiculars	175 feet (53.34 m)
Beam	43.5 feet (13.26 m)
Draught	23 feet (7.01 m) (best sailing draught)
Tonnage	2,200 td
Sail area	42,720 sq. feet (3,969 m^2), including stun'sails
Engine	None
Complement	about 450 officers and men during the War of 1812
Armament	main battery = 30 long 12-pounder guns; topside batteries = 22 32-pounder carronades + 2 18-pounder guns
Photograph date	1990
Photograph location	Boston, Massachusetts, USA

CREOLE

The magnificent *Creole* is one of the world's big classic vintage yachts. She was designed and built by Camper & Nicholson's for Mr Alex Smith Cochrane but she was sold before completion to Major Maurice Pope and Sir Connop Guthrie. The *Creole* is composite-built with 4 in. (10 cm) teak planking over steel frames and her bottom is copper-sheathed.

The yacht was requisitioned by the Admiralty during the Second World War, for use as an auxiliary naval vessel. Her masts were cut off and she was demagnetized for mine sweeping and anti-submarine patrols off Scotland. After the war she was returned in a very beaten-up condition to the Camper & Nicholson's yard at Southampton where she remained laid-up until 1951 when she was bought by Mr Stavros Niarchos, the Greek shipping magnate. He had her registered in Bermuda. In 1956 he lent her to a British crew who entered her in the first Tall Ships Race, from Torbay to Lisbon, and the *Creole* won second place in that race. Niarchos made much use of the *Creole*, living aboard much of the time and running his shipping business from the yacht at such times.

After the tragic death of his wife, Niarchos lost interest in the *Creole* which remained laid-up in Piraeus until she was sold, in August 1978, to the Danish firm Thomas Brockelbank, the shipowning branch of the Nyborg Søfartskole (Nyborg Seamanship School). This is a cooperative of 15 private schools and 400 teachers which also owned and operated a number of other tall ships. The *Creole* was, for a very short while after the purchase, renamed *Mistral*, but she quickly reverted to her original name, under the same ownership. She was given a perfunctory refit at Piraeus and sailed on 17 August for Nyborg, Denmark, where she arrived on 13 September. There she was also given a rebuild which was also partly a demolition job as the fine yacht accommodations were converted to schoolship dormitories. She set sail on her first training voyage on 4 June 1979, to West Africa, the West Indies and Spain. Her second course, in 1980, was from Malaga to Santo Domingo and Boston, where she joined the Tall Ships Race to Kristiansand, Norway, and from Frederikshavn, Denmark, to Amsterdam. At that time she had 12 crew including two teachers, and 38 trainees half of whom were professional trainees who paid for their own berths, the other half being 'problem kids' who were community sponsored.

In September 1983 the *Creole* was sold to a Panamanian company representing Mr Maurizio Gucci, the Italian fashion designer. By that time the old yacht, which had suffered a fair share of technical mishaps under the Nyborg management, was fairly run down and needed just the sort of owner she had just acquired. The *Creole* was given a three-week provisional refit at Nyborg and sailed on 22 October on delivery to Monte Carlo, a passage that should have taken 21 days but which ended up taking 47, with heavy weather and exhaust problems. From Monte Carlo the *Creole* went to La Spezia, Italy, for a two-year, £2 million refit, from which she emerged once again as a luxury yacht. She was photographed at the 1991 Nioulargue vintage yacht event at St Tropez and she is usually based at the Club de Mar at Palma de Mallorca. In early 1992 she set sail for San Diego for the *America's* Cup events.

Name of vessel	Creole, ex-Mistral, ex-Creole
Year built	1927
Designer	Camper & Nicholson's
Builder	Camper & Nicholson's, Southampton, England
Current Owner	Mr Gucci, Italy
Current flag	British registered in the Bahamas
Rig	Three-masted staysail schooner
Construction	Composite
Length extreme	214.2 feet (65.30 m)
Length of hull	189.6 feet (57.80 m)
Length between perpendiculars	166.7 feet (50.80 m)
Beam	30.8 feet (9.40 m)
Draught	16.4 feet (5.00 m)
Tonnage	433.91 grt; 272.06 nrt; 697 td
Sail area	21.958 sq. feet (2,040 m^2) (total)
Engines	2 × 1,250 hp; twin propellers
Complement	25 crew + 10 Owner's party
Photograph date	1991
Photograph location	St Tropez, France (Nioulargue)

CUTTY SARK

Today the *Cutty Sark* is the sole preserved and restored example of the ultimate sailing ships that were the clippers. She was built for the tea trade for Jock 'White Hat' Willis, a shipmaster turned owner and established in London. He had commissioned a young architect, Hercules Linton, to design and build him a clipper capable of outpacing the *Thermopylae*, allegedly the fastest clipper on the China run. In earlier days big premiums were paid to the first clipper to bring the new season's tea from China and although that premium had been discontinued, the spirit of racing and consequent big wagers lived on.

The *Cutty Sark* was first home on her first voyage, in 1870, and second home the following year, but the *Thermopylae* had not been in the running those years. Both 'raced' in 1872 but the *Cutty Sark* lost her rudder and lost ten days jury-rigging at sea a makeshift rudder. She sailed into London only seven days after her rival. The following year the *Thermopylae* did beat the *Cutty Sark* in a fair race but on that voyage the *Cutty Sark* was commanded by a master who was not made of racing-skipper stuff.

The *Cutty Sark* made her last tea voyage in 1875–76: the opening of the Suez Canal the very year she was launched opened up the tea trade to the steamers; the clippers could not avail themselves of that shorter route on account of prevailing winds. By 1877 it was no longer economical to carry tea in clippers and the *Cutty Sark* was engaged in Indian Ocean and Far East tramping with general and varied cargoes until 1883 when she entered the Australian wool trade. That trade, the clippers' last refuge, involved circumnavigating voyages by way of Good Hope, Leeuwin and the Horn and lots of 'easting down' the Roaring Forties. Consequently the *Cutty Sark*'s rig was shortened: her

skysail was removed and her masts were shortened. This actually improved her sailing performance in all but the lightest of airs. In that trade she proved more than a match for the *Thermopylae*, particularly from 1884 onwards when she was under the command of her best master, Captain Richard Woodget.

In 1895 the *Cutty Sark* was sold to J.A. Ferreira of Lisbon who renamed her *Ferreira* and engaged her in the Portuguese colonial trade. Following a dismasting in a cyclone in 1916 she was re-rigged as a barquentine. In 1920 she was sold to the Companha Nacional de Navegação who renamed her *Maria do Amparo*. It was under that name that she was recognized as the former *Cutty Sark* by Captain Wilfred Dowman. He brought her back under British ownership in 1922 and turned her into a stationary schoolship. In 1938 after his death his widow presented the ship to the Thames Nautical College which kept her in the same employment.

In 1951 she was donated to the Cutty Sark Preservation Society (since then shortened to Cutty Sark Society) and in 1954 she was placed in a dry dock specially built for her, the one where she now is. She was restored to the appearance she had in her tea clipper days and was opened to the public by Queen Elizabeth II on 25 June 1957. In her 'tween deck there are exhibits relating to her history and the China tea trade, and her lower hold houses the world's finest collection of merchant ship figureheads. The *Cutty Sark* is one of London's most popular tourist attractions, welcoming almost half a million visitors a year at her permanent dock in Greenwich. In 1989 her management merged with that of the Maritime Trust. In March 1992 a £2 million public appeal was launched to renew her masts, her weather deck and her keel.

Name of vessel	Cutty Sark, ex-Maria do Amparo, ex-Ferreira, ex-Cutty Sark
Year built	1869
Designer	Hercules Linton
Builder	Scott & Linton at Dumbarton; completed by William Denny & Bros., Leven, Scotland
Current Owner	Maritime Trust, Greenwich, London
Current flag	United Kingdom
Rig	Full-rigged ship
Construction	Composite; teak deck
Length extreme	280 feet (85.34 m)
Length of hull	224 feet (68.28 m)
Length between perpendiculars	212.5 feet (64.77 m)
Beam	36 feet (10.97 m)
Draught	20 feet (6.10 m) (load)
Tonnage	963 grt; 921 nrt; 2,100 td
Sail area	32,800 sq. feet (3,047 m²)
Engine	None
Complement	19–28 men (24 on average, in her sailing days)
Photograph date	1981
Photograph location	Greenwich, England

DANMARK

Following the tragic disappearance of the five-masted barque *København* and all her seventy-five souls aboard, during a passage from Argentina to Australia around New Year 1929, and the sale later that year of the four-masted barque *Viking* to the Åland shipowner Gustaf Erikson, Merchant Navy sail training in Denmark was taken over by the State. They ordered the construction of a new ship to be named *Danmark*. She was launched on 19 November 1932 and commissioned in June 1933.

For six years she carried out her duties for Denmark until 1939 when the outbreak of war found her attending the World Trade Fair at New York. She was ordered by her management not to return to Europe. She was laid up at Jacksonville, Florida. When the United States entered the war in December 1941 she was put at the disposal of the United States Coast Guard which used her as a training ship. She trained more than 5,000 Coast Guard cadets. Her performance was so appreciated by the USCG that they decided to carry on sail training after the war with the German war prize barque *Horst Wessel* which they renamed *Eagle* (see p. 80).

As for the *Danmark*, she returned to her home country on 13 November 1945 and resumed her normal peace time duties the following year.

The *Danmark* operated a very regular annual routine until 1990. She ran two five-month training cruises a year, one for apprentices (midshipmen) and the other to teach basic seamanship. The first cruise would start in January from La Spezia, Italy, and the ship would sail via the Canaries and sometimes the West Indies to the East Coast of the United States (where she is always assured of an excellent welcome by the Coast Guard), thence back home to Denmark where she would spend a couple of months in refit. The second cruise would start from Copenhagen in August and, with a number of calls on the way, would proceed to the Canaries, thence to La Spezia where the crew and cadets would head for their homes shortly before Christmas. With such a busy turnaround the *Danmark* had two masters and two crews, one for each cruise.

Some years the schedule was somewhat altered in order to participate in Tall Ships Races and sail parades. The *Danmark* usually takes part in the trans-Atlantic Tall Ships Races and events (such as the 1976 Tall Ships Race and the 1986 New York OpSail) and she will be taking part in the 1992 Columbus trans-Atlantic 'Regatta'.

The *Danmark* has mixed trainee crews since 1983.

In 1990 she underwent the third of a major refit — the remainder to be scheduled in future years as funds become available. The hull was sandblasted and completely repainted from bare steel; new generators were fitted; the mizzen mast was completely overhauled and the fore and main mast shrouds were replaced. The trainees still sleep in hammocks.

The training programme is now reduced to one cruise a year — the basic seamanship training course — following the non-renewal of a contract with the shipowning firm A.P. Møller which had to give up the expense of having its young officers trained under sail. This also means that the *Danmark* now only has one permanent crew.

Name of vessel	Danmark
Year built	1932
Designer	Aage Larsen, Denmark
Builder	Nakskov Shipyard, Lolland, Denmark
Current Owner	Direktoratet for Søfartsuddannelsen, Copenhagen
Current flag	Denmark
Rig	Full-rigged ship
Construction	Steel; teak deck
Length extreme	252.6 feet (77.00 m)
Length of hull	212.3 feet (64.70 m)
Length between perpendiculars	178.8 feet (54.50 m)
Beam	32.8 feet (10.00 m)
Draught	14.7 feet (4.47 m)
Tonnage	790 grt; 216 nrt; 845t TM; 150 tdw
Sail area	17,610 sq. feet (1,636 m²)
Engine	486 hp Frichs
Complement	19 crew + 80 cadets
Photograph date	1972
Photograph location	Kiel, Germany

DAR MŁODZIEŻY

The *Dar Mlodziezy*'s name (pronounced 'Dar Mwajy-ezhy') means 'Gift of Youth' because the financing of the ship's construction was largely funded by contributions from the youth of Poland. This vessel was built as replacement for the ageing *Dar Pomorza* (see next spread) and she is appreciably larger. The *Dar Mlodziezy* trains up to 150 students from Gdynia's Merchant Marine Academy, to which she belongs, although she sometimes also provides berths for students of the Szczecin Merchant Navy school. In recent years she has also been accepting some foreign fare-paying adventure trainees and passengers to supplement her hard currency budget.

With some counselling by the late Captain Kazimierz Jurkiewicz, former master of the *Dar Pomorza*, the *Dar Mlodziezy* was designed by the naval architect Zygmunt Choreń. She incorporates lots of modern and novel ideas. The masts are made of a single tapered tube. The tops, instead of being half-moon shaped, are nearly triangular. Similar but smaller platforms are set over the topgallant and royal cross-trees, and rattled royal shrouds lead to the royal tops. Such shrouds (and tops) do not exist on traditional rigs but with standing yards it is necessary to climb all the way up the royal mast to furl its sail. All the yards on the *Dar Mlodziezy* are standing, obviating the need to hoist them when setting sail. There are three decks, with a flush upper or spardeck linking the poop to the fo'c's'le, and the accommodation is on two decks. Gone is the open plan berth deck with hammocks (or in some modernized ships, with tiers of bunks), a legacy from the men-o'war: the cadets sleep in six 25-bunk dormitories so that watches and their divisions can go about their work without disturbing the others. There are purpose designed class rooms and a separate cadets' mess. The spacious officers' mess and saloon is in the stern of the main deck and has square stern windows — a more spacious version of the great cabin of olden times. The accommodation and equipment are to modern merchant ship standards and style.

The *Dar Mlodziezy* is the first of a numerous class: she has five sisterships built from 1987 to 1990 for the Soviet Union: *Mir, Druzhba, Pallada, Khersones* and *Nadezhda*. These were also built at the same shipyard in Gdansk, the birthplace of the Solidarity movement, originally named after Lenin but now just named the Gdansk Shipyard.

The *Dar Mlodziezy* was launched sideways on 4 March 1981 and commissioned on 4 July 1982, and her maiden voyage included that year's Tall Ships Race. She is a very regular participant in these races and other tall ships gatherings. In 1983 she sailed to Japan for the Osaka Sail Festival and in 1984 she took part in the trans-Atlantic Tall Ships Race St-Malo — Bermuda — Halifax — Quebec — Sydney (Newfoundland) — Liverpool. In 1987–88 she sailed to Australia to take part in that country's Bicentennial Tall Ships Race and sailed home by way of Cape Horn. In 1989 she was in the London and Rouen festivals. In 1990 she made some fare-paying passenger cruises out of Marseilles in order to earn some hard currency. In 1992 she will be taking part in the trans-Atlantic Columbus Regatta where she will be carrying some fare-paying 'adventure' trainees.

Name of vessel	Dar Mlodziezy
Year built	1981
Designer	Zygmunt Choreń
Builder	Stocznia Gdanska im. Lenina, Gdansk, Poland
Current Owner	Wyzsza Skola Morska (Merchant Marine Academy), Gdynia, Poland
Current flag	Poland
Rig	Full-rigged ship
Construction	Steel; wood-clad deck
Length extreme	357.0 feet (108.80 m)
Length of hull	311.0 feet (94.80 m)
Length waterline	259.8 feet (79.20 m)
Beam	45.9 feet (14 m)
Draught	21.7 feet (6.60 m)
Tonnage	2,385 grt; 335 nrt; 3,791 td
Sail area	32,453 sq. feet (3,015 m²)
Engines	2 × 750 hp Sulzer; 1 propeller
Complement	40 crew + 4 instructors + 150 cadets
Photograph date	1984
Photograph location	Bermuda

DAR POMORZA

The *Prinzess Eitel Friedrich*, built in 1909, was one of three square riggers owned and operated by the Deutsche Schulschiff-Verein (German Schoolship Association). She was seized by the French in 1918 and, under the name of *Colbert*, was to languish for the next 11 years in a laid-up state. There were plans to recommission her as a French schoolship but these came to naught. So did the plans of her next owner, the Baron de Forrest, to convert her to a private yacht.

In 1929 the Merchant Marine Academy at Gdynia was searching for a replacement for the old 1869 British-built barque *Lwow* which they had been using. The people of Pomerania raised the money to buy the *Colbert* and she was towed to Denmark for repairs under the name of *Pomorze* ('Pomerania') – a delivery during which she was very nearly lost. She was rebuilt at the Nakskov yard where the *Danmark* (p. 74) was to be built. Upon her arrival in Poland the ship was renamed *Dar Pomorza* (pronounced 'Dar Pomozha' and meaning 'Gift of Pomerania'), and the Polish flag was hoisted on her for the first time on 13 July 1930.

The *Dar Pomorza* sailed to New York in 1931, to the West Indies in 1932 and to Brazil and South Africa in 1933. In September 1934 she set sail from Gdynia for a round-the-world voyage. In 1936 she transited the Panama Canal for a second visit to the Pacific Ocean and called at the Galapagos and Tahiti. In 1937 she became the first Polish windjammer to round Cape Horn. She spent the war years laid up as a refugee in neutral Sweden.

The Dar Pomorza returned to Gdynia in 1945 and resumed her former employment. She operated in the Mediterranean and the Atlantic. She returned to the West Indies for the first time since the war in 1972 and later that year she was the first ship from Eastern Europe to take part in a Tall Ships Race. She was to become a regular participant in those races until her retirement.

In the 1974 Tall Ships Race the *Dar Pomorza* was visited by HRH the Duke of Edinburgh in Portsmouth and she took part in the trans-Atlantic American Bicentennial Tall Ships Race in 1976. She was one of the most popular and respected ships in the fleet. It was also the last voyage before his retirement of the late Captain Kazimierz Jurkiewicz who had been with her since before the war. In 1980 the *Dar Pomorza* was awarded the biggest prize of that year's Tall Ships Race, the Cutty Sark Trophy. This has nothing to do with winning a race; this is a distinction awarded by secret ballot of all the masters and skippers in the race to the ship which has most contributed to the spirit of international friendship. It was a bittersweet occasion as this was the last Tall Ships Race before the ship's retirement. The 'White Frigate', as she was affectionately called by her crew, made one last voyage in 1981, calling in West Germany, Plymouth, Gibraltar, Santa Cruz de Tenerife, Rotterdam and back to Gdynia.

She was retired in Gdynia as a museum ship, once more under the command of Captain Jurkiewicz – who said, with his typical sense of humour, that 'he was one of the exhibits'. He has since slipped his cable but the *Dar Pomorza* lives on, a monument to Polish seafaring.

Name of vessel	Dar Pomorza, ex-Pomorze, ex-Colbert, ex-Prinzess Eitel Friedrich
Year built	1909
Designer	Blohm & Voss
Builder	Blohm & Voss, Hamburg
Current Owner	Dar Pomorza Trust, Gdynia, Poland
Current flag	Poland
Rig	Full-rigged ship
Construction	Steel; wooden deck
Length extreme	298.6 feet (91 m)
Length of hull	266.6 feet (81.25 m)
Length waterline	230.3 feet (70.10 m)
Beam	41.3 feet (12.60 m)
Draught	18.7 feet (5.70 m)
Tonnage	1,561 grt; 525 nrt; 1,784 t TM
Sail area	22,604 sq. feet (2,100 m^2)
Engine	430 bhp MAN
Complement	39 (incl. 12 officers) + 150 cadets
Photograph date	1976
Photograph location	Plymouth, England

EAGLE

The *Eagle* was the second of the German Reichsmarine's three schoolships (see *Tovarishch*, p. 190) and the first of a series of four sisterships (see *Gorch Fock*, p. 106). She was launched on 30 June 1936 under the name of *Horst Wessel*, which was that of a hero of the Nazi Party. The *Horst Wessel*'s career as a German naval schoolship ended with the outbreak of war. She was converted to a cargo ship used mainly in the Baltic to ferry supplies and passengers between East Prussia and other German ports. She carried a light armament and is said to have shot down four Soviet aircraft.

When the US Coast Guard returned the *Danmark* to her owners after the war (p. 74) they decided they wanted a schoolship of their own. They obtained the *Horst Wessel* as a war prize in 1946 and renamed her the USCG cutter *Eagle*. All USCG boats are traditionally called cutters, even the *Eagle* although she was and remained a barque. The Coast Guard replaced her German-style double spanker (as can be seen on pp. 21, 107 and 191) by the usual style spanker seen in the picture opposite, although they have reverted to a double spanker since January 1990. The eagle figurehead was replaced (see frontispiece p.17).

The *Eagle* normally sails three-and-a-half to four months per year, in the summer, running three classes or cruises known as 'phases'. The first and second phases last one-and-a-half months each and train cadets from different years; the final phase is a short fourteen-day cruise with freshmen. Thus Coast Guard students get to sail two or three times on the *Eagle* in the course of their studies.

The *Eagle* usually operates along the East Coast of North America but not unfrequently sails further afield. Along with the *Black Pearl* (p. 52) she was the first American ship to enter a Tall Ships Race in Europe, in 1972.

In 1981–82 the *Eagle* was fitted with many additional water-tight bulkheads to comply with US safety rules (which are enforced by the USCG but for many years the *Eagle* had sweeping exemptions!) At the same time the present engine was installed and the cadets' hammocks were replaced by bunks in 'berthing areas', with a separate mess 'deck'.

The present day complement of the *Eagle* consists of 35 permanent crew (including five officers) who are supplemented by 5 temporary officers and 15 temporary enlisted men during the phases, and 150 cadets, all students at the USCG Academy at New London. For some years girls have been admitted and there is an average of 20 girls among the *Eagle*'s cadets.

In 1988 the *Eagle* took part in the Australian Bicentenary Tall Ships Race and in 1989 she paid her first visit to the Soviet Union, calling at Leningrad prior to attending a tall ship festival at Rouen marking the bicentennial of the French Revolution. 1990 was the bicentenary year of the USCG and the *Eagle* made a special cruise to mark the anniversary, visiting a number of US ports from Maine to Florida. In 1991 she sailed to Europe, calling at Cherbourg, Weymouth and Lisbon. In 1992 she will not be racing in the Columbus Regatta but will meet the fleet in Puerto Rico and host it in New York and Boston.

Name of vessel	Eagle, *ex*-Horst Wessel
Year built	1936
Designer	Blohm & Voss
Builder	Blohm & Voss, Hamburg, Germany
Current Owner	United States Coast Guard, New London, Connecticut, USA
Current flag	United States of America
Rig	Barque
Construction	Steel; teak clad deck
Length extreme	294.4 feet (89.73 m)
Length of hull	264.7 feet (80.70 m)
Length waterline	230.5 feet (70.26 m)
Beam	39.1 feet (11.92 m)
Draught	17.0 feet (5.18 m) (load)
Tonnage	1,500 grt; 1561 t TM; 1,634 td (standard); 1,816 td (load)
Sail area	21,345 square feet (1,983 m^2)
Engine	1,000 hp Caterpillar
Complement	35 permanent crew + 20 temporary crew + 150 cadets
Photograph date	1976
Photograph location	Newport, Rhode Island, USA

EENDRACHT

Het Zeilend Zeeschip's first *Eendracht* was built and commissioned in 1974. She was a 105 ft. (32 m) (hull length) steel two-masted foreyard schooner and she had a trainee capacity of 25. By 1985 it had become clear that she was too small for the demand and moves were started to replace her by a larger ship. Funds for the building of the new vessel were mainly raised through private and corporate donations. She was to cost £2.7 million. The keel was laid on 15 September 1988 at the de Vries Lentsch Damen yard. This new *Eendracht* was commissioned on 29 August 1989. The old schooner was sold to the German youth training organisation 'Clipper' (which also operates the *Amphitrite* — see p. 28) and was renamed *Johann Smidt*.

The name *Eendracht* means 'Union' and was also the name of a famous Dutch man-o'-war in the 17th century.

The *Eendracht* is an adventure sail training schooner that takes ordinary members of the public, young and mature, on adventure cruises where they are put into watches and take part in running the ship. She operates 330 days a year. From May to November she sails in North European waters and from December to April she operates in the Canaries and sometimes out of Malaga. During the summer and autumn holiday season and in the Tall Ships Races she only takes young men and women between the ages of 15 and 26. At other times the upper age limit is removed. Some cruises are on a head-berth basis; others are block-booked by groups, clubs and companies. The cruises vary in length from day trips to 16 days, the most common durations, apart from one and two-day trips,

being 8 and 10 days. The *Eendracht* took part in the 1990 and 1991 Tall Ships Races and will be taking part in the 1992 Tall Ships Race in the Baltic.

The afterguard crew of 13 includes only four paid permanent crew: the bosun, his mate, the engineer and the cook. The others, including the master, the mates and the ship's doctor, are drawn from a body of qualified volunteers and they pay for their expenses.

There are 40 trainee berths arranged in 8 two-bunk and 6 four-bunk cabins, all fitted with a washbasin.

The *Eendracht* is a typical de Vries Lentsch yacht design, high sided, very beamy and with heavy-looking deckhouses, but with good underwater lines. There is a long, shallow fin keel and the rudder hangs from a skeg. There is a 100 hp bow thruster. The *Eendracht* was built and is maintained to Lloyds' class ⊹100 A1 + LMC. The masts are aluminium; the fore and main masts are gaff-rigged; the mizzen sets a Bermudan sail. The schooner can reach 15 knots in Force 5 winds.

The saloon and galley are in the deckhouse; the saloon has table places for the entire complement in one sitting. The raised bridge with enclosed wheelhouse is like on a motorvessel. Abaft it there is an open air sailing bridge which is stepped up so that the helmsman can see over the wheelhouse. Under and abaft this sailing bridge there is an open air deck saloon or cockpit with benches and four tables. The lower deck is entirely taken up by the crew's and trainees' cabins, arranged along the ship's sides, and by the toilet and shower blocks positioned along the centreline. The engine room is below this deck.

Name of vessel	Eendracht
Year built	1989
Designer	De Vries Lentsch, The Netherlands
Builder	Damen shipyard, Gorinchem, The Netherlands
Current Owner	B.V. Rederij 'de Twaalf Provincien', The Hague
Operator	Stichting 'Het Zeilend Zeeschip', The Hague
Current flag	The Netherlands
Rig	Three-masted schooner
Construction	Steel. Wood-clad deck
Length extreme	193.8 feet (59.08 m)
Length of hull	180.4 feet (55.00 m)
Length waterline	137.6 feet (41.95 m)
Beam	40.4 feet (12.30 m)
Draught	16.4 feet (5.00 m)
Tonnage	606 grt; 181 nrt; 457.5 td (light); 519.7 td (load)
Sail area	11,119 sq. feet (windward); 12,981 sq. feet (total) (1,033/1,206 m^2)
Engine	540 bhp Caterpillar
Complement	13 crew + 40 trainees
Photograph date	1990
Photograph location	Off the Isle of Wight, England

ELINOR

This schooner was launched in 1906 under the name of *Alta*. She was unengined and had the same rig as now — a type called 'Newfoundland rig' by the Danes as it was mostly used by those Danish schooners engaged in the salt fish trade from Newfoundland. It is three-masted and with a single yard on the foremast. When the wind is abaft the beam and not too strong a single square sail is set flying (hoisted from deck) to that yard. In addition the *Elinor*, like many other Newfoundland-rigged schooners, carries a triangular 'square' topsail known as a raffee; hers is unusual in that it is a split raffee, cut down the middle because of the arrangement of the jib stays.

The *Alta* was registered at Marstal, Denmark, and was engaged in the Newfoundland trade.

She was sold in 1916 to a Norwegian owner and became the *Sørkyst I* of Christiania (now Oslo) and she was engaged in Arctic whaling and sealing. A small auxiliary engine was installed at that time. In 1928 she was sold back to Denmark, becoming the *Agnete* of Aalborg. Her rig was reduced to that of a galease (two-masted schooner) and a more powerful auxiliary was installed. She was put to work as a stone fisher — dredging up stones and gravel from the sea floor for the building trade. She was sold again in 1938 and was renamed *Elinor*, which name she retained through a number of new ownerships and new ports of registry in Denmark. She was converted at the start of that period into motor freighter and engaged in the Baltic trade.

She was bought out of trade in 1967 by a syndicate forming the share company Sejlksibs K/S 'Alta'. This company is still the owner although individual shareholders have come and gone since then. The *Elinor* was restored for charter work, a process that took until 1971. She was chartered in the late 1970s by various Danish social service agencies to sail-train problem youngsters who joined for lengthy periods in groups of ten plus a teacher. In 1978, with such a 'cargo', the *Elinor* undertook a ten month voyage to the Mediterranean, but she usually sailed in the Baltic and North Sea.

The *Elinor* joined the 1980 Baltic Tall Ships Race. She had almost reached the finishing line off Karlskrona at night when a Swedish motor fishing boat steaming on autopilot and without lights or lookout, collided into her, completely demolishing the starboard quarter and tearing off the transom to within a couple of inches of the waterline. The *Elinor* managed to limp into Karlskrona and later was put into a yard for repairs.

In 1981 she set out on a voyage to Jamaica with some paying participants and a cargo of Portuguese wine; she sailed back, with paying trainees and a cargo of rum, as part of the 1982 Tall Ships Race from Venezuela to Southampton via Philadelphia, Newport, Lisbon and Vigo. She sailed back that same year to the Virgin Islands and in 1983 and 1984 she was chartered by the Quebec social work group Cap Espoir for youth training work. She attended the tall ships gathering in Quebec in the summer of 1984 and sailed back to Denmark via Oporto where she picked up a cargo of Port wine. In 1985 and '86 she was chartering out of the Virgin Islands (including a film charter for which she was mocked up as a galleon) and she took part in the New York OpSail '86. She remained based in the Virgins and in 1989 went in for refit at Cumana, Venezuela. At the time of writing, early 1992, she is still operating charters out of the Virgin Islands.

Name of vessel	Elinor, ex-Agnete, ex-Fuur, ex-Sørkyst I, ex-Alta
Year built	1906
Designer	Otto Hansen
Builder	Otto Hansen yard, Stubbekøbing, Denmark
Current Owner	Sejlskibs K/S 'Alta', Gentofte, Denmark
Current flag	Denmark
Rig	Three-masted foreyard schooner
Construction	Wood
Length extreme	118.1 feet (36.0 m)
Length of hull	82.0 feet (25.0 m)
Beam	19.7 feet (6.0 m)
Draught	6.6 feet (2.0 m)
Tonnage	71 grt; 38 nrt; 120 td
Sail area	4,844 sq. feet (450 m^2)
Engine	155 hp Deutz
Complement	5—6 crew + 10 passengers or trainees
Photograph date	1984
Photograph location	Quebec, Canada

ELISABETH LOUW

This schooner was built in 1910 as a pilot schooner based on the sailing logger type with an elegant counter and more rake than usual in the stem. She was bought under the name of *Tonijn* ('Tunny') by Captain H.J. Hoogendoorn who had just sold to Ireland his previous charter vessel, the gaff ketch *Flyvholm*. Captain Hoogendoorn converted the *Tonijn* in 1985–86 into this very good looking charter schooner and he re-named her *Elisabeth Louw*. The schooner is in Dutch class BZ 1234 Class 3, meaning that she is licensed to sail worldwide. The crew consists of the skipper-owner and his wife, who live aboard year round, and of two seasonal deckhands. There are 23 guest bunks in 8 cabins.

The *Elisabeth Louw* operates charter cruises out of Enkhuizen; her sailing area extends from Brittany to Scandinavia and the Baltic. Most cruises are self-catering and the guests are the sort who expect to take an active part in the sailing. In 1986, 87 and 88 the schooner was chartered by a Belgian sail training organization, an operation which was sponsored by Schweppes. A special suit of pale yellow sails was cut for this, the same colour as the label on the well-known Indian tonic bottles.

The riveted steel hull has four watertight bulkheads. In the conversion the raked but straight stem was transformed into a false clipper bow by flaring out the steel bulwarks above the deck (which requires no structural alterations) and by adding a false clipper bow-plate. The steel deck was clad with laid iroko. The windlass is both manual and electric. The main wheel and binnacle are located on the stepped-up poop deck, abaft the wheelhouse.

The masts, bowsprit and booms are made of solid larch. The gaffs and yards are lightweight aluminium tubes painted white. Both yards are standing. The square fore-topsail is set flying from the deck. Above it a raffee can be set which brails to the topmast pole.

The wheelhouse is open plan but has two distinct areas. The fore part is the wheelhouse proper, with an 'inside' wheel, engine controls, chart table, navigational instruments and a ladder leading down to the skipper-owner's suite under the poop; the after part is the crew's saloon with table, settee and a fully equipped galley.

The midship deckhouse is sunk-in, with its floor a few feet below deck level. The entrance is through the after side. This is the guests' saloon and galley, all open plan. There are two large tables to port, a long settee and the galley corner to starboard. Stairs lead down respectively to the midship accommodation and to the fore accommodation.

The midship accommodation consists of six passenger cabins, 3 WCs and 2 showers. Five of the cabins have three bunks each (athwartship upper and lower bunks and a fore-and-aft mid-level bunk); the sixth has two bunks. All cabins have a washstand with hot and cold running water and a hanging locker. The central companionway of this compartment leads through a watertight door to the fore accommodation which consists of a further two 3-berth passenger cabins and a 2-berth crew cabin, appointed as above, a WC and a shower and, forward, a store room and laundry.

Name of vessel	Elisabeth Louw, ex-Tonijn
Year built	1910. Converted 1985–86
Designer	Vigé
Builder	Vigé yard, Haarlem, Holland
Current Owner	Mr J.H. Hoogendoorn
Current flag	The Netherlands
Rig	Topsail schooner
Construction	Steel; Iroko-clad deck
Length extreme	131.2 feet (40.00 m)
Length of hull	94.1 feet (28.69 m)
Beam	21.6 feet (6.58 m)
Draught	8.9 feet (2.70 m)
Tonnage	110 grt; 33 nrt; 160 td
Sail area	4,040/6,000 sq. feet (374/520 m^2)
Engine	300 Henschel
Complement	4 crew + 23 passengers
Photograph date	1988
Photograph location	Cowes, England

ESMERALDA

The schoolship *Esmeralda* is the sixth Chilean Navy ship to bear that name. The first was a Spanish frigate captured during the Chilean War of Independence. She had been blockading Valparaiso and was boarded in 1818 by the Chilean frigate *Lautaro* commanded by Commander O'Brien who died in the exploit. The *Esmeralda* got away that time but was finally captured in 1820 at Callao (Peru) by an expedition led by Lord Cochrane — the new Chilean Navy was trained by ex-Royal Navy officers. The second *Esmeralda* was built in 1855 and successfully engaged the Bolivian Navy a number of times in 1879 during the Chile-Bolivia War. The third *Esmeralda* was a light cruiser commissioned in 1889; the fourth was a heavy cruiser laid down in 1898. The fifth was an anti-submarine frigate commissioned in 1946 and which was renamed when her name was transferred to the present *Esmeralda*.

Neither is the *Esmeralda* the first schoolship of the Chilean Navy, a navy which has always valued sail training. Her predecessors include the auxiliary steam barque *General Baquedano* built in Britain, and the four-masted barque *Lautaro*, formerly the *Priwall* of Hamburg.

The *Esmeralda* was laid down in 1942 under the name of *Juan de Austria*. She had been ordered by the Spanish Navy as a sistership of the *Juan Sebastian de Elcano* (p. 116) and was built in the same yard. But before completion the *Juan de Austria* suffered a very serious fire and construction was halted. In 1951 the Spanish Navy approved the sale of the damaged vessel to the Chilean Navy; repairs were done and work resumed. The vessel, renamed *Esmeralda*, was launched in 1952 and commissioned in 1954.

There are differences between the two sisterships. The most noticeable concerns the rig: the *Juan Sebastian de Elcano* is a typical four-masted topgallant schooner but on the *Esmeralda* the gaff foresail has been replaced by staysails between the main and fore masts which, in view of the four square sails carried on the foremast, causes many people to call this vessel a barquentine. However the square sails are exactly the same as on the *Juan Sebastian de Elcano*: they are rigged schooner-fashion with a very tall lower mast and a foreyard standing much higher than on a conventional square rigged mast. This arrangement is that of a topsail-staysail schooner; It is similar to the one on the 'brigantine' *Outlaw* (p. 150). The correct terminology for such hybrid rigs is a constant source of heated debates among sailors and we propose the hybrid name of schooner-barquentine.

The other main difference with the Spanish ship concerns the hulls' superstructures: the *Juan Sebastian de Elcano* has a normal length fo'c's'le forward of the foremast and a long waist divided by two Liverpool houses; the *Esmeralda* has a very long fo'c's'le extending to the main mast and a correspondingly short waist with deckhousing that is not built out to the ship's sides.

The *Esmeralda* trains both ordinary seamen and midshipmen. Her complement consists of 237 officers and crew and 100 midshipmen or cadets.

The *Esmeralda* is one of the training ships that sails the most sea miles per year. She frequently sails on very long voyages and she has sailed around the world a number of times, often by way of Cape Horn or the Magellan Straits. She frequently crosses the Pacific and frequently visits Europe. She took part in the 1964 and 1976 Tall Ships Races to New York, in the Osaka Sail Festival of 1983, in the 1986 New York OpSail and the 1988 Australian Bicentennial Tall Ships Race. She will be joining the Columbus Regatta in 1992.

Name of vessel	Esmeralda, ex-Juan de Austria
Year built	1942–52
Designer	Camper & Nicholson's, Gosport, England
Builder	Echevarrieta y Larriñaga, Cadiz, Spain
Current Owner	Chilean Navy
Current flag	Chile
Rig	Four-masted schooner-barquentine
Construction	Steel; teak-clad deck
Length extreme	370.7 feet (113.00 m)
Length of hull	308.4 feet (94.00 m)
Length waterline	259.2 feet (79.00 m)
Beam	42.7 feet (13.00 m)
Draught	19.7 feet (6.00 m)
Tonnage	2,276 t TM; 3,222 td (standard); 3,673 td (load)
Sail area	30,892 sq. feet (2,870 m²)
Engine	1,500 hp Fiat
Complement	237 officers and men + 100 cadets
Photograph date	1976
Photograph location	Newport, Rhode Island, USA

EUGENIOS EUGENIDIS

The *Eugenios Eugenidis* was until recently the schoolship in which the future merchant navy officers and seamen of Greece were trained. The cadets, most of whom were 18 or 19 years old, came from fifteen different nautical colleges around the country. Some 1,500 to 2,000 trainees were trained each year on the schooner. From 1979 this number included some female cadets who sailed on all-female cruises. The *Eugenios Eugenidis* operated mostly in the Eastern Mediterranean. She made one long cruise each summer and a number of shorter ones at other times. However since 1989 Greek cadets are no longer trained under sail and the schooner is now laid up at Zea, near Piraeus. As of early 1992 no decision concerning her future had yet been made.

The *Eugenios Eugenidis* is built of riveted steel. The lower deck is watertight. The rig is described as a topgallant schooner because the foremast staying arrangement has the topmast shrouds fixed to the topmast below the upper yard — the latter therefore hoists along a topgallant pole. The *Eugenios Eugenidis* has a powerful rig and an excellent turn of speed and she can reach 16 knots under sail.

The schooner was designed by G.L. Watson & Co. of Glasgow (who still are leading naval architects today) for Sir Walter Runciman, later Lord Runciman (1847–1937), as a replacement for his yacht *Sunbeam*, a three-masted topgallant schooner that had originally been built for Lord Brassey. The new yacht was built in 1929 at Dumbarton by William Denny & Brothers, the same yard that had completed the building of the clipper *Cutty Sark* in 1869 (p. 72). The schooner, launched in August 1929, was named *Sun-beam II*. She remained Lord Runciman's private yacht until his death in 1937.

During the Second World War the *Sunbeam II* was requisitioned by the Admiralty for use as a naval auxiliary vessel. At the end of the war she was returned to the estate of Lord Runciman and put up for sale. She was bought in 1946 by the Abraham Rydberg Foundation of Stockholm for use as a schoolship, in replacement for its four-masted barque *Abraham Rydberg*. The Foundation refitted the schooner and shortened her name to *Sunbeam*. She was operated in the Baltic and the North Sea and made a voyage to the West Indies. She was laid up for sale at the end of 1952 for financial reasons.

The *Sunbeam* did not find a buyer until 1954, when she was bought by Einar Hansen's Clipper Line of Malmö, Sweden. She was renamed *Flying Clipper* and was used as a schoolship for the midshipmen and apprentices of the Clipper Line. She took part in the first two Tall Ships Races, from Torbay to Lisbon and from Brest to Las Palmas. In 1961–62 she was the star of the film *Flying Clipper*. She also featured in *Lord Jim*, the film based on Joseph Conrad's novel of the same title. Her primary purpose remained however sail training. By the time she was sold on, she had trained 200 deck officers, 60 engineers and 27 catering staff for the Clipper Line.

The *Flying Clipper* was bought on 4 June 1965 by the Greek Merchant Navy Ministry, her current owner, mostly with funds provided for the purpose by the heirs of Mr Eugenios Eugenidis, a Greek shipowner who had died in 1954. The *Flying Clipper* was re-named in his memory.

Name of vessel	Eugenios Eugenidis, *ex*-Flying Clipper, *ex*-Sunbeam, *ex*-Sunbeam II.
Year built	1929
Designer	G.L. Watson & Co., Glasgow, United Kingdom
Builder	William Denny & Brothers Ltd, Dumbarton, United Kingdom
Current Owner	Merchant Navy Ministry, Piraeus, Greece
Current flag	Greece
Rig	Three-masted topgallant schooner
Construction	Steel. Teak deck
Length extreme	217.2 feet (66.20 m)
Length of hull	195.0 feet (59.44 m)
Length waterline	150.0 feet (45.72 m)
Beam	30.1 feet (9.17 m)
Draught	18.0 feet (5.49 m)
Tonnage	636.34 grt; 225.71 nrt; 659 t TM; 1,300 td
Sail area	15,005 sq. feet (1,394 m^2)
Engine	400 bhp Polar Atlas
Complement	24 crew + 54 trainees
Photograph date	1976
Photograph location	Poros, Greece

EYE OF THE WIND

The *Eye of the Wind* was built and launched as the German trading topsail-schooner *Friedrich*. Until the start of the Great War she made two voyages a year from Hamburg to the River Plate carrying general cargoes out, hides to Cornwall and Cornish clay to Germany. From 1923 to 1969 she was engaged in general trade, under successive ownerships and names, across the North Sea and the Baltic, becoming a motor coaster along the line.

She was found in Sweden by her present owners who bought her in 1973. The owners are Australian and British members of a syndicate, some of whom had previously owned the wooden three-masted topsail schooner *New Endeavour* which they had sold in Sydney. They repaired the vessel in Sweden, re-named her *Eye of the Wind* and motored her to her new port of registry, Faversham in Kent, England, where they re-rigged her as a hermaphrodite brigantine — that is, the rig commonly called brigantine today, without yards on the mainmast.

The refit and conversion were completed in 1976 and the *Eye of the Wind* went on an adventure cruise (with participating paying guests) around the world via Australia. She returned home to England in 1978.

Later that same year she set sail on her second circumnavigation, under charter to Operation Drake, a British inspired and led youth adventure project during which she embarked a total of 400 young 'Venturers'. She returned to England in December 1980. After a summer spent sailing around Britain and the Narrow Seas she set sail again for the Pacific in October 1981. While in New Zealand she was chartered for the filming of *Savage Islands*. For that production she was rigged as a true brigantine, a rig she has retained ever since. Compared to the common or garden brigantine, prop-erly known as a hermaphrodite brig, she has square sails on her main topmast; compared to a brig, her gaff mainsail is much taller and larger, her mainmast being rigged like that of the foremast of a topsail schooner.

The *Eye of the Wind* reached Australia in December 1982. From 1983 to 1985 she operated an annual pattern of short cruises out of Hobart followed by long cruises among Western Pacific Islands (including Fiji, Vanuatu and New Guinea) and ending with short cruises along the Great Barrier Reef. In late 1985 she sailed for China for the filming, early 1986, of the film *Tai Pan*.

She sailed back to Australia via Micronesia and Melanesia, reaching Cairns in August 1986 and then sailed around 'the top' to Perth in connection with the *America's* Cup, and back around 'the bottom' to Hobart and Sydney. From April to October 1987 she underwent a refit to meet new Board of Trade regulations.

Having satisfied the Board of Trade, the *Eye of the Wind* sailed from Sydney to meet and join the First Fleet Re-enactment at Perth on 20 December 1987. She sailed as part of the Fleet to Sydney, arriving there on Australia's Bicentenary Day (26 January 1988), and then taking part in Fleet cruises up and down the East Coast until the end of May. She then resumed her own scheduled cruises in the Pacific, calling, among numerous other places, at Pitcairn for the bicentenary of the burning of the *Bounty* (23 January 1990).

On 6 October 1991 she sailed from Sydney with the *Søren Larsen* (p. 182) on a voyage to Lisbon round Cape Horn, which she rounded on 10 December 1990. She will be taking part in the Columbus Regatta '92 from Lisbon and Cadiz to New York and Liverpool, and then she will be sailing back to Australia.

Name of vessel	Eye of the Wind, *ex*-Merry, *ex*-Rose Marie, *ex*-Merry, *ex*-Sam, ex-Friedrich
Year built	1911
Designer	C. Lühring
Builder	Lühring shipyard, Brake, Unterweser, Germany
Current Owner	Adventure Under Sail Syndicate, Annandale, NSW, Australia
Current flag	United Kingdom
Rig	True brigantine
Construction	Iron; teak-clad deck
Length extreme	132 feet (40.23 m)
Length on deck	103 feet (31.40 m)
Length waterline	90 feet (27.43 m)
Beam	23 feet (7.01 m)
Draught	9 feet (2.74 m)
Tonnage	149.96 grt; 115.07 nrt; 260 tdw
Sail area	6,000 sq. feet to windward (557 m^2); 8,500 sq. feet total (790 m^2)
Engine	230 hp Gardner
Complement	10 crew + 18 passage participants
Photograph date	1986
Photograph location	Perth, W. Australia

FALLS OF CLYDE

The *Falls of Clyde* is the only remaining rigged and restored four-masted full-rigged ship in the world. Only two other examples of the type are still in existence: the *County of Peebles*, still afloat as a hulk used as a breakwater in Punta Arenas, Chile, under the name of *Muñoz Gamero*, and for which the Clyde Maritime Trust in Glasgow is trying to raise finance for her purchase and restoration in Govan (Glasgow); and the *County of Roxburgh* which is a wreck high and dry on a coral reef at Takaroa atoll in the Tuamotu islands. The *Falls of Clyde*, another Clyde-built ship, was built at Port Glasgow and was launched in December 1878, seven months after the laying of her keel.

She was the first of nine ships that made up the Falls Line, six of which were full-rigged four-masters, and all of which were named after waterfalls in Scotland. The *Falls of Clyde* was credited by her captain, C. Anderson, as 'making no fuss at fifteen knots'. For the next twenty years she sailed under the British flag carrying general cargo.

In 1898 she was sold to the Matson Shipping Line of San Francisco and became the first ship to fly the Hawaiian flag. Her rig was altered to a barque and she traded until 1907 between San Francisco and Hilo, Hawaii, carrying general cargo (including livestock) to Hilo and mostly sugar (and sometimes small quantities of coffee) to San Francisco. She also carried up to 12 adult passengers and 6 children.

In 1907 the *Falls of Clyde* was converted to a sailing oil tanker and ownership was assumed by the Associated Oil Co. in 1908 when the Matson and Associated fleets were divided. Ten large wing tanks were built in the hold, with a totel capacity of more than 700,000 US gallons (2,650 m³) and cans of petrol were also carried. For the next fourteen years she carried bulk and case oil from Gaviota, California, to Hilo or Honolulu, with return cargoes of sugar and molasses. The passages averaged 17 days; her best passage from Honolulu to Gaviota was 8 days, in 1908.

In 1921 the *Falls of Clyde* was sold to the General Petroleum Company and, after her last voyage in 1922, she was converted into a floating oil depot at Ketchikan in Alaska.

In 1958, when there was no further use for the ship, plans were made to sink her in Vancouver Harbour to form a breakwater. However she was sold to a private buyer who wanted to save her, but his bank foreclosed on him in 1963 and she was put up for sale again. Fortunately she was saved when the people of Hawaii managed, by public donations, to purchase her and she was towed to Honolulu. The Bernice P. Bishop Museum undertook to restore her and fitted her with four new masts, decking and rigging, plus a new figurehead carved by the famous woodcarver Jack Whitehead of the Isle of Wight. She is open to the public at Pier 7, Honolulu harbour.

In 1980 the Bernice P. Bishop Museum, primarily an ethnographical museum, considered the disposal of the ship due to financial cutbacks. However some State money was made available to maintain her under the aegis of the Museum until a more suitable management structure was found. Eventually, in 1986, her ownership was transferred to the Hawaii Maritime Center, a private non-profit organization. Recently the Hawaii Maritime Center has obtained a grant for the renewal of the deck and the restoration of the upper pump room where there is machinery for the pumping out of her cargoes of petroleum. The *Falls of Clyde* is not restored to a given period in time but so as to display the most remarkable features in her career: the four-masted full rig (the jigger-mast yards were not crossed at the time of the picture) and the tanks and pumps in her hold that make her the sole surviving example of an early oil tanker that did not depend on the benighted stuff for her own propulsion.

Name of vessel	Falls of Clyde
Year built	1878
Builder	Russel & Co., Port Glasgow, Scotland
Current Owner	Hawaii Maritime Center, Honolulu, Hawaii
Current flag	USA
Rig	Four-masted full-rigged ship
Construction	Iron; steel and wood deck
Length extreme	323 feet (98.45 m)
Length of hull	280 feet (85.34 m)
Length waterline	266 feet (81.08 m)
Beam	40 feet (12.19 m)
Draught	21 feet (6.40 m)
Tonnage	1,809 grt; 1748 nrt; 1,195 td
Engine	None
Complement:	14 crew (period 1907-21)
Photograph date	1977
Photograph location	Honolulu, Hawaii, USA

FANTOME III

The *Fantome III*, the flagship of Captain Mike Burke's Windjammer fleet, has a most unusual history. Her keel was laid down during the First World War for the Italian Navy: she was intended as a destroyer. The war ended before completion and further work was halted. Eight or nine years later the Duke of Westminster bought the half-built vessel and had her completed in 1927 as a private sailing yacht with a four-masted foreyard schooner rig. He named her *Flying Cloud* and used her for cruises in the Mediterranean. In 1932 the yacht was sold to Mr Nelson B. Warden, of Philadelphia, who had her refitted with more powerful engines and who sailed her in the Mediterranean with two cows on board to ensure a fresh milk supply. In 1937 the *Flying Cloud* was sold to Mr H.J.P. Bomford, an Englishman, and later the same year to Lord A.E. Guinness who renamed her *Fantome III*. He already owned the *Fantome II* (the *Belem*, p. 44), and he kept both big yachts until his death in 1948. The *Fantome III* was refitted and modernized and sailed to the Pacific. She arrived at Seattle in 1939 and was laid up at anchor there for the war years and beyond, with little maintenance. In 1951 she was sold to William and Joe Jones of Seattle. They held conducted tours of the luxury yacht. In 1953 the *Fantome III* finally left Seattle under tow, bound for Montreal. In 1956 she was bought by Aristotle Onassis who had her refitted at the Howaldt yard in Kiel, Germany. He had the intention of giving her as a wedding present to Prince Rainier of Monaco and Grace Kelly but since he was snubbed by not receiving an invitation to the wedding, the yacht was not delivered. She remained laid up at Kiel for thirteen years.

She was bought by Captain Mike Burke in 1969. He had her towed to Skagen Denmark, and then to Spain, for conversion to a sailing passenger vessel. Two bachelor and bachelorette quarters for six passengers each, 15 deck cabins and 42 regular cabins were built, along with bars, a main saloon, new crew quarters, etc., with air conditioning. She was rigged with a labour-saving staysail-trysail rig.

The *Fantome III* joined the other windjammers of Mike Burke in the West Indies (see p. 158). These ships operate year-round cruises from the Bahamas, the British Virgin Islands, St Martin, Antigua and Grenada. The *Fantome* (as she is called in the brochures, without the 'III') has been based at most, if not all these islands, running six-day cruises that alternate itineraries, giving passengers the option of booking a double cruise without repeated calls. In 1991 she operated out of Antigua, calling at St Barts, St Martin, St Kitts and Monserrat in the first and third weeks of each month, and at Dominica, Guadeloupe and the Saints in the second and fourth weeks. In August 1991 she began a $5 million overhaul and upgrading, spending only three months out of service for the heavy yard work, including new engines and new tanks with a saving of space making a new lower deck available for cabins. The old cabins on the main and upper decks are being made more comfortable and spacious. The total number of passenger beds is only increased from 126 to 128. Work on the cabins is continuing at sea as the schooner sails with a number of passengers reduced to 84. By May 1992, the *Fantome* will have the finest appointments in the fleet.

Name of vessel	Fantome III, *ex*-Flying Cloud
Year built	1927
Builder	Ansaldo S.A., Leghorn, Italy
Current Owner	Fantome S.A.
Current flag	Honduras
Operator	Windjammer Inc., Miami Beach, Florida, USA
Rig	Four-masted topsail staysail schooner
Construction	Steel
Length extreme	282 feet (86.0 m)
Length of hull	235 feet (71.6 m)
Length between perpendiculars	193 feet (58.9 m)
Beam	40 feet (12.2 m)
Draught	19 feet (5.8 m)
Tonnage	676 grt; 310 nrt
Sail area	21,000 sq. feet (1,951 m^2)
Engines	2 × 399 hp Caterpillar; twin propellers
Complement	45 crew + 128 passengers
Photograph date	1988
Photograph location	Antigua

GEORG STAGE

The first *Georg Stage* was a small full-rigged iron ship built in 1882 with money donated by the Danish shipowner Frederik Stage in memory of his son Georg who had died at the age of 22. This vessel trained Danish merchant navy cadets until 1934 when her replacement, the slightly bigger ship shown here, was ordered to be built. The old ship was bought by the well known Australian sailor and author Alan Villiers who renamed her *Joseph Conrad* and sailed her round the world by way of Cape Horn. Since 1948 this vessel has been preserved next to the *Charles W. Morgan* at Mystic Seaport, Connecticut.

The new *Georg Stage* was commissioned in 1935. She was, and still is, a very traditional schoolship where the cadets, aged from 15 to 18 years, sleep in the open-plan berth deck in hammocks that are stowed during the day in lockers along the inside of the bulwarks. The small deckhouse between the main and fore masts contains the galley and the crew's mess and the poop deck is not disfigured by any wheelhouse or charthouse. Of all the square-rigged training barques and ships sailing today, including those that were actually built as merchantmen, the *Georg Stage* is the one that most looks like a merchant ship of the latter half of the 19th century. As one of her former masters puts it, 'she is the smallest of the biggest, but the prettiest!' It is hard to disagree with him.

The *Georg Stage* only has a permanent crew of 2, the master and the chief mate. Eight more afterguard, professional officers and seamen, and a cook, nearly always themselves former trainees of the *Georg Stage* or of the *Danmark* (p. 74), are signed on for the six-month-long operational season. The cadets, who are training in seamanship in view of seafaring careers, are sixty in number. Since 1981 the ship also accepts girl cadets (two years before the *Danmark*). They are treated no differently from the boys. The mix ratio is variable and there are usually from 15 to 20 girls. The afterguard has also become mixed.

There is only one course per year, lasting six months. The new cadets join the ship at the end of March and their first job is to send up the yards, bend the sails and reeve the running rigging. This and other instruction keeps them in Copenhagen harbour for the first month. Then the ship sets sail, at first doing only short day hops between the Danish islands and anchoring at night. The cadets do all the shipboard maintenance and frequently practise boatmanship with the ship's boats prior to weighing anchor in the morning. Short cruises follow, with night watches, and the end of the seagoing course is marked by a voyage with at least a couple of long passages – although the ship usually remains in the Baltic and North Sea. The *Georg Stage* returns to Copenhagen late August and during the last two weeks of the course the cadets lay-up the ship for winter, taking the sails off the yards and sending the yards down on deck.

The *Georg Stage* takes part in the North Sea and Baltic Tall Ships Races when these are compatible with her programme and schedules. In 1989 the ship made her first trans-Atlantic voyage, sailing to the West Indies and then 'up' the American East Coast to Mystic Seaport where, for the first time ever, the two *Georg Stages* were berthed side by side. In 1992 the *Georg Stage* will be sailing on a second trans-Atlantic voyage, with the Colombus Regatta '92.

Name of vessel	Georg Stage
Year built	1935
Designer	Å. Larsen
Builder	Frederikshavn Værft & Flydedok A/S, Frederikshavn, Denmark
Current Owner	Stiftelsen Georg Stages Minde, Copenhagen
Current flag	Denmark
Rig	Full rigged ship
Construction	Steel. Wood clad deck
Length extreme	170.6 feet (52.00 m)
Length on deck	136.5 feet (41.60 m)
Length between perpendiculars	117.8 feet (35.90 m)
Beam	27.9 feet (8.50 m)
Draught	13.8 feet (4.20 m) (load)
Tonnage	297.77 grt; 185.61 nrt; 396 t TM; 455 td (light); 505 td (load)
Sail area	9,257 sq. feet (860 m²)
Engine	220 hp Burmeister & Wain Alpha
Complement	11 crew + 60 cadets
Photograph date	1986
Photograph location	Newcastle, England

GLADAN and FALKEN

The *Gladan* ('Kite') and her sistership *Falken* ('Falcon') were built for the Swedish Navy as replacements for its full-rigged training ships *Najaden* and *Jarramas*. The *Najaden*, launched in 1897, is composite-built and used to carry a crew of 22 plus 100 cadets although she measures only 131.4 feet (40.1 m) along the hull! Her near-sistership *Jarramas*, three feet shorter and built of iron, was launched in 1900 and had a crew of 27 plus 92 cadets. Perhaps one of the reasons why so many cadets could be embarked was that they must have been small: on *Najaden*, at least, they were extraordinarily young, from 13½ to 15 years of age. The *Najaden* was in active service until 1938 and was saved in 1946 from the breakers by the town of Halmstadt which has preserved her to the present day as a museum ship. The *Jarramas* last sailed in 1946 and was sold in 1950 to the town of Karlskrona where she is presently also preserved as a museum ship.

The *Gladan*'s keel was laid on 28 May 1946. This schooner was launched on 14 November and commissioned on 2 June 1947, ten days before the launch of the *Falken* which was herself completed on 1 October 1947. The two schooners are very much alike and the easiest way to distinguish them is by their sail numbers – S 01 for *Gladan* and S 02 for *Falken*. Their lines and rig are inspired from the German North Sea pilot schooners. They cross a single yard which has a permanently bent-on square sail. The galley is in the fore deckhouse and the officers' mess in the after deckhouse. The cadets, whose complement was originally 38 on each schooner but which has been reduced to 30, sleep in bunks and hammocks.

Originally, and still in 'normal' years, the schooners each operate five one-month training cruises per year, mostly in the Baltic and North Sea. When the Abraham Rydberg Foundation's training three-masted schooner *Sunbeam II* was laid up due to lack of funds for necessary repairs (see *Eugenios Eugenidis*, p. 90) they chartered the *Falken* from the Navy in 1952, and each subsequent year until 1956, for six-month winter cruises to the Caribbean for the training of merchant seamen. Both schooners took part in the first Tall Ships Race in 1956 and they are 'semi regulars' in these races. The *Gladan* took part in the American Bicentennial Tall Ships Race in 1976.

The normal employment of the schooners is with midshipmen from the Naval Academy at Karlskrona, who embark on four-week training courses. Only one schooner is necessary for the job nowadays and in recent years budget cuts have frequently led to the laying-up of one or the other schooner, although both were in commission in 1990 and 1991. On a number of occasions the 'spare' schooner has been sailing with civilian school groups and the like. In 1992 the *Gladan* will be taking part in the Baltic Tall Ships Race but it looks likely that the *Falken* will be laid up unless she finds a sponsor to take part in the Columbus Regatta.

Names of vessels	Gladan *and* Falken
Years built	1946 (Gladan), 1947 (Falken)
Designer	Capt. Tore Herlin
Builder	Naval Dockyard, Stockholm
Current Owners	Swedish Navy
Current flag	Sweden
Rigs	Foreyard schooners
Construction	Steel; wood-clad teak
Length extreme	129.9 feet (39.60 m)
Length of hull	112.6 feet (34.30 m)
Length between perpendiculars	92.8 feet (28.30 m)
Beam	23.8 feet (7.25 m)
Draught	13.8 feet (4.20 m)
Tonnage	232 t TM; 220 td (standard)
Sail area	6,523/7,567 sq. feet (606/703 m^2) (plain/total)
Engine	128 hp Scania Vabis
Complement	14 crew + 30 cadets
Photograph date	1984
Photograph location	Cowes, England

GLORIA

The Colombian government decided in 1966 to provide its Navy with a square-rigged schoolship. The plans were made by Senermar in Madrid, and the ASTACE yard in Bilbao, Spain, was contracted for the construction. The ship, named *Gloria*, was launched during the last quarter of 1967. After completion and trials off Bilbao the Colombian Navy took delivery of the *Gloria* at Bilbao in September 1968. With her Colombian crew and a full complement of cadets, the *Gloria* sailed from Bilbao on 5 October and arrived at Cartagena, her base port, on 8 November. Only then was she formally commissioned into the Colombian Navy.

The *Gloria* has a conventional barque rig where all yards, except the lowers and lower-topsail yards, have halyards and are hoisted up to their respective mastheads for sailing. The lower masts and topmasts are in one piece but the topgallant masts (with their royal poles) are fidded. The wheel is located in a motorvessel-style bridge just abaft the mainmast. It is so high that the view forward is completely obscured by the mainsail — which is why the latter is usually either not set or only half-set, partly trussed up by the buntlines, to allow the helmsman and the watch officer to see where the ship is going. The ship's figurehead is a gilded Winged Victory.

The *Gloria*'s usual complement consists of 10 commissioned officers, 30 warrant officers, 12 deck seamen, 8 other personnel (galley, etc.), 5 teachers, and 80 midshipmen who are aged about 19.

The *Gloria* serves the dual purpose of training naval midshipmen under sail and of being Colombia's itinerant goodwill ambassador, also promoting Colombian trade and industry abroad, which is why she frequently takes part in international windjammer events.

In 1970 she sailed around the world via La Guaira (Venezuela), Rio de Janeiro, Buenos Aires, Capetown, Sydney, Wellington, Valparaiso, Callao, Guayaquil (Ecuador), the Panama Canal and thence back to Cartagena. In 1971–75 she sailed mostly in the Caribbean and in 1976 she joined the US Bicentennial Tall Ships Race in Bermuda, to sail to Newport, New York and Boston. She then sailed on to Europe outside the Race.

The *Gloria* took part in the 1980 Tall Ships Race ending in Amsterdam, in the 1982 Philadelphia Tricentennial, in the 1983 Festival of Sail at Osaka, in the 1984 Tall Ships Race from Puerto Rico to Bermuda and Halifax and in the subsequent gathering at Quebec City, in the 1986 New York OpSail, in the 1988 Australian Bicentenary Tall Ships Race from Hobart to Sydney, in the 1989 French Revolution Bicentennial tall ship festival at Rouen, in Sail Amsterdam '90, etc. She is expected to take part in the Columbus Regatta in 1992.

The *Gloria* is the first of a series of four barques built by ASTACE for Latin American navies, each subsequent one being a bit bigger than her predecessor but all showing a family resemblance: the *Gloria* was followed by the *Guayas* of Ecuador (1976, p. 110), the *Simon Bolivar* of Venezuela (1979, p. 178 and cover picture) and the *Cuauhtémoc* of Mexico (1982).

Name of vessel	Gloria
Year launched	1967
Year commissioned	1968
Designer	Sener Sistemas Marinos SA (Senermar), Madrid, Spain
Builder	Astilleros y Talleres Celaya (ASTACE), Bilbao, Spain
Current Owner	Colombian Navy
Current flag	Colombia
Rig	Barque
Construction	Steel; teak clad deck
Length extreme	249.3 feet (76.00 m)
Length of hull	211.9 feet (64.60 m)
Length between perpendiculars	184.1 feet (56.10 m)
Beam	34.8 feet (10.60 m)
Draught	16.4 feet (5.00 m)
Tonnage	1,150 td (standard), 1,300 td (load)
Sail area	15,070 sq. feet (1,400 m^2)
Engine	530 hp Naval Stork
Complement	50–65 crew + 80 cadets
Photograph date	1984
Photograph location	Quebec, Canada

GOLDEN HINDE

There never were any plans of the *Golden Hind*, the galleon on which Francis Drake sailed around the world in 1577–80: in those days ships were built without plans, by eye and rule of thumb. The present *Golden Hinde* (spelt the way used by Drake) is a serious reconstruction of Drake's ship, based on all available historical data, shipbuilding rules of the period, contemporary pictorial representations and other circumstantial evidence.

The *Golden Hinde* was built as a fully working 'museum' ship for educational purposes, for the Crowley Maritime Corporation of San Francisco. Shipbuilding methods and materials of the period were followed in most respects although the hull planking is iroko, more durable than oak. The original suit of sails was hand-sewn flax but as these sails are wearing out they are being replaced by sails in Duradon, a synthetic cloth that looks like flax but is lighter and more durable. The ship is armed with 18 working replica guns. Except for a small and well concealed engine room, the ship is also period style below decks and carries replica furniture, carvings, artefacts and navigational instruments. The only visible anachronism is the wheel — well into the 18th century tillers on galleons were actuated by a vertical lever, the whipstaff, which was awkward to use. As the *Golden Hinde* frequently sails, she was given a modern wheel. Many millions of visitors have explored her five levels of decks and experienced the feel, noises and smells of a working Elizabethan galleon.

After opening her gangplank to the public in several English ports, including London, the *Golden Hinde* set sail in 1974 for San Francisco, her intended permanent port. Drake had sailed past the Bay of San Francisco in 1579 and had anchored just to the north of it. However, after good initial gates, the number of visitors began to fall as the years went by, and the owners were glad to charter the galleon for the filming in Japan of the television serial *Shogun* (in which she played the role of the *Erasmus*). She sailed to Japan via Hawaii in 1979. After filming, she sailed back to England via Hong Kong and the Mediterranean. She arrived at Plymouth in the spring of 1980, having sailed round the world like her namesake but via Panama and Suez.

From 1980 to 1985 she visited a large number of British ports, taking part in various harbour festivals and commemorations. She was sold to her present owners, John Carter and Roddy Coleman, in October 1984. They use her as an itinerant exhibition. On 25 October 1985 the *Golden Hinde* left England for the West Indies where she arrived before Christmas. She opened up to the public in Charlotte Amalie and St Thomas from January to March 86, after which she went to Vancouver for Expo '86 — under tow to save time. She was in Vancouver from May to October 86. Then, until July 1990, she visited 60 US West Coast ports, before sailing to the US East Coast. There she visited a number of ports until 13 September 1991 when she sailed homeward bound from Philadelphia. She arrived at Penzance late October and now winters at Salford near Manchester, open to visits by school parties and individuals. She will be touring UK harbours during the 'sailing season'. This is likely to be her pattern for the foreseeable future.

Name of vessel	Golden Hinde
Year built	1973
Designer	Loring Christian Norgaard, California
Builder	J. Hinks & Son, Appledore, Devon, England
Current Owner	Golden Hinde Ltd
Current flag	United Kingdom
Type	Galleon
Construction	Wood
Length extreme	120 feet (36.60 m)
Length on deck	102 feet (31.10 m)
Length waterline	75 feet (22.90 m)
Beam	23 feet (7.00 m)
Draught	13 feet (4.00 m)
Tonnage	156 grt; 96 nrt; 290 td
Sail area	4,150 sq. feet (386 m^2)
Engine	295 hp Cummins
Complement	18 crew (on voyages)
Photograph date	1974
Photograph location	Cowes, England

GORCH FOCK

Germany operated a large number of splendid merchant and naval schoolships from the beginning of our century until the Second World War. Most of the pre-1914 schoolships were seized as war prizes by the Allies in 1919 but were replaced between the wars. The German Navy ordered the construction of four sister school barques in the 1930s from the Hamburg yard of Blohm & Voss.

The first of these was the first *Gorch Fock*, built in 1933. She was named after the pen-name of the German maritime author Hans Kinau who had perished during a naval combat in the Skagerrak in 1916. She was seized by the Soviet Union after the Second World War and is still sailing under the name of *Tovarishch* (p. 190). The second, the *Horst Wessel*, was built in 1936 and was some 24 feet (7.5 m) longer; she is nowadays the *Eagle* (p. 80). The third was another 'big sister', the *Albert Leo Schlageter* of 1937 (now the *Sagres*, p. 168). Then, in 1938, Blohm & Voss built the 'little sister' *Mircea* for Romania (p. 140). A fourth 'big sister' class barque, the *Herbert Norkus*, was launched for the German Navy in 1939 but she was never completed on account of the war. In 1947 she was loaded by the Allies with wartime surplus explosives and ammunition, towed out to sea and blown up.

Once again the Federal Navy had to start from scratch: the *Gorch Fock* (II), a big-sister class barque, was ordered from Blohm & Voss. She was built, launched and commissioned in 1958, the year after the tragic sinking of the *Pamir* and the final retirement of the *Passat*. Both these German four-masted barques had been put back in service after the war as cargo-carrying merchant schoolships but they were to have

been laid up in 1957 anyway, even without the *Pamir's* disaster. But an unbroken continuity of ships and men, of know-how and skills, was thus just achieved and nowadays a number of retired captains of the *Gorch Fock* skipper German youth training ships, thus passing on square rigger 'lore'.

The *Gorch Fock* is an excellant traditional design. Although equipped with up-to-date gadgets and, since 1985, a cafeteria and a watermaker (etc.), she still spends more time under sail (as opposed to under power) than most other schoolships. Her cadets still sleep in hammocks. Since 1989 some of her cadets are female.

The *Gorch Fock* trains midshipmen from the Naval Academy at Kiel — Kiel is her base port and the harbour where she winters. She operates long seasons. In normal years she runs three cruises. The first is a short one in home waters; the second sees her sailing to foreign destinations in the Baltic or North Sea; the third is a long voyage, often to the Caribbean and North America.

The *Gorch Fock* is a very regular participant in the Tall Ships Races and associated windjammer gatherings. She sailed around the world in 1987–88, leaving Kiel west-abouts on 23 July 1987 and operating her first crew changeover in Honolulu in November. She then sailed on to Samoa and Auckland and took part in the Bicentenary parade of sail in Sydney in January 1988, prior to another crew changeover in Melbourne. She then sailed back via Suez, and arrived home at Kiel on 22 June. She took part in the tall ship gatherings at London, Rouen and Hamburg in 1989 and in the 1990 Tall Ships Race. In 1992 she will be taking part in the Columbus Regatta.

Name of vessel	Gorch Fock
Year built	1958
Designer	Wilhelm Süchting, Germany
Builder	Blohm & Voss, Hamburg, Germany
Current Owner	German Federal Navy
Current flag	Germany
Rig	Barque
Construction	Steel; teak deck
Length extreme	293.0 feet (89.32 m)
Length of hull	266.6 feet (81.26 m)
Length between perpendiculars	230.3 feet (70.20 m)
Beam	39.4 feet (12.00 m)
Draught	16.4 feet (5.00 m)
Tonnage	1,499 grt; 882 nrt; 1,727 t TM; 1,760 td (standard); 1,870 td (load)
Sail area	21,011 sq. feet (1,952 m^2)
Engine	800 hp MAN
Complement	80 crew + 160 cadets
Photograph date	1988
Photograph location	Cowes, England

This vessel was ordered from the Jan Smit yard by a Dutch merchant shipowner and she was launched in 1909 as a three-masted auxiliary trading schooner. She was fitted from the start with a diesel engine and she is said to have been the first vessel in the world to be thus powered. Her original name was *San Antonio* and for thirty years she traded to North and West Africa. She was unrigged in the 1940s and converted to a motor-coaster, with a more powerful diesel engine. In 1947 she was sold to Sweden and renamed *Buddi* and traded across the Baltic and North Sea. She was subsequently resold several times and was renamed *Santoni* and, once more, *San Antonio*.

She was found in 1973 in a small Swedish harbour by Captain Hartmuth Paschburg of Hamburg, who was later to put back in service the four-masted barque *Sea Cloud* (p. 170) and to convert a lightvessel to the barquentine *Atlantis* (p.38). He found shipping agents in Hamburg willing to finance the purchase, restoration and conversion of the old schooner for the luxury charter trade. The vessel was given back her original rig with a fore-yard. The three holds separated by water-tight bulkheads were subdivided into a total of 18 en-suite cabins with air conditioning and heating, for 36 to 46 passengers. The cargo hatches were removed and a very long deckhouse, with deck saloon, bar, dining room and galley, was built from the poop to within three feet of the fo'c's'le. The crew of 11 lived forward in the fo'c's'le and aft in the poop accommodation over the engine room. Under the new name of *Ariadne* and under Panama registry she operated charters in the Baltic, the Mediterranean and the West Indies. In 1977 she was used as support ship for the German Admiral's Cup team which had entered three ocean-racing yachts in the contest off Cowes. In 1979 a controlling interest in the schooner was acquired by the Paris sailing holiday agency Mondovoile which operated her in the Caribbean.

The present owners bought the schooner in 1983 for use as a stationary schoolship and as a sailing training ship. They renamed her *Grossherzogin Elizabeth* after the name of a full-rigged ship which had been built in 1901 as a schoolship for the Deutsche Schulschiff-Verein and which had been seized by France for war reparations at the close of the Second World War (and which is now being restored in Dunkirk as a museum ship bearing the name *Duchesse Anne*; the two other schoolships of the Deutsche Schulschiff-Verein are also still in existence as the *Dar Pomorza*, p. 78, and as the Norwegian adventure training barque *Statsraad Lehmkuhl*).

The schooner *Grossherzogin Elizabeth* is registered and homeported at Elsfleth, on the left bank of the Weser between Bremerhaven and Bremen, and she is attached to the Elsfleth nautical school (Elsfleth Seemannsschule). During school terms she is used as residential accommodation for student seamen. During the summer recesses (June to August) the *Grossherzogin Elizabeth* is available for cruises with fee-paying participants and sails in the North Sea and Baltic.

Name of vessel	Grossherzogin Elizabeth, ex-Ariadne, ex-San Antonio, ex-Buddi, ex-Santoni, ex-San Antonio
Year built	1909
Designer	Poul Benzon
Builder	Scheepswerven Jan Smit, Alblasserdam, the Netherlands
Current Owner	Landkreis Wesermarsch, Brake, Germany
Current flag	Germany
Rig	Three-masted fore-yard schooner
Construction	Steel; teak deck
Length extreme	209.0 feet (63.70 m)
Length of hull	174.1 feet (53.07 m)
Length between perpendiculars	151.0 feet (46.20 m)
Beam	27.0 feet (8.23 m)
Draught	11.6 feet (3.53 m)
Tonnage	462 grt; 217 nrt; 540 tdw
Sail area	10,760 sq. feet (1,000 m^2)
Engine	400 hp Caterpillar
Complement	11 crew + 40 trainees (when sailing)
Photograph date	1977
Photograph location	Cowes, England

GUAYAS

The *Guayas* is the second of the four ASTACE-built barques, slightly longer than the first, the *Gloria* (p. 102) and a bit smaller than the last two, the *Simon Bolivar* (p. 178 and cover picture) and Mexico's *Cuauhtémoc*, the last of this series, built in 1982 and measuring 258 feet (78.50 m) hull length and 1,662 tons standard displacement.

The *Guayas* was built as a schoolship for the Ecuadorian Navy. Her keel was laid down at Bilbao on 1 June 1976 and she was launched on 22 October that same year. She was completed the following year and delivered at Bilbao to the Ecuadorian Navy in July 1977.

The *Guayas* is named after Ecuador's main river by which is built the city of Guayaquil. The barque is attached to the Naval Superior School in Guayaquil, a school that was founded by the country's Liberator Simon Bolivar.

The *Guayas'* cadets are aged around 21 years. Their number and the number of the regular crew and instructors appear to vary from voyage to voyage but, as for most Latin countries, the ratio of crew to cadets is very high.

The *Guayas* is easily distinguished from her near sistership the *Gloria* by the open flying bridge instead of the covered wheelhouse — but that station is still pretty much at the same height and there are the same problems of forward vision obscured by the mainsail when the latter is set. There is another wheel traditionally placed on the poopdeck aft but its forward view is blocked by the charthouse and flying bridge structure. Another difference is the figurehead which, on the *Guayas*, represents an Andean condor (the *Esmeralda*, p.88, also has a condor for figurehead).

The first couple of years after her arrival in Ecuador the *Guayas* sailed in the Eastern Pacific and in the Caribbean. She sailed back to Europe in 1980, sailing from Guayaquil on 16 April to join the start of the American Tall Ships Race at Cartagena, Venezuela, racing to Norfolk, Virginia, (where she arrived first, winning the second prize on corrected time), then carrying on in the Race from Boston to Kristiansand, Norway, in which she was third. From Kristiansand she joined the Cutty Sark Tall Ships Races Kiel – Karlskrona – Frederikshavn – Amsterdam. She was the only tall ship to have taken part in the whole series from Cartagena through to Amsterdam. On that voyage she carried 13 officers, 10 warrant officers, 94 crew and 36 midshipmen. In the harbours she was not only seen but heard, with frequent performances by her brass band with a non-martial repertoir of Latin American music and jazz. She returned to Guayaquil on 21 October 1980.

The *Guayas* also took part in the 1986 Operation Sail in New York which actually brought together all four of the Senermar/ASTACE barques. On that voyage the *Guayas* had 14 officers, 73 seamen and 60 cadets.

In 1987 the *Guayas* sailed to Australia, first to Brisbane then to Hobart, to join the Tall Ships Race ending at Sydney on Australia's Bicentennial Day, 26 January 1988. On that voyage the barque carried 63 cadets.

She is expected to take part in the Columbus Regatta '92, the Tall Ships Race series marking the 500th anniversary of Christopher Columbus' first voyage to the New World.

Name of vessel	Guayas
Year built	1976
Designer	Sener Sistemas Marinos SA (Senermar), Madrid, Spain
Builder	Astilleros y Talleres Celaya (ASTACE), Bilbao, Spain
Current Owner	Ecuadorian Navy
Current flag	Ecuador
Rig	Barque
Construction	Steel; teak clad
Length extreme	257.5 feet (78.48 m)
Length of hull	219 feet (66.75 m)
Length between perpendiculars	184.1 feet (56.10 m)
Beam	34.8 feet (10.60 m)
Draught	15.4 feet (4.70 m)
Tonnage	934 grt; 1,397 t TM, 1,153 td (standard) 1,300 td (load); 234 tdw
Sail area	15,177 sq. feet (1,410 m²)
Engine	700 hp General Motors
Complement	87 crew + 63 cadets
Photograph date	1980
Photograph location	Kiel, Germany

HELGA

The *Helga* was built in 1908 as a fore-and-aft schooner primarily intended for carrying agricultural cargoes on Lakes Vänern and Vättern and associated waterways. She has a spoon bow and a transom stern with typically Swedish lines. Her frames, beams and hull planking were all oak and her deck was pitchpine.

In 1959 her rig was cut down to the foremast which was kept only for use as a derrick to load and unload cargo. She traded under power until 1969 and was then laid up.

In 1971 she was bought by a Swede who converted her to a houseboat and motorsailer. In 1975 she was sold to an Englishman who brought her over to England with the intention of converting her back to sail. However his project did not mature and he resold the ship to Mr Alan Reekie, the owner and skipper of the Thames sailing barge *Ironsides*.

Alan Reekie did a lot of work on the *Helga* in Faversham, Kent, from 1978 to 1983: new ceilings (the internal hull planking), removal of the large cargo hatch, laying a new deck made of ¾ in. (20 mm) laid teak on ply over the original pitchpine, renewing all the timberheads, some frames and the covering board, renewing the planking to below the waterline in pitchpine, renewing the bulwarks and rails and building a new cabin trunk aft, in iroko, etc.

He re-rigged the *Helga* as a schooner, with steel lower masts and Douglas fir topmasts, bowsprit and spars, and had Duradon sails made. In 1984 he rigged a square topsail fitted with roller-furling gear allowing it to be handled from the deck. The *Helga* can be sailed by a crew of just two.

The *Helga* is a small vessel but she looks and feels much bigger than she is. Externally, because of her lines and rig; on deck because the flush deck is exceptionally uncluttered (the saloon is lighted by flush deck-deadlights), and below deck because cabin space has been sacrificed in favour of a large saloon which is made to feel even bigger by an optical illusion provided by the wide passage entrance leading forward – it feels a part of a saloon while its narrowing forward gives the perspective of a long passageway. On the port side of this passage there is a two-berth cabin and a study with a built-in walnut desk; to starboard there is another two-bunk cabin (the lower being wide enough to count as a double for very good friends) and a shower cubicle. The passage ends with a double door decorated with a lovely lacquered painting of irises, anemones and birds on a black background – but it mundanely leads to the heads! Abaft the saloon there is a galley to port and the owner's cabin to starboard (with double bed). Alan Reekie and his wife Ronda lived aboard. The trunk cabin is the chart room.

They sold *Helga* in August 1986 to Mr Patrick Keen who already owned the Thames sailing barge *Kitty* based at Southampton. The *Helga* joined the *Kitty* at the Ocean Village Marina and was given an expensive refit and was equipped with modern navigational electronics. The deck was relaid, in teak. She was used for day charters in the Solent, corporate receptions, wedding parties, etc. In the spring of 1991 she left Southampton for the Mediterranean but ran into a Channel gale and had problems. She took shelter at Guernsey and fell against a wall at low water. Repairs were done in Guernsey and the schooner sailed back to England. She was wintering at St Katharine's Dock, London, in 1991–2.

Name of vessel	Helga
Year built	1908
Designer	J. Hugerman
Builder	J. Hugerman yard, Viken, Malmöhuslän, Sweden
Current Owner	Mr Patrick E. Keen, UK
Current flag	United Kingdom
Rig	Topsail schooner
Construction	Wood
Length extreme	81 feet (24.69 m)
Length on deck	61.7 feet (19.26 m)
Beam	19.5 feet (5.94 m)
Draught	8 feet (2.44 m)
Tonnage	53.04 grt; 28.53 nrt
Sail area	3,000 sq. feet (280 m²) (approx.)
Engine	125 hp Scania
Complement	8 berths
Photograph date	1988
Photograph location	Off Isle of Wight, England

HENRYK RUTKOWSKI

The *Henryk Rutkowski* was originally built, in 1943–44, as a German Navy *vor Posten Kutter*, a naval patrol boat or 'cutter', one of a class built by the hundreds on plans derived from the 1910 Dutch pilot schooner design (see *Vrouwe Geertruida Magadalena*, p. 200). After the war many of these boats were converted to motor fishing vessels, notably in the Netherlands, East and West Germany and Poland. With their pilot schooner lines these hulls are ideal for conversion to sail and a number have indeed been converted to sailing yachts when their fishing days were over. The *Henryk Rutkowski* is perhaps the only one to have been directly converted from a laid-up naval patrol boat to sail.

The patrol boat was built in the German Baltic port of Swinemünde (nowadays Świnoujście in Poland). She was seized by Poland in 1945 for war reparations and was renamed *Henryk Rutkowski* after a wartime Resistance fighter. She was converted in 1950–51 at the Rybacka yard in Gdynia to a gaff ketch with wooden pole masts. She retained her wooden flush deck and was given a large wheelhouse aft. She was owned by the national League for Sport and Technology and was used for sail-training apprentice fishermen. She was registered in Gdynia under the fishing fleet number GDY-180. She was put into service in the spring of 1951 and sailed in the Baltic.

She was laid up in 1976, in need of a major overhaul. Funds were not immediately available. By 1984 the decision had been taken to rebuild her as a brigantine along plans made by Bohdan Leonczuk. The work was done at the Rybacka repair yard at Wldadislawowo.

The wooden deck was replaced by a steel deck painted blue with non-skid sanded paint. The after third of the hull's sides were raised 75 cm (2½ feet) with steel plates to build a raised poop in place of the old wheelhouse. Right in the stern there is a cockpit with the wheel, and in front of it, sunk into the poop deck, a chart room. The poop accommodation contains the afterguard's quarters and the galley. The trainees' quarters are forward of the engine compartment and include a saloon, 2 four-berth and 2 six-berth cabins.

The rig is typically 'modern Polish' with steel masts in one piece, standing yards (three in number) and much use of fishing boat orange polypropylene rope for the running rigging.

The *Henryk Rutkowski* was put back into service in July 1986. Her management had been transferred to the Trzebiez Sailing Centre. She has a permanent crew of three (skipper, engineer and cook/purser) supplemented by two volunteer passage watch officers. Some cruises are scheduled cruises sold by the berth but many are chartered by clubs, associations and youth groups. The ship herself does not operate an upper age limit, and Westerners, paying in much needed hard currency, have always been welcome from the start. Even before the change of regime in Poland the *Henryk Rutkowski* made frequent cruises to Western Europe.

The brigantine took part in the London – Hamburg Tall Ships in 1989 and in the Plymouth–Corunna–Bordeaux–Amsterdam Tall Ships Race in 1990. In addition to her regular cruises she has been doing some rehabilitation cruises for juvenile delinquents. Recently she has operated joint US-Polish 'school at sea' cruises.

Name of vessel	Henryk Rutkowski
Year built	1944. Converted in 1986
Rebuild and conversion architect	Bohdan Leonczuk, Poland
Builder	at Swinemünde, Germany (today Świnoujście, Poland)
Current Owner	Centralny Ośrodek Zeglarstwa Trzebiez, Poland
Current flag	Poland
Rig	Brigantine
Construction	Composite; steel deck
Length extreme	97.4 feet (29.70 m)
Length of hull	79.7 feet (24.30 m)
Length waterline	70.2 feet (21.40 m)
Beam	21.1 feet (6.43 m)
Draught	10.5 feet (3.20 m)
Tonnage	99.43 grt; 24.29 nrt
Sail area	3,633 sq. feet (337.51 m²)
Engine	121 hp Delfin
Complement	3 permanent crew + 2 volunteer watch officers + 20 trainees
Photograph date	1990
Photograph location	Plymouth, England

JUAN SEBASTIAN DE ELCANO

The *Juan Sebastian de Elcano* is the schoolship of the Spanish Navy. Her plans were designed by Charles E. Nicholson of Camper & Nicholson's of Gosport, England. The ship was built in Spain, at Cadiz.

The *Juan Sebastian de Elcano* and her younger near-sistership the Chilean *Esmeralda* (p. 88) were, until the advent of the *Wind Star* class sail-liners, the biggest fore-and-aft vessels in existence, and they still have the greatest sail area within the schooner class. By any yardstick of length, tonnage or sail area these two Hispanic vessels are among the largest sailing vessels in service today or in the past.

The sail plans of the two vessels are slightly different and are discussed in the text for the *Esmeralda*. While some people may still prefer to call the *Esmeralda* a barquentine, there is no such argument about the correct term for the *Juan Sebastian de Elcano*: she is typically a topgallant schooner — that is, a topsail schooner setting a topgallant above her square topsails.

The lower masts, fidded topmasts, bowsprit and spars are made of steel. The engine's exhaust is led through the lower jiggermast. When she was built the schooner had two large deckhouses on the main deck, in the waist; these were widened at a later date so that their sides became flush with the hull's sides. Such full-beam deckhouses are known as 'Liverpool houses' because they were first seen on some Liverpool ships in the late 19th century. These two 'islands' divide the waist deck into three short decks almost like well decks. Catwalks allow an easy level passage from the poop deck to the fo'c's'le, via the tops of these islands.

The schooner, being a naval vessel, is armed with four 5.7 cm quick-firing guns used for salutes. The figurehead is a crowned female figure. The vessel is named after the Spanish navigator who was the first to circumnavigate the world. In 1519 Magellan set out from San Lucar with five ships and 270 men. He was killed in the Philippines and de Elcano, the senior officer left, assumed command of what remained of the expedition. He completed the voyage in 1522 with just one ship, the *Victoria*, and a mere eighteen survivors.

The *Juan Sebastian de Elcano* spends much of her time at sea on training voyages. She trains naval midshipmen or *Guardias Marinas*. In addition to seamanship and sail handling they follow theoretical and practical courses in navigation, astronomy, meteorology, maritime history, English, marine engineering, radio and marine electronics, etc.

The *Juan Sebastian de Elcano* frequently undertakes long cruises. Her maiden voyage, in 1928, was a circumnavigation. She has taken part in a number of Tall Ships Races and tall ship festivals. In 1976 she was in the American Bicentennial Tall Ships Race. At the start of the leg from Bermuda to Newport the Argentinian *Libertad* bore down on her from windward and caught the Spaniard's outer and flying jib stays with her bowsprit, causing the fore-topmast to bend in two. The schooner withdrew from the race for repairs and managed to make these in time for the big sail parade in New York on 4th of July.

In 1988 the *Juan Sebastian de Elcano* was at Sydney for Australia's Bicentennial, and in 1992 she will be the flagship of the Columbus Regatta which will be starting from her home port of Cadiz.

Name of vessel	Juan Sebastian de Elcano
Year built	1927
Designer	Charles Ernest Nicholson, Camper & Nicholson's, England
Builder	Astilleros Echevarrieta y Larrinaga, Cadiz, Spain
Current Owner	Spanish Navy
Current flag	Spain
Rig	Four-masted topgallant schooner
Construction	Steel; teak deck
Length extreme	370.1 feet (112.80 m)
Length of hull	308.8 feet (94.11 m)
Length between perpendiculars	259.6 feet (79.12 m)
Beam	43.1 feet (13.15 m)
Draught	22.6 feet (6.89 m)
Tonnage	2,478 grt; 3,420 td (standard); 3,754 td (load)
Sail area	26,555 sq. feet (2,467 m^2)
Engine	1,500 hp Sulzer-Bazan
Complement	208 officers and crew + 80–100 cadets
Photograph date	1976
Photograph location	New York, USA

KALIAKRA

The *Kaliakra* was built on order from Bulgaria as a near sistership of the Polish Navy barquentine *Iskra*, herself a slightly enlarged sister of the *Pogoria* (p. 156). Construction began on 5 October 1983 at Gdynia. The hull was built upside down in a shed and after launching, on 28 January 1984, was towed to Gdansk for completion. A crew of Bulgarians, who had been trained the previous year on the *Iskra*, took delivery of the Kaliakra on 29 June 1984 and sailed her to her home port of Varna. She began her training cruises that autumn.

Compared to the *Iskra* and *Pogoria*, the *Kaliakra* had a shorter foremast, without a royal. This was because, unlike the two Polish vessels which have a bare steel deck, she has a teak-clad deck and it was thought that the extra weight would be detrimental to stability, hence the reduction of weight and sail area aloft. The picture opposite and the sail area below correspond to that original rig. In fact the stability fears were quite unfounded and when the *Kaliakra* returned to Poland in early 1989 for her first quinquennial refit, her foremast was lengthened and a royal yard was crossed. Other differences include the transom which is vertical on the *Kaliakra*, and which has stern windows, whereas the Polish barquentines have reverse transoms, and the absence of a fore deckhouse on the new barquentine (the small structure left is a companionway). The *Kaliakra* has a cast bronze figurehead representing the maiden Kaliakra, a 14th century Bulgarian heroine who jumped to her death from a headland rather than be taken captive by the invading Turks.

The *Kaliakra* is primarily intended for the training of students preparing for sea careers in the merchant navy or the Bulgarian Navy. They come from three different nautical colleges all located in Varna. At times when she is not required on professional training cruises she is made available to youth organizations.

From the start the *Kaliakra* was also intended as a goodwill ambassador of her country and she has been a regular participant in the Tall Ships Races despite the distances involved to take part in these races from her home waters – she was often the training vessel that had sailed the longest distance to join the STA events. Her first appearance in a Tall Ships Race was in the 1986 Race in the North Sea. She also took part in the 1987 Race in the Baltic, which she won in her class, beating the *Iskra* in the process. She took part in the 1988 Tall Ships Race, again in the Baltic, and on her way home she took part in an international traditional sail festival at Douarnenez, France. In 1989, with her new rig, she came to London for the start of the North Sea Tall Ships Race but sailed from the Thames to Rouen for a gathering of windjammers for the bicentennial of the French Revolution. From Rouen she re-joined the STA racing fleet at Hamburg. In 1990 she took part in the Plymouth – La Corunna – Bordeaux Tall Ships Race. In all those races she had cadets under professional training; the youth and adventure training cruises were operated in the Black Sea, often with calls at Constanţa in Romania and at Odessa and Sochi in the USSR.

Owing to the economic crisis following the collapse of the old order she was laid up in 1991 except for a two-week youth training cruise to Piraeus, Greece, and back. However in 1992 she will be representing Bulgaria in the Columbus trans-Atlantic Tall Ships Race.

Name of vessel	Kaliakra
Year built	1984
Designer	Zygmunt Choreń, Poland
Builder	'Paris Commune' yard at Gdynia; completed at the Lenin Shipyard at Gdansk, Poland
Current Owner	Water Transport Corporation, Varna, Bulgaria
Operator	Navigation Maritime Bulgare, Varna, Bulgaria
Current flag	Bulgaria
Rig	Barquentine
Construction	Steel; teak-clad deck
Length extreme	160.4 feet (48.90 m)
Length of hull	140.5 feet (42.81 m)
Length between perpendiculars	118.1 feet (36.00 m)
Beam	26.3 feet (8.00 m)
Draught	12.3 feet (3.75 m)
Tonnage	247 grt; 74 nrt; 341 td (light); 392 td (load)
Sail area	9,526 sq. feet (885 m²)
Engine	310 bhp Wola Warszawa
Complement	21 permanent crew + 30 cadets or trainees
Photograph date	1986
Photograph location	Newcastle-upon-Tyne, England

KASKELOT

The *Kaskelot* was launched in 1948 under that name which means 'Sperm Whale' in Danish. She was built by the J. Ring Andersen yard at Svendborg, the best-known wooden sailing ship yard in Denmark. The *Kaskelot* was however built as a motor vessel although her lines and construction are those of the Greenland whaling barques and barquentines that had preceded her in her intended trade. The frigate-style raised fo'c's'le and poop deck are original features.

The *Kaskelot* was built for the Danish Royal Greenland Company as a supply vessel servicing scattered settlements along the coasts of Greenland. Because of the ice conditions she was built with extra strong framing and ice plating at and below her waterline. Later she underwent several changes of ownership and names, working for a while in the Faroe Islands.

She was bought in Denmark in 1983, in a very run-down condition, by Clearwater Holdings Ltd of Jersey, for a conversion to the likeness of Robert F. Scott's polar expedition barque *Terra Nova* (a former whaling ship) for a film project. The rebuild, conversion and management of the ship were contracted to Square Sail of Colchester which had already converted and operated several Baltic traders and, at that time, already owned or managed the brigantine *Søren Larsen* (p. 182) and the three-masted schooner hulk *Orion*. All these vessels are still in the Square Sail fleet since then increased by the gaff schooner *Carrie* and the brigantine *Phoenix* (p. 154). The *Kaskelot's* rebuild and conversion was done at the Troense shipyard, just across the water from the yard where she had been built. The work was completed in 1984. The ship was given back her original name and was registered in Jersey.

Although mainly converted for film charter work, the *Kaskelot* is no movie mock-up prop but a superbly rigged and seaworthy barque. The accommodation under the poop is original and consists of 11 berths in five cabins plus galley, saloon and heads. There are a further 8 bunks in the fo'c's'le and another five can be quickly rigged up. Her sailing complement is 14; she can take 12 passengers on offshore cruises or up to 100 on day trips, but her main business is film work and chartering for harbour events such as festivals, corporate promotions, etc. Her vast hold, 66 × 26 feet (20 × 8 m), is unconverted and provides an ideal venue for exhibitions or receptions for up to 200 guests. In 1988 the barque was bought out by Mr Robin Davies, one of the directors of Square Sail, and re-registered at Bristol.

Her first contract, in 1984, was the filming of the TV dramatized documentary serial *The Last Place on Earth*, for which she made two voyages, to Greenland and to the Faroes, to play the parts of the *Terra Nova* and of Amundsen's *Fram*. That same year she also 'acted' in *The Stamp of Greatness*. In 1985 she was mocked-up to an 18th century appearance for the filming of *Revolution* and *Sea Dogs*. She has appeared in many movies since then, including *Rock around the Dock*, and has done some commercials. In 1988 she was chartered by the organisers of the Douarnenez Traditional Sail Festival; in 1989 she was chartered for the Rouen windjammer gathering, etc. In 1991 she sailed to Iceland for the filming of a dramatized documentary on Jean Charcot and his polar exploration barque *Pourquoi Pas?*. She will be at the Brest and Douarnenez Traditional Sail Festivals in 1992.

Name of vessel	Kaskelot, ex-Anne-Marie Grenius, ex-Anne Marie, ex-Arctic Explorer, ex-Kaskelot
Year built	1948. Converted 1983−84
Designer	J. Ring Andersen
Builder	J. Ring Andersen, Svendborg, Denmark
Current Owner	Square Sail (Mr Robin Davies), Colchester, England
Current flag	United Kingdom
Rig	Barque
Construction	Wood
Length extreme	155 feet (47.24 m)
Length on deck	127 feet (38.71 m)
Beam	28 feet (8.53 m)
Draught	12.5 feet (3.81 m)
Tonnage	226 grt; 350 tdw
Sail area	9,500 sq. feet (883 m^2)
Engine	380 hp Burmeister & Wain Alpha
Complement	14 crew + 12 passengers or 100 day passengers
Photograph date	1987
Photograph location	Cowes, England

KRONWERK

The Grand Duchy of Finland had been part of the Russian Empire since 1809. Finland declared her independence in 1917, during the Russian Revolution, and it was recognized by the Soviet Union in 1920. This did not prevent Stalin from attacking Finland in November 1939, in the days of the Molotov-von Ribbentrop Non-Aggression Pact, as the Western democracies were otherwise occupied with Germany. Stalin seized Eastern Karelia and parts of Finnish Lapland. When Hitler attacked Stalin in the summer of 1941 Finland allied herself to the Third Reich in a bid to recover her lost territories. She was defeated in 1944. Not only did the Soviet Union retain Eastern Karelia and other parts of Finland but Stalin exacted heavy war reparations from Finland. Finland, which had suffered very heavy damages in the war had nothing to offer in way of compensation except her timber and shipbuilding skills. Thus it was that from 1946 to 1952 Finland built many hundreds of wooden merchant barquentines, three-masted schooners, galeases (two-masted schooners) and a few ketches. The *Kronwerk*, opposite, is one of these vessels. Most of these vessels were engaged in transporting sand, gravel, timber and other building supplies to assist the reconstruction of the devastated towns of the Eastern Baltic shore, where even the roads had been rendered useless. The *Kronwerk*, ex-*Sirius*, was however one of a number of these vessels that were turned into training ships for Soviet sailors.

Those Finnish vessels were not long-lived: they were built of pine and fir, poor shipbuilding timbers in the first place and furthermore much of the timber used at the time was unseasoned; one can also suspect that the

Finnish shipwrights did not put all their hearts and the best of their skills in the building of those vessels and Soviet maintenance did the rest . . . Anyway, such vessels quickly became obsolete: they were already so when built.

The *Sirius* was laid up under the name of *Kronwerk* in Leningrad and is preserved afloat as a restaurant ship. The figurehead representing a lion's head obviously dates from that conversion.

Only one vessel of that fleet remains in service today: the *Zarja* (pronounced 'Zarya'). She was built as a three-masted foreyard gaff schooner in 1952, using only non-magnetic materials as she was intended for use as a geomagnetic research vessel. She is (or was, until any current name changes or developments) operated by the Leningrad Institute of Oceanography. She was converted to a Bermudan rig in 1975 and underwent a major refit at Antwerp in 1983. Aluminium Proctor masts were fitted at that time. The three-masted Bermudan schooner *Kodor*, which was still sailing in 1982 as a training vessel for the Leningrad Higher Engineering School, has been moved by way of canals and the Volga to Baku, in Azerbaijan, on the inland Caspian Sea and is used there as a restaurant ship. The barkentine *Vega II*, built in 1952, which was operated by the Tallinn Seamen's School, was laid up in 1979; the barquentine *Kihnu John* was laid up at Tallinn by 1982 and the schooner *Nadeszda* was laid up at Nakhodka: these vessels, if they are still in existence today, are all that remain of the reported 6 or 800 windjammers built in Finland between 1946 and 1952 for the Soviet Union. The story of this last great sailing fleet in Europe has yet to be written up.

Name of vessel	Kronwerk, ex Sirius
Year built	1948
Builder	Laivateollisuus yard, Åbo, Finland
Current flag	Russia
Rig	Barquentine
Construction	Wood
Length of hull	144.3 feet (44.0 m)
Beam	29.2 feet (8.90 m)
Draught	10.8 feet (3.30 m)
Tonnage	322 grt; 41 nrt; 55 tdw
Engine	Removed (originally had an East German auxiliary diesel)
Photograph date	1976
Photograph location	Leningrad (now St Petersburg), Russia

KRUZENSHTERN

The four-masted barque *Padua* was built in 1926 for the Hamburg shipowners F. Laeisz, to replace war losses. She is the last Cape Horner to have been built. Although carrying full cargoes, she also had accommodation for 40 boys or apprentices. She first worked on the Chilean nitrate route but that trade was at an end. She was briefly laid up in 1932 but was recommissioned with a government subsidy and she operated in the Australian grain trade until the Second World War which she spent laid-up at Flensburg.

In January 1946 she was towed to Swinemünde and handed over to the Soviet Navy as a war prize. She was renamed after the Russian navigator and explorer Adam Johann von Krusenstern (1770–1846), an Estonian Prussian whose name has been re-transliterated phonetically from the Cyrillic alphabet as *Kruzenshtern*.

Until 1959 the *Kruzenshtern* was officially in commission as part of the Soviet Baltic Fleet, but she remained in harbour. In 1959–61 she underwent a major refit and was given her first set of engines. From 1961 to 1965 she was operated by the Soviet Navy's Hydrographic Department, conducting hydrographic surveys and oceanographical surveys for the Academy of Sciences of the USSR in the Atlantic, Caribbean and Mediterranean, while at the same time serving as a schoolship for naval cadets. In those days she had a white livery.

In 1965 she was transferred to the USSR Ministry of Fisheries, registered at Riga, and began her career as a training ship for future fisheries officers. In 1968–72 she underwent another refit and modernization. Her poop was extended forward to merge with the Liverpool house and the current set of engines was installed. The hull was painted in the current livery, black with a white band with painted gunports. She resumed her training cruises (normally two-months long) in 1972. Her cadets came from Fishery schools in Baltic ports and Murmansk.

In 1974 she was the first Soviet ship, with the *Tovarischch* (p. 190), to take part in a Tall Ships' Race and was awarded the Cutty Sark (friendship) Trophy. In 1976 she took part in the US Bicentennial trans-Atlantic Tall Ships Race where, under orders from 'up above' to win at all cost, she cheated with her engines and got dubbed '*Dieselstern*'. Her prize was nonetheless awarded, but without any clapping of hands from the assembled crews at the Prizegiving. The message got through to the owners and since then the *Kruzenshtern* has been a frequent, fairplaying and popular participant in the Races and other international windjammer gatherings. Following the lead set by the *Sedov* (p. 172) the *Kruzenshtern* began accepting some hard-currency paying Western trainees from the 1990 Tall Ships Race onwards.

Around 1980 the *Kruzenshtern*'s registry was changed to Tallinn, without change of purpose. In April 1991, when Estonia was about to break away from the Soviet Union, her registry was transferred to Kaliningrad, Russia. The USSR Ministry of fisheries which owned her was abolished in November 1991 but she is expected to be taken over in February 1992 by the new Russian Ministry of Fisheries. The operators are raising the finance for a refit, including through the sale of hard currency berths, for a refit in order to take part in the Columbus Regatta.

Name of vessel	Kruzenshtern, *ex*-Padua
Year built	1926
Designer	J.C. Tecklenborg
Builder	J.C. Tecklenborg, Wesermünde, Germany
Prospective owner	Russian Ministry of Fisheries (see text)
Current Operator	Kaliningrad Nautical College
Current flag	Russia
Rig	Four-masted barque
Construction	Steel, wood-clad deck
Length extreme	375.7 feet (114.50 m)
Length of hull	342.2 feet (104.30 m)
Length between perpendiculars	313.3 feet (95.50 m)
Beam	46.1 feet (14.05 m)
Draught	23.5 feet (7.17 m)
Tonnage	3545 grt, 607 nrt, 3185 t TM; 3,760 td (light) 5725 td (load)
Sail area	39,342 sq. feet (3,655 m^2)
Engines	2 × 800 hp Russky Diesel; twin propellers
Complement	76 crew + 202 cadets
Photograph date	1974
Photograph location	Cowes, England

LADY ELLEN

This spectacular yacht was designed by her original owners, Lars and Lars-Erik Johansson (father and son), owners of a merchant shipping firm and of a wooden Baltic schooner converted for charter, the *Hamlet*. They come from an old shipowning family and the lines and rig of the *Lady Ellen* were derived from those of a wooden trading schooner, the *Ellen*, built in 1909, which used to be owned by the Johansson family. She was fast, handy and much loved. She used to carry timber and other cargoes between Scandinavia and the United Kingdom. She was sold to America and has long since disappeared.

The *Lady Ellen* however is no wooden trading schooner. She was built of steel under Norske Veritas inspection and class; her deck and deckhouses are clad in teak and there is enough tropical hardwoods on her to have caused a minor ecological disaster. A reminder of her oaken ancestry can however be seen in grooves cut with a milling grinder along the smooth-welded hull plates to simulate plank seams, as well as in the general lines of the hull with its clipper bow, elliptical stern, marked sheer, good deadrise and long keel. The traditional lines and rig were not kept at the expense of speed: the *Lady Ellen* has reached almost 18 knots under favourable conditions.

Her rig is entirely traditional. Although the bowsprit and jibboom are in one piece, the topmasts are fidded. All the masts and spars are made of Oregon pine. She can set 14 sails totalling 13,000 sq. feet (1,200 m²): 5 headsails, 3 square sails, 3 gaff sails, 2 gaff topsails and a main topmast staysail. In addition she can set a square foresail.

The foredeck is agreeably spacious and uncluttered; the poop deck is raised by about 2.5 feet (75 cm). The midship deckhouse is of moderate dimensions and contains a deck saloon, a deck shower and toilet, and companionways to below-deck compartments. Just abaft this deckhouse, on the poop deck, there is a deck cockpit with the wheel and padded benches. The whaleback deckhouse at the stern of the poop deck is the chartroom; it has a pilot berth and a ladder down to the skipper's quarters.

Below decks there are cabins for up to 14 guests, a very spacious saloon (554 sq feet — 51.5 m²), a good-size galley, two big cold rooms, and accommodation for 8 crew.

The *Lady Ellen*'s keel was laid down in 1980 at the Kockums yard at Malmö, which built the hull and installed the engine. The accommodation was made by Vindö Marin which also rigged the schooner. The terylene sails were made in Denmark. The *Lady Ellen* was extensively fitted with modern electronics and guest amenities (including a video library and equipment for various water sports) and later she was fitted with an INMARSAT direct-dial telephone.

The *Lady Ellen* was completed in 1982 and chartered in the West Indies. In 1984 she sailed to Quebec City for a two-month charter in connection with the windjammer gathering marking the 450th anniversary of the discovery of Canada by the French navigator Jacques Cartier. In the following years she chartered both in the Caribbean and the Mediterranean — upmarket charters.

In 1990 her accommodation was completely renewed and then the owning company went bankrupt. Since mid-1990 the schooner has been laid-up at San Remo, Italy, in the hands of the receivers.

Name of vessel	Lady Ellen
Year built	1982
Designer	K.B. Lars Johansson Shipping, Sweden
Builder	Kokums yard, Malmö; completed by Vindö Marin, Sweden
Current Owner	Ackordscentralen, Göteborg, Sweden (receivers)
Current flag	Sweden
Rig	Three-masted topgallant schooner
Construction	Steel; teak-clad deck
Length extreme	178.8 feet (54.50 m)
Length of hull	141.1 feet (43.00 m)
Length between perpendiculars	118.1 feet (36.00 m)
Beam moulded	25.8 feet (7.85 m)
Draught	11.0 feet (3.35 m)
Tonnage	229 grt, 130 nrt
Sail area	12,917 sq. feet (1,200 m²)
Engine	550 hp Fiat-Allis
Complement	8 crew + 14 guests
Photograph date	1984
Photograph location	Quebec, Canada

The *Leeuwin*, as she is called without the *II* except on official documents, is Australia's largest sail training vessel. She derives from a 1974 project to build for Western Australian youth a sistership of New Zealand's brigantine *Spirit of Adventure*. The project faltered at first through lack of support but was revived in 1981 with an eye on the Australian Bicentennial celebrations in 1988. Fund raising was long and laborious but got an AUS $700,000 grant in 1985 from the Australian Bicentennial Authority. More funds were raised on paper when, in the wake of Alan Bond's victory in the 1983 *America's* Cup, the 1986–87 Cup challenges were to be held at Fremantle: the Project was offered AUS $600,000 for a five month charter of the ship for use as a spectator vessel. Other funds were raised from various sources by members of the supporters' association, the Sail Training Association of Western Australia (STAWA), and the yard offered to build the barquentine at cost price.

The hull was built upside down and launched that way in early 1986. She was righted in the water and slipped for completion. The second and official launching was held on 2 August. The barquentine was named after the Dutch vessel *Leeuwin* ('Lioness') which, in 1622, first rounded the southwestern point of Australia to which her name was given. The barquentine bears the *II* after her name not on account of that early Dutch galleon but because the name of *Leeuwin* was already taken on the Registry by a small private yacht.

The *Leeuwin* was commissioned on 12 September 1986 as a 'gin palace' for day trips to watch the Cup races and for smart in-harbour receptions. She had an oak-panelled interior that was later stripped and rebuilt to accommodate five professional crew, eight volunteer crew and forty trainees. The *Leeuwin* made her maiden sail training voyage in May 1987, to Albany.

The *Leeuwin*'s normal activities are ten-day sailing courses for young men and women with a minimum age of 15. Initially the emphasis was on seamanship training but in 1989, under a new captain, the character training aspect was increased and more responsibilities were given to the trainees. From the seventh day until the end of the cruise they elect officers from among their own ranks and run the ship themselves. The regular crew stand aside and intervene only if the safety of the ship and her company are at risk. Youth cruises account for 90% of all training cruises; the remainder are character training and team-building courses for corporate executives. Recently the *Leeuwin* has been training the crew of the new Polish-built Japanese sail training brigantine *Kaisei*.

The *Leeuwin* also runs fund-raising day cruises called 'Half Sea Days' crewed by competent volunteers at times when the permanent crew are on shore leave. This helps keep the youth training berth prices down — five years after her launch the ship had repaid all debts incurred during the building phase.

Running mostly ten-day cruises with 12,000 miles of Western Australian coastline to cruise along, the barquentine seldom leaves home waters. In January 1988 she took part in the Hobart to Sydney Tall Ships Race and in the Bicentennial parade of sail at Sydney. In 1990 she took part in the Fremantle to Bali Race.

Name of vessel	Leeuwin II
Year built	1986
Designer	Len Rendell
Builder	Australian Shipbuilding Industries Pty Ltd, South Coogee, Western Australia
Current Owner	Leeuwin Sail Training Foundation Ltd
Current flag	Australia
Rig	Barquentine
Construction	Steel; teak-clad deck
Length extreme	180.4 feet (55.00 m)
Length on deck	136.2 feet (41.50 m)
Length waterline	109.6 feet (33.40 m)
Beam	29.5 feet (9.00 m)
Draught	11.2 feet (3.40 m)
Tonnage	236 grt, 99 nrt; 300 td (standard)
Sail area	10,150 sq. feet (943 m^2)
Engines	2 × 230 hp Detroit; twin propellers
Complement	5 permanent crew + 8 volunteer crew + 40 trainees
Photograph date	1986
Photograph location	Perth, Western Australia

LIBERTAD

The Argentinian Navy has always believed in training its officers under sail. Its first schoolship was the corvette *La Argentina* (1884 to 1891). She was succeeded by a purpose-built steam corvette with a full-ship rig, the *Presidente Sarmiento*. That ship was built by Cammell-Laird in 1897, at Birkenhead, England, and was commissioned the following year. When she was finally laid up as a museum ship in Buenos Aires, after 63 years of service, she had logged 1,100,000 miles, which has to be a record for a schoolship.

The *Libertad* is the replacement of the *Presidente Sarmiento*. Her keel was laid down on 11 December 1953 and she was launched on 30 May 1956. She was commissioned on 28 May 1960 and sailed on her maiden voyage on 28 May 1963 — almost ten years after her construction had begun. In many ways she is the last to be commissioned of the second generation of big professional schoolships directly derived from un-engined windjammers: the building of the *Gloria* in 1967 (see p. 102) heralded the third and current generation of big schoolships with 'decadent' features, notably in the matter of excessive, windage-causing deckhousing, indicating an increasing reliance on the engines. The *Libertad* has a clipper bow with a figure-head representing an effigy of Liberty in a long flowing robe, and a cruiser stern bearing a crest with the arms of Argentina. She is spardecked, with a flush deck linking the fo'c's'le to the poop deck, to increase accommodation space. She already showed the trend to come, with a couple of big deckhouses on the spardeck, the forward one being surmounted by a covered bridge in turn surmounted by a flying bridge . . .

The *Libertad* is however a very fast sailing ship in quartering winds. In 1966 she made a record-breaking passage from Cape Race (Canada) to the line Dublin-Liverpool, sailing 2,059 miles in 8 days and 12 hours, an average speed of just over ten knots. In that same passage she obtained the 124-hour run record for a sail training ship (1,335 miles), for which she was awarded the Boston Teapot Trophy, and she logged her best speed at 18.5 knots.

The *Libertad* sails on a yearly six-month voyage of instruction and her cadets come from the Naval School at Rio Santiago. Her maiden cruise in 1963 took her to Puerto Rico, the Bahamas, Lisbon, Le Havre, Hamburg, London, Cadiz and Dakar. In 1964 she joined the Tall Ships Race from Lisbon to Bermuda and on to the New York OpSail. In 1970 she sailed to Sydney for the 200th anniversary of the discovery of New South Wales. In 1976 she joined the US Bicentennial Tall Ships Race at Bermuda (with the *Juan Sebastian de Elcano* incident, p. 116). She paid courtesy visits in London in 1975 and 1979 and her last call there and in the UK to date was in July 1981, in the course of a voyage that took her to Brazil, the West Indies, the USA, Canada, Denmark, Germany, France, Portugal, Spain, Tunisia and Uruguay: the following year Argentina and Britain were at war over the Falklands. The *Libertad* joined the 1984 Tall Ships Race from Bermuda to Halifax and called later at Quebec; she took part in the 1986 OpSail in New York from which she joined the North Sea Tall Ships Race at Bremerhaven later the same month. The Libertad will be taking part in the Columbus Regatta in 1992.

Name of vessel	Libertad
Year built	1956
Builder	A.F.N.E. (Naval Dockyard), Rio Santiago, Argentina
Current Owner	Argentinian Navy
Current flag	Argentina
Rig	Full-rigged ship
Construction	Steel; teak-clad deck
Length extreme	345.1 feet (105.20 m)
Length of hull	301.0 feet (91.75 m)
Length between perpendiculars	262.5 feet (80.00 m)
Beam	45.3 feet (13.80 m)
Draught	21.8 feet (6.65 m)
Tonnage	2,587 t TM; 3,025 td (standard), 3,720 td (load)
Sail area	28,546 sq. feet (2,652 m^2)
Engines	2 × 1,200 hp Sulzer; single propeller
Complement	263 crew + 88−150 cadets
Photograph date	1976
Photograph location	Newport, Rhode Island, USA

The *Lord Nelson* is a square-rigged training ship specially designed and fitted out to allow people with a variety of physical disabilities to participate fully in the ship's handling alongside 'able-bodied' trainees. Of the forty trainee berths, half are reserved for 'PHs' (Physically Handicapped) and half for 'ABs' (Able-Bodied). The trainees operate a 'buddy' system whereby PHs and ABs are paired. The minimum age for both categories of trainees is 16 and there is no upper age limit.

The *Lord Nelson*'s decks are wide, horizontal and flat and are fitted with tracks along which six specially adapted wheelchairs can run without the risk of tipping over or fetching up against a bulwark in a lurch. They can even go on the bowsprit which is horizontal, wide and flat. There are no coamings (sills) across the wide accommodation entrances; instead there are large gratings over sump boxes, with drains, that catch any water sloshing on deck. The bridge is accessible to all and it is possible to steer from a sitting position. There is an audio-compass for the blind and the chart table can be used by paraplegics. The radio has 'tactile' controls so it can be operated by the blind and the radar has an extra bright screen for the partially sighted. There are light signals to translate major commands or instructions ('all hands on deck', 'meal time', etc.) for the deaf and the latter have vibrators under their pillows to wake them up when alarms are sounded. The galley and even the engine room are accessible to wheelchairs and the washrooms and toilets are also specially fitted for use by paraplegics. There is a specially equipped surgery and the permanent crew includes a State Registered Nurse.

There are electrically-operated lifts allowing wheelchair-bound trainees to move from one deck to the other. The running rigging is so arranged that chair-bound trainees can haul with the rest of them. The staysails and upper topsails are roller-furled from deck (the upper topsails roll up inside the yards). There are self-operated lifting devices to allow those who cannot use the ratlines to go aloft. The barque also has a specially designed tender.

The *Lord Nelson* sailed on her maiden voyage on 28 October 1986 but she had a lot of teething problems and needed repairs and alterations that were carried out at Cole's yard in Cowes. She began normal operations in 1987 and was laid-up for winter in her home port of Southampton at the end of that season.

The *Lord Nelson* operates 3 to 15-day cruises around the British coasts from around Easter to the end of October. Most of these cruises involve a call abroad. In 1988–89 the barque operated a winter season in the West Indies. She sailed with some Operation Raleigh Young Venturers to the Turks and Caicos and then operated regular cruises out of Grand Bahama, with British and Bahamanian PH and AB trainees. Since then the barque operates in the winter out of Puerto Rico in Gran Canaria. Paraplegics are not embarked on the long ocean passages. The *Lord Nelson* does not race in the Tall Ships Races but sometimes accompanies them as support and communications vessel; in 1992 she will be calling at Liverpool at the time when the Columbus Regatta ships are scheduled to arrive there from Boston.

Name of vessel	Lord Nelson
Year built	1984–86 (launched 1985)
Designer	Colin Mudie
Builder	James W. Cook & Co., Wyvenhoe; completed by Vosper Thornycroft UK Ltd., Southampton – England
Current Owner	The Jubilee Sailing Trust, Southampton, England
Current flag	United Kingdom
Rig	Barque
Construction	Steel; teak-clad deck
Length extreme	197.5 feet (54.70 m)
Length of hull	140.4 feet (42.80 m)
Length waterline	121.4 feet (37.00 m)
Beam	29.5 feet (9.00 m)
Draught	13.5 feet (4.12 m)
Tonnage	368 grt; 110 nrt; 490 td
Sail area	10,755 sq. feet (1,000 m^2)
Engines	2 × 260 hp Mitsubishi Herald; twin propellers
Complement	8 permanent crew + 2 volunteer officers + 40 trainees
Photograph date	1989
Photograph location	Cowes, England

MALCOLM MILLER

The background and inception of this schooner are covered in the entry for her sistership, the *Sir Winston Churchill*, p. 180. The building of the *Malcolm Miller* was made possible by the generosity and dedication of Sir James Miller, then Lord Mayor of London and former Provost of Edinburgh, who donated half the £175,000 building cost and who organized the fund raising for the other half. The schooner was named in memory of his son Malcolm who had died in a car accident in 1966.

The keel was laid down on 23 March 1967 and the schooner was launched on 5 October. She was commissioned at Leith on 10 March 1968 and sailed on her maiden voyage the same day.

Both schooners met for the first time in August that year, for the Tall Ships Race from Gothenburg to Kristiansand. They are near-identical. Externally they can only be told apart by their sail numbers (TS/K1 for *SWC*; TS/K2 for *MM*), the shape of their deckhouse doors (arched on *SWC*, square on *MM*), their figureheads and, of course, their nameboards. The '*Churchill*'s' figurehead is a red English lion holding the STA's crest with a Cross of St George; the figurehead of the '*Miller*' is a red Scottish lion holding the coat of arms of Sir James Miller.

The crews on both schooners consist of five permanents and eleven volunteers. Each permanent crew consists of a master, a first officer, a bosun, an engineer and a cook. Each schooner has her own permanent crew and share with the other a relief permanent crew. The volunteers (who pay for the privilege) are called 'afterguard' and consist of three watch officers and a navigator (all with professional qualifications), a purser and his assistant (who are adults), and three watch leaders, a bosun's mate and a cook's assistant who are hand-picked ex-trainees between the ages of 17 and 24.

The trainees are aged 16 to 24 inclusive. Girls were first admitted in 1972, on a few all-girl cruises, and the *Sir Winston Churchill* caused quite a sensation when she turned up with an all-girl crew of trainees in the 1972 Tall Ships Race. Nowadays about half the segregated cruises are reserved for girls, and there are a few mixed cruises for 18–24 year-olds. The trainees come from all walks of life. The berths are on a paying basis but many of the trainees are sponsored by their employers or have other forms of sponsorship.

The youth training cruises are usually 2 weeks long. Apart from the first and last cruise of each season, six-days each, which are traditionally reserved for adults, they used to be the only cruises on offer. In recent years however the number of young applicants has dropped, for economic and study reasons, as a result of which there are now a number of off-peak 6-day mixed adult cruises.

The schooners seldom sail together outside the Tall Ships Races: they tend to work their way around Britain on opposite coasts. They youth cruises usually include a call in a foreign port. The schooners are of course stalwarts on the European Tall Ships Races, but only once did one of them, the '*Churchill*' in 1976, take part in a trans-Atlantic Race, as the length of some of the legs and incidental travel expenses would result in charges that are beyond the reach of most of the young people the schooners were built to serve.

Name of vessel	Malcolm Miller
Year built	1967
Designer	Camper & Nicholson's, Southampton, England
Builder	John Lewis & Sons Ltd., Aberdeen, Scotland
Current Owner	Sail Training Association Schooners, Portsmouth, England
Current flag	United Kingdom
Rig	Three-masted topsail schooner
Construction	Steel; teak deck
Length extreme	150.0 feet (45.72 m)
Length of hull	135.0 feet (41.15 m)
Length waterline	105.0 feet (32.00 m)
Beam	26.7 feet (8.13 m)
Draught	15.8 feet (4.82 m)
Tonnage	219.16 grt; 40.33 nrt; 299 t TM; 284 td
Sail area	8,794 sq. feet (817 m²)
Engines	2 × 135 bhp Perkins; twin propellers
Complement	5 permanent crew + 11 volunteer afterguard + 39 trainees
Photograph date	1972
Photograph location	Kiel, Germany

MARIA ASUMPTA

The *Maria Asumpta* was built in Badalona, near Barcelona, in 1858. When sailing on the *Maria Asumpta* today it is not hard to believe, but somewhat awesome to realize, that she first went to sea in days when extreme clippers battled with Cape Horn, when hundreds of whaling ships plied the South Seas, before the age of iron-built ships and barques, and when the cotton fields of the American South were worked by slaves.

Claims that the *Maria Asumpta* herself engaged in slaving are unsubstantiated but similar vessels were caught carrying slaves from West Africa to Cuba well into the 1860s. The *Maria Asumpta* was built as a brig or a brigantine for the trans-Atlantic trade between Spain and her West Indian colonies, (of which Cuba was the most important), carrying wine, oil, wheat and manufactured products out, and sugar, molasses, rum and tobacco back.

She traded under sail only until the 1930s, by which time she had been re-rigged as a schooner for the European and Mediterranean coasting trades. Then an auxiliary engine was installed and she became a *motovelero*, a motorsailer.

At some point her name had been changed to *Pepita* and about 1953 her name was changed again to *Ciudad de Inca*. She was still trading when Neil Armstrong landed on the moon, although by then she had become a motorcoaster, with a double storey deckhouse aft and no masts. She was finally retired in 1978.

In 1980 she was about to be scuttled by her owner when she was discovered by two Englishmen, Mark Litchfield and Robin Cecil-Wright, already the owners of the barque *Marques* (see next spread), and they bought her for the price of her engines. They motored her from Malaga to Barbate de Franco, just west of Gibraltar, where she was rebuilt and re-rigged over 18 months, in 1981–82.

A third of her frames and half her planking were renewed. In June 1982, a reborn brig, she set sail for England and performed remarkably well. That summer she sailed around Britain in company with the *Marques*, on a sail-training voyage. The following year she was chartered for a film production (*The Master of Ballantrae*), sailed to Portugal and back, ran a number of adventure training cruises and set sail, with the *Marques*, to the Canaries and, in January 1984, on to the West Indies.

Later that year she was in the Tall Ships Race Puerto Rico – Bermuda – Halifax but sailed back to Bermuda while in the second race, when her master, Mark Litchfield, got the awful news about the loss of the *Marques*. Some days later, with a relief skipper, the *Ciudad de Inca* sailed again, directly for Toronto to honour an engagement. She spent more than three years in the Great Lakes before sailing back to sea, to Halifax, in November 1987. The following spring she sailed across the Atlantic back to England, probably the oldest ship to have made such a passage. To mark her 130th birthday she was given back her original name of *Maria Asumpta*. She took part in the 1988 traditional sail festival at Douarnenez, France, and will be taking part in the repeat event there and in nearby Brest, in 1992. Since her return to Europe she has been chartering to harbour festivals, been used for promotional events, and been sailing on adventure training cruises.

Name of vessel	Maria Asumpta, *ex*-Ciudad de Inca, *ex*-Pepita, *ex*-Maria Asumpta
Year built	1858. Rebuilt 1981–82
Builder	at Badalona, Spain
Current Owner	Mr Mark Litchfield, England
Operator	Yalefleet Ltd., Maidstone, Kent
Current flag	United Kingdom
Rig	Brig
Construction	Wood
Length extreme	125.0 feet (38.10 m)
Length on deck	98.0 feet (29.87 m)
Length between perpendiculars	88.0 feet (26.82 m)
Beam	25.0 feet (7.62 m)
Draught	10.0 feet (3.05 m)
Tonnage	127.03 grt; 72.6 nrt; 260 td
Sail area	8,500 sq. feet (790 m^2)
Engines	2 × 175 hp Dorman; single propeller
Complement	8–16 crew and cruise participants
Photograph date	1988
Photograph location	Cowes, England

MARQUES

The *Marques* was built as a two-masted 'Mallorcan' schooner for trade mainly in the Mediterranean. Her first engine was installed in 1928. She was bombed during the Spanish Civil War but was rebuilt in the 1940s and carried on sailing, mainly carrying cargoes of beer from Tarragona to Mallorca. In the 1960s her engine was replaced by twin Kelvins and her sails were no longer used. She was retired from trade at La Palma in 1970.

She was bought there in 1972 by an Englishman, Robin Cecil-Wright, who refitted her and re-rigged her as a polacca-brigantine. From 1974 to 76 she was based in Cornwall and was used for a number of film productions, including *The Onedin Line* and the *Poldark* television serials.

In 1976 Mark Litchfield became half-owner and the *Marques* was re-rigged as a barque to represent HMS *Beagle* for the BBC TV production *The Voyage of Charles Darwin*, for which she circumnavigated South America (by way of the Magellan Strait) in 1977−78. Upon her return to Britain she took part in the Great Yarmouth to Oslo Tall Ships Race and appeared in the TV production *Kidnapped* and the feature movie *Dracula*. In 1979 she underwent a refit followed by TV work in Belgium (*Robinson Crusoe*), a pilot cruise for the Jubilee Sailing Trust's *Lord Nelson* project (p. 132) and a cruise to Wales, Ireland, Brittany and the Scillies for an art gallery. She spent seven months operating two-week cruises in the Canaries in 1980, followed by a two-month round-Britain cruise for an art gallery. In 1981 she was refitted at Barbate de Franco in Spain, and was fitted with royals and stun'sails; she did more film work and a series of cruises in the Western Mediterranean. From 1982 she operated in tandem with her owners' new brig, the *Ciudad de Inca* (previous spread) and in 1984 both entered the Tall Ships Race Puerto Rico−Bermuda−Halifax.

She won the first race, Puerto-Rico to Bermuda, and had a trainee crew changeover in Bermuda. The second race, to Halifax, started at 14:00 hours on 2 June with no bad weather forecast. At 4 am on 3 June, when the watch on deck was relieved, the barque was sailing comfortably at 7 knots on the port tack in a steady Force 6 wind; fortunately not all the relieved crew went immediately below. About 8 minutes later the *Marques* was hit by an extremely violent squall coming out of the darkness. She heeled over, her topsail lee yard arm almost in the water; the helmsman tried to bear off but was thrown overboard. The gust eased and the barque started to right herself when a second and more sustained gust pushed her back down, lee rail under; the sea poured in through the partially submerged companion; the weight of the water thus shipped caused loss of stability and then of buoyancy and the *Marques* went down by the head. It was all over in barely a minute from the time the first gust had struck. The squall had been very localised; ships a few miles away did not experience it but one saw distress flares fired by survivors in a liferaft. Nineteen lives were lost including the master, his wife and their fifteen-month old baby; there were nine survivors, none of whom had been below deck at the time of the squall. This is the first tragedy of the kind to hit the Tall Ships Races, and only the third instance since the Second World War of a training ship going down with loss of trainee lives.

Name of vessel	Marques
Year built	1917
Builder	at Pueblo Nuevo del Mare, Valencia, Spain
Last owners	Mark Litchfield and Robin Cecil-Wright, England
Last operator	*The China Clipper Society, Kent, England*
Last flag	United Kingdom
Rig	Barque
Construction	Wood
Length extreme	117 feet (35.7 m)
Length on deck	86 feet (26.2 m)
Length waterline	75 feet (22.9 m)
Beam	24.7 feet (7.53 m)
Draught	10.5 feet (3.20 m)
Tonnage	82 grt; 57 nrt; 150 td (approx.)
Sail area	7,500 sq. feet (698 m^2) (with stun'sails)
Engines	2 × 127 hp Gardner; twin propellers
Complement	9−15 crew; total complement: 32 max.
Photograph date	1984
Photograph location	Bermuda

MIRCEA

Romania sided with Russia in the 1877–78 war against Turkey and she recovered as a result her ancient coastal province of Dobrugea, between the Danube and the Black Sea and with the seaport of Constanţa. Having regained a seafront, Romania set up a Navy and decided to have a schoolship. A brig was ordered built at Blackwall, London. That brig, launched in 1882, was aptly named *Mircea* (pronounced 'Mircha') after the Romanian prince Mircea Staria, ruler (1383–1418) of Muntenia (Eastern Walachia), who reconquered Dobrugea from the Turks and reinstated Romania as a sea trading country.

By the 1930s the brig *Mircea* was ageing and due for retirement. Romania ordered a replacement from the yard of Blohm & Voss, to be built on the plans of the first *Gorch Fock* (now the *Tovarishch*, p. 190). These two barques are the slightly smaller sisters of the *Eagle* (p. 80), *Sagres* (p. 168) and the new *Gorch Fock* (p.106).

The keel of the Romanian barque was laid down on 15 April 1938. The barque was launched on 22 September and was named *Mircea* after her predecessor in the Romanian service. She had (and still has) a splendid figurehead representing Prince Mircea, a sculpture derived from a mural painting of the prince found in the Romanian monastery of Kosia. The barque was delivered on 16 January 1939 and sailed to Constanţa where she was commissioned in April. She was operated by the Merchant Marine Nautical College at Constanţa. She originally had a complement of 223 souls, consisting of 43 officers, 40 seamen and 140 cadets.

The *Mircea* however only made one 'regular' training voyage in 1939, in the Mediterranean, before the outbreak of war. After Romania had entered the war in 1940, fighting Russia on the Axis side, the *Mircea* only made short inshore training cruises, purely for the training of naval cadets. When the Red Army occupied Romania (from 27 August 1944) the *Mircea* was seized at Constanţa and the Soviet flag was raised on her. However, six months or so later, the Soviet Union gave the barque back to Romania in which a pro-Moscow regime was being installed.

From 1946 to 1965 the *Mircea* only operated near the coast, in the Black Sea and Mediterranean. From January to September 1966 she underwent a major refit at her builder's yard in Hamburg. Her masting and rigging were overhauled; new, additional, water-tight bulkheads were built; the electrical systems and wiring were renewed and modernized; the accommodation was completely renewed and a new suit of sails was made.

The *Mircea* trained 20 to 21-year old cadets intending to become officers in the naval or mercantile services. The barque sailed mainly in the Black Sea and Mediterranean but she visited other regions of Europe, Africa and North and South America. In 1975 she took part in the tall ships gatherings in London and Amsterdam and in 1976 she entered the US Bicentennial trans-Atlantic Tall Ships Race in which her complement consisted of 23 officers, 57 seamen and 107 cadets.

The *Mircea* carried on sailing after the December 1989 revolution and is currently undergoing part of a $5 million refit which is to be recouped by income from adventure training cruises with (Western) trainees paying in hard currency. She is scheduled to attend a traditional sail festival in Brest in July 1992.

The *Mircea* is shown here lying astern at her exact-sister, the *Tovarishch* ex-*Gorch Fock*, ahead of which is the latter's replacement in the German Navy, the *Gorch Fock* (II), a slightly longer sister. The full-rigged ship at the head of the trot is the *Dar Pomorza*.

Name of vessel	Mircea
Year built	1938
Designer	Blohm & Voss
Builder	Blohm & Voss, Hamburg, Germany
Current Owner	Romanian Navy
Current flag	Romania
Rig	Barque
Construction	Steel; teak-clad deck
Length extreme	266.7 feet (81.28 m)
Length of hull	241.8 feet (73.70 m)
Length between perpendiculars	203.4 feet (62.00 m)
Beam	41.0 feet (12.50 m)
Draught	17.1 feet (5.20 m)
Tonnage	1,312 grt, 1,723 t TM; 1,630 td (standard), 1,760 td (laden)
Sail area	18,837 sq. feet (1,750 m^2)
Engine	1,100 hp MaK
Complement	65 crew + 120 cadets
Photograph date	1976
Photograph location	Newport, Rhode Island, USA

MOSHULU

This imposing Cape Horn barque was built in Scotland for the shipowning firm of G.H.J. Siemers of Hamburg, and she was named *Kurt* after the firm's director, Dr Kurt Siemers. She was engaged in the South American nitrate trade. On her tenth voyage she unloaded her outward-bound cargo of coal at Santa Rosalia, Mexico, and was on passage to Portland, Oregon, to load grain, when the First World War broke out. On her owners' instructions she was laid up at Astoria, Oregon, for the duration.

She was seized there by the American government when the United States entered the war in 1917. She was put under the management of the US Shipping Board Emergency Fleet Corporation, first under the name of *Dreadnought* and then under the name of *Moshulu*, an American-Indian name also meaning 'dread naught'. She was used to transport freight between the American West Coast, the Philippines and Australia. In 1922 she was bought by James Tyson, of San Francisco who immediately re-sold her to Charles Nelson & Co., also of "Frisco". She sailed in the sawn timber trade between the American Northwest, Australia and Africa, until 1928. She was then laid up first at Seattle and later at Winslow, Washington.

She was bought, in 1935, by Captain Gustaf Erikson of Mariehamn, in the Åland Islands (Finland). He was the last big sailing ship fleet owner who managed to make these ships pay where their previous owners had to give up. At that time he owned 25 tall ships, including the *Moshulu*. He operated most of them in the Australian grain trade. The *Moshulu* was refitted on the spot and sailed to South Australia where she loaded a cargo of grain. She then set sail for Europe where she arrived in July 1936. Her last voyage under sail, with a cargo of grain, ended at Kristiansand, Norway, in the summer of 1940.

She was commandeered by the German occupation forces which used her as a depot ship first at Horten, near Oslo, and later at Kirkenes, in the far north, where she stranded and capsized. She was raised in 1947 and converted to a motor vessel but, in the event, she was used as a grain storage hulk at Stockholm from 1948 until 1952 when she was sold to Heinz Schliewen of Lübeck, Germany. Under the new name of *Oplag*, it was Schliewen's intention to refit her as a cargo-carrying schoolship. This project had to be abandoned for financial reasons. The *Oplag* went back to Stockholm for use as a grain store, and from 1961 to 1968 she served in the same capacity at Naantali in Finland.

In 1968 she was purchased by Specialty Restaurants, her present owners. Renamed *Moshulu*, she was towed to Amsterdam where work was begun on her conversion to a restaurant ship. In 1972 she was towed to New York, where it had originally been intended to exploit her, and in 1974 she was towed to her permanent berth at Penn's Landing, in Philadelphia. Work began on her re-rigging and she was opened for business in December 1976. Her 'tween deck, which has a 450-seat restaurant and a bar, is lighted by rows of windows cut in the ship's sides — not a very nice thing to do to a Cape Horn windjammer, but at least the use of smoke-tinted glass has the merit of making these windows not too conspicuous. In addition to the restaurant there are a couple of bars (one on deck), and a Maritime Exhibit (Museum) which can be visited without necessarily being a client of the restaurant or bars.

Name of vessel	Moshulu, ex-Oplag, ex-Moshulu, ex-Dreadnought, ex-Kurt
Year built	1904
Designer	William Hamilton & Co.
Builder	William Hamilton & Co. Ltd., Port Glasgow, Scotland
Current Owner	Specialty Restaurants Inc., Philadelphia, USA
Current flag	United States of America
Rig	Four-masted barque
Construction	Steel; wooden deck
Length extreme	393.0 feet (119.80 m)
Length of hull	364.2 feet (111.00 m)
Length between perpendiculars	334.3 feet (101.90 m)
Beam	46.9 feet (14.30 m)
Depth in hold	28.2 feet (8.60 m)
Tonnage	3,116 grt; 2,911 nrt; 5,393 tdw
Sail area	45,000 sq. feet (4,180 m^2) (in past)
Engine	None
Complement	26–34 men (in past)
Photograph date	1982
Photograph location	Philadelphia, Pennsylvania, USA

NIPPON MARU

When the first *Nippon Maru* and her sistership *Kaiwo Maru* were launched in 1930, the use of sailing schoolships was already well established in Japan. *Nippon* means, of course, Japan, and *Kaiwo* is the Japanese equivalent of Neptune; *Maru* is suffixed to most Japanese merchant ships' names and means 'endeavour'. These two vessels are four-masted barques and carried 75 crew and 120 cadets. Their sails, yards and gear are somewhat scaled down compared to the norm, on account of the small stature of pre-War Japanese trainees. They performed a long and successful service training for generations of Japanese merchant navy officers and could have continued to do so for an indefinite period but in the early Eighties the decision was taken to replace them by two new ships.

The new design was done with computers and tank and wind tunnel tests on models, but the requirements being pretty much the same as those met by the old ships, the new barques are in fact very similar. The most obvious differences are that the new ships are completely spar-decked, doing away with the well deck, have double spankers instead of single ones, and do not have a funnel. The yards and gear are 'full size', the spectacular increase in living standards in post-War Japan having led to an equally spectacular increase in the average height of the new generations of Japanese. The masting and rigging are traditional, with the lower masts and topmasts in one piece but with fidded topgallant masts; the upper topsail, upper topgallant and royal yards are hoisting (but hoist along mast tracks).

Compared to the *Nippon Maru* (I) the *Nippon Maru* (II) is 42.6 feet (13 m) longer from the jigger boom to the tip of the bowsprit, 25.5 feet (7.8 m) longer on the waterline and 2.8 feet (85 cm) beamier; the gross tonnage is increased by 287 tons and the load displacement by 687 tonnes; the sail area is increased by 3,870 sq. feet (360 m^2). The number of cadets remains the same and the number of staff crew is decreased by 5.

The spar deck carries three deckhouses, the forward one having a bridge above it; there is a wheel abaft the jigger mast which is used when under sail. The upper deck contains the officers' quarters, the galley, a large lecture room and some crew quarters; the lower deck contains the cadet's quarters (mostly eight-berth cabins, as on the old ships, and there are provisions for female cadets), the crew's mess and more crew accommodation. The 'tween deck below, apart from another lecture room, is entirely taken up by the engine room, tanks and store rooms.

The *Nippon Maru* (II) was laid down in April 1983, was launched in February 1984 and was delivered the following September. At that time the *Nippon Maru* (I) was taken out of service; she is berthed today in Yokohama as a museum ship under the management of the Nippon Maru Commemorative Foundation.

The *Nippon Maru* (II) represented Japan in the Australian Bicentenary events; in fact she carries on exactly the same duties of training officers and of promoting Japan abroad as her predecessor. Her sistership, the new *Kaiwo Maru*, took over from the old one in September 1989, and in 1990 she won the Boston Teapot Trophy for the best 124-hour run under sail, having logged 1,350 miles in that time.

Name of vessel	Nippon Maru
Year built	1984
Designer	Sumitomo Heavy Industries
Builder	Sumitomo Heavy Industries Uraga Shipyard, Yokosuka, Japan
Current Owner	Ministry of Transport, Institute of Sea Training, Tokyo
Current flag	Japan
Rig	Four-masted barque
Construction	Steel; teak-clad deck
Length extreme	361.2 feet (110.09 m)
Length of hull	325.3 feet (99.15 m)
Length between perpendiculars	282.2 feet (86.00 m)
Beam	45.3 feet (13.80 m)
Draught	20.6 feet (6.29 m)
Tonnage	2,570 grt; 2,150 nrt; 3,274 td (light); 4,730 td (load)
Sail area	29,708 sq. feet (2,760 m^2)
Engines	2 × 1,500 hp Daihatsu; twin propellers
Complement	24 officers + 46 seamen + 120 cadets

NONSUCH

For much of the 17th century France, which control-led Quebec and the St Lawrence river, had a monopoly on the lucrative Canadian fur trade. In time, two French traders, Radisson and Groseilliers, discovered an overland route to the southern shores of Hudson's Bay. They tried, but failed, to persuade the authorities in France to develop a direct trade route to that bay. They found however an enthusiastic backer in the person of Prince Rupert. With some London mer-chants they formed, in 1668, the Hudson's Bay Company, to trade in furs and, if possible, to discover the elusive Northwest Passage. King Charles II lent a ship, the *Eaglet*, and the company bought for £290 a second, similar but slightly smaller vessel, the *Nonsuch*.

The *Nonsuch* is believed to have been built in 1650 at Wivenhoe, Essex, by a Mr Page. She had been acquired by the Commonwealth's Navy in 1654, had been captured by the Dutch in 1658 and had been recaptured in 1659. The *Eaglet* and the *Nonsuch* set sail from London on 3 June 1668. During the Atlantic crossing the *Eaglet* suffered storm damage and turned back; the *Nonsuch* reached Hudson's Bay after a 44-day passage. She came back to London after a 15 month voyage, laden with £1,379-worth of beaver skins and other pelts. Her success led to the incorpora-tion by Royal Charter of the Hudson's Bay Company on 2 May 1670.

To commemorate their tercentenary, the Hudson's Bay Company commissioned the yard of J. Hinks & Son at Appledore to build a full-size sailing reconstruc-tion of their first ship, the *Nonsuch*. A team led by Rodney Warrington-Smyth drew up plans from data in the Company's archives and at the National Maritime Museum in Greenwich. At the yard, which five years later was to build the *Golden Hinde* (p. 104), period tools had first to be made and old skills re-learnt. The hull was built the traditional way and the planks are fastened with trunnels (wooden pegs), not nails.

This vessel astonishes us by her small size but most 17th century merchantmen were no bigger. Few had such elaborate carvings, but the *Nonsuch* had been in the Navy and had investors at Court. The catheads in the bows are supported by mermaids; the gun ports are framed with garlands and the stern windows are sur-rounded by elaborate gilded carvings; there is also plenty of 'gingerbread' on deck. The carvings were done on the Isle of Wight by Jack Whitehead.

The *Nonsuch* has the original ketch rig, two-masted with a main mast forward of the smaller (mizzen) mast, and with square sails. Typical features of the period are the round top, futtock shrouds made fast to the lower shrouds, the lateen mizzen, and the lack of a bobstay under the bowsprit which is instead bowsed down by a gammon lashing holding its base to the stem.

The new *Nonsuch* cost £70,000 to build and would cost £300,000 or more to replicate today: the 1668 purchase was a bargain! In 1969, after having paid a visit to a few English ports including London, the *Nonsuch* crossed the Atlantic as deck cargo on a freighter. Back in the water, she sailed along the East Coast of North America and in the Great Lakes, and was also transported to the West Coast as a sailing itinerant exhibition, until 1974 when she was en-shrined under cover at the Manitoba Museum of Man and Nature in Winnipeg.

Name of vessel	Nonsuch
Year built	1968
Designer	Rodney Warrington Smyth
Builder	J. Hinks & Son, Appledore, Devon, England
Current Owner	Hudson's Bay Company
Preserved at	Manitoba Museum of Man and Nature Winnipeg, Canada
Current flag	Canada
Rig	Square-rigged ketch
Construction	Wood
Length extreme	74.8 feet (22.80 m)
Length of hull	53.5 feet (16.30 m)
Length between perpendiculars	50.2 feet (15.30 m)
Beam	15.4 feet (4.70 m)
Draught	6.9 feet (2.10 m)
Tonnage	65 td
Sail area	1,894 sq. feet (176 m^2)
Engine	95 hp Perkins (now removed)
Complement	12 (on sailings)
Photograph date	1969
Photograph location	Plymouth, England

OUR SVANEN

The *Our Svanen* was launched under the name of *Mathilde*, a three-masted fore-and-aft Danish schooner for the Baltic trade. With changes of ownership she was successively renamed *Pacific* in 1926, *H.C. Andersen* in 1930 and *Svanen* in 1938. It was in the latter year that she was first engined, with a 34 hp diesel. She changed owners several times under that name. In 1969 she had been employed for some years to deliver bulk cargoes of malt to the Tuborg brewery in Copenhagen and she was given a more powerful 134 hp engine. Later that year she was bought out of trade by Doug and Margaret Havers, an Anglo-Canadian couple.

They spent eight years rebuilding her in a Danish shipyard, and re-rigging her as a barquentine. In 1977 they registered her at Stornoway, in the Hebrides, under the name *Our Svanen*, the name *Svanen* being already taken up in the register. They sailed her from Denmark to Poole, England, where a further two years were spent fitting her out. On 22 November 1978 she left England bound for Victoria, British Columbia, via the West Indies and Panama. In 1980 she was given a long charter by the Royal Canadian Sea Cadets for sail training. At that time she had a permanent crew of 8, including the Havers, and carried 16 Sea Cadets of both sexes, aged 17–20. She sailed to Alaska in the summer and out of Baja California in winter. In 1981 she sailed from Mexico to Hawaii and back to Victoria and, still with Sea Cadets, left Victoria in October on a long voyage that included the 1982 Tall Ships Races Venezuela–Philadelphia–Lisbon–Southampton. She had a winter refit (1982–83) at Troense, Denmark. In 1983, still with Sea Cadets, she sailed to England, Florida, Nova Scotia, Newfoundland and to the West Indies for winter cruises. She took part in 1984 in the Puerto Rico – Bermuda – Halifax – Quebec Tall Ships Races and wintered at Halifax.

In 1985 the Havers sold the *Our Svanen* to Sail Pacific Charters Ltd of Vancouver, a consortium of five part-owners. She had recently arrived in Vancouver in 1986 when she was contracted to take part in the Australian Bicentenary First Fleet Re-enactment. Being still British-registered, her owners refitted her to current British Department of Transport requirements for the loadline certificate necessary for that charter. She was also re-engined with a 250 hp Caterpillar. When she arrived in England shortly before the First Fleet departure in May 1987, her owners were informed by the DoT that the loadline rules had been changed while she was at sea and she had to sail without a loadline certificate and without fare-paying participants. The matter was not solved by the time she and the fleet reached Mauritius, so the owners transferred her registry to the Cayman Islands and the *Our Svanen* obtained a passenger licence from the Australian authorities on arrival at Perth in November so she could participate normally in the First Fleet cruises in Australian waters. After these were over she was sold to the Sail Training Association of New South Wales as a replacement of their barquentine *New Endeavour* that had been scrapped in 1987. The STANSW was however unable to keep up with mortgage repayments and the *Our Svanen* was resold at auction in May 1990. She was bought by a Sydney businessman, Mr Laurie Kalnin, and she now runs day trips in Sydney Harbour and whale-watching trips off the coast of Queensland.

Name of vessel	Our Svanen, ex-Svanen, ex-H.C. Andersen, ex-Pacific, ex-Mathilde
Year built	1922
Designer	K. Andersen
Builder	K. Andersen, Frederikssund, Denmark
Current Owner	Svanen Charters Pty. Ltd., Redfern, NSW, Australia
Current flag	Australia
Rig	Barquentine
Construction	Wood
Length extreme	137.0 feet (41.76 m)
Length on deck	92.0 feet (28.04 m)
Length waterline	84.0 feet (25.60 m)
Beam	22.1 feet (6.74 m)
Draught	9.5 feet (2.90 m)
Tonnage	119.26 grt; 81.1 rt; 250 tdw
Sail area	5,900 sq. feet (548 m²)
Engine	250 hp Caterpillar
Photograph date	1984
Photograph location	Bermuda (star of Tall Ships Race to Halifax)

OUTLAW

The *Outlaw* is a former Mallorcan trading schooner, one of the last to be built. Her building took six years partly because of government hostility to traditional wooden shipbuilding – the policy was to encourage 'modern' steel motorvessel building.

The *Outlaw*'s original name was *Cala Millo*, and she was a gaff schooner fitted with a 140 hp engine. She was engaged in the Mediterranean trade, carrying local agricultural products: wine, olives, olive oil, cereals, oranges and other fruits, etc. In the 1960s the *Cala Millo* was sold to Abel Matutes of Ibiza, the owner of several other Mallorcan schooners. He renamed her *Antonio Matutes* and kept her in the same trade until 1974 when he sold her to the Overseas Tramps company of Valletta, Malta. The new owners registered the schooner in Malta under the name of *Outlaw*. They re-rigged her as a staysail schooner and converted her for holiday charter cruises.

In 1977 the *Outlaw* was bought by the German social work organization Jugendschiff Corsar e.V. for use as a rehabilitation ship for convicted juvenile delinquents, as an alternative to borstal. The schooner's name was appropriate for her new purpose, so it was not changed; neither was the Maltese registry although the ship was put under German Ship Inspectorate inspection. The engine was replaced by a 200 hp Deutz.

The *Outlaw* had a professional crew of five: master, first and second mates, bosun and engineer. She also carried four social work staff: three social workers and one teacher plus, on a temporary basis, a psychologist. The crew and staff quarters consisted of three single cabins, five double cabins and a saloon aft. The trainee complement was up to 16 and consisted of boys and girls aged 15 to 18. They were berthed in two berth cabins. There was also a 'club room' (open communal space) below deck, around the foot of the foremast. The galley and messroom were in the deckhouse abaft the foremast.

The *Outlaw* operated two rehabilitation courses a year, each 5 to 6 months duration. The winter courses were held in the Mediterranean, Canaries and Red Sea and the summer courses were held in the North Sea and Baltic. Shore leave for trainees was very restricted and subject to strict rules and the discipline aboard was strict. The programme was not intended as an easy option or a holiday.

The *Outlaw* took part in the Baltic and North Sea Tall Ships Races in 1980, 82, 84 and 86. In 1982 three yards were crossed on the foremast. Because of this and of the existence of main staysails, some people say the *Outlaw* is a brigantine. However she was a staysail schooner and the rigging of her foremast was not changed when the yards were added: it still is a schooner mast, not a square-rigged mast, hence the nomenclature of schooner-brigantine is preferable.

In 1987 Jugendschiff Corsar had their funding cut for a while and the *Outlaw* subsequently failed to pass survey by the German Ship Inspectorate. The hull was in reasonable condition but the rig and mechanics were not. In 1988 or 1989 she was sold for DM 140,000 (approx. £45,000) to a social service organization in Bremen for use as a static drug therapy hostel. If funds can be found, she will be refitted for active sailing service.

Name of vessel	Outlaw, *ex-*Antonio Matutes, *ex-*Cala Millo
Year built	1946–52
Builder	Astilleros Naviera Mallorquina, Palma de Mallorca, Spain
Current Owner	Outlaw Verein, Germany
Current flag	Germany
Rig	Schooner-brigantine
Construction	Wood
Length extreme	129.9 feet (39.60 m)
Length of hull	109.9 feet (33.50 m)
Length waterline	98.1 feet (29.90 m)
Beam	26.3 feet (8.03 m)
Draught	10.5 feet (3.20 m)
Tonnage	171.29 grt; 141 nrt; 277 t TM; 183 td (load)
Sail area	6,460 sq. feet (600 m²) (approx.)
Engine	200 hp Deutz
Complement	5 crew + 4–5 social workers/teachers + 16 trainees (prior to lay-up)
Photograph date	1986
Photograph location	Newcastle, England

PALINURO

The *Palinuro* was one of two fishing barquentines built in 1934 for the Société des Pêcheries Malouines of St Malo, France. She was named *Commandant Louis Richard*; her sistership (which no longer exists) was the *Lieutenant René Guillon*. Since the last quarter of the 19th century the French had favoured barquentines for the Newfoundland fisheries and these two were the last sailing Newfoundland fishing boats to be built. They were also the biggest and the only ones to be built in steel, and they had auxiliary propulsion. The *Palinuro* still displays her original sail plan. The squat rig is not the result of having an engine but the hallmark of the fishing barquentines, on account of frequent gales on the fishing grounds and for reducing rolling motion at anchor. Those ships were normally anchored at sea while their dories were out fishing. Some of the 'lost' sail area was made up by extra wide square sails bent to very long yards.

The two barquentines were atypical not only by their size and their steel construction, but also in their general arrangement. They had a very long poop extending almost to the mainmast and the 44 men as well as the 5 officers had their quarters under the poop deck. Under the raised fo'c's'le were the windlass, paint locker, etc., and hen coops and a pig pen. The fishroom or hold was mostly for carrying fish salted the traditional way but also had a couple of cold stores in which a small part of the catch could be frozen.

The two barquentines fished until the Second World War and were put back in service after the war. There were still 26 French barquentines fishing in 1947 but within two years they were all replaced by motor trawlers. The *Commandant Louis Richard* was sold in 1948 to a Frenchman who renamed her *Jean Marc Aline* and who tried to operate her in the south Indian Ocean, around the islands of St Paul and Amsterdam (38°S) which were beyond the reach of trawler competition, but the distance raised the costs and the ship and fishing methods were unsuited to local conditions. One trip was enough. The *Jean Marc Aline* was put up for sale.

She was sold in 1951 to the Italian Navy for conversion to a schoolship. The poop was extended forward of the mainmast to increase accommodation space and the fishroom became a trainee halfdeck. The hull was painted black and white, with painted gun ports. The stem was decorated with a gilded figurehead representing Palinuro holding the tiller of a steering oar. Palinuro was the pilot of Aeneas' ship when they fled from defeated Troy to eventually land and settle in Italy. The ship was named *Palinuro* and commissioned on 16 June 1955.

The *Palinuro* is the schoolship of the Italian Navy's NCO school at La Maddalena, Sardinia. Her cadets are aged 17–18 years. The *Palinuro* mostly sails in home waters, along the Tyrrhenian and Adriatic coasts of Italy. She sometimes hosts traditional sail events in those waters, such as the Classic Yacht Regattas at Porto Cervo, Sardinia.

In the early Eighties there was talk of replacing her by a new ship, but when the cost of building a new ship was compared to that of refitting the *Palinuro*, she won a reprieve. She was given a major refit in 1984–86 at the Messina Dockyard and was recommissioned thereafter.

Name of vessel	Palinuro, *ex*-Jean Marc Aline, *ex*-Commandant Louis Richard
Year built	1933–34
Builder	Anciens Chantiers Dubigeon, Nantes, France
Current Owner	Italian Navy: Naval Training School at La Maddalena, Sardinia
Current flag	Italy
Rig	Barquentine
Construction	Steel; wood-clad decks
Length extreme	226.2 feet (68.95 m)
Length of hull	193.5 feet (58.98 m)
Length between perpendiculars	164.0 feet (50.00 m)
Beam	33.1 feet (10.09 m)
Draught	15.9 feet (4.84 m)
Tonnage	858 grt; 1,042 td (standard); 1,341 td (load)
Sail area	11,517 sq. feet (1,070 m^2)
Engine	450 hp Fiat
Complement	48 crew and instructors + 70 trainees
Photograph date	1982
Photograph location	Sardinia, Italy

PHOENIX

The *Phoenix* was originally the Danish evangelical mission schooner *Anna*. She had been built like a trading schooner and had a 78 hp diesel auxiliary engine. She was sold in 1941 to become a cargo schooner and in 1942 she was re-rigged as a galease; in 1964 she became an unrigged motorcoaster. She was laid up in 1972 following a fire that destroyed her engine room.

She was bought in 1974 by an Anglo-Dutch couple, John and Frederika Charles. They took her to Holland for rebuilding as a brigantine which they aptly named *Phoenix* and they registered her in Ireland. The *Phoenix*'s first work as a brigantine was a club charter to take part in the 1976 American Bicentennial Tall Ships Race. She was the smallest entry in the big square rigger Class A and the only one in that class not to be a government-subsidized schoolship. She had a mixed international crew of up to 28 persons and 20 egg-laying hens. The *Phoenix* was the only Class A vessel in the return Race, Boston-Plymouth, which she therefore won in her class. That was not a foregone conclusion: she would have been disqualified had she retired to finish under power, as did most of the Class B and C yachts, because of lack of wind. The passage took 32 days instead of the expected 18 to 24, and in good British nautical tradition (the purser being English) she had been penny-pinchingly provisioned for 18 days!

In 1977 and 1978 the *Phoenix* operated charters in the Channel and North Sea and, also in 1978, the Charleses transferred her registry to Holland and entered her under their own name in the Tall Ships Race, in the Baltic. In 1979 the *Phoenix* was chartered to an American educational institution which sailed her, *inter alia*, to Leningrad. In 1980 the *Phoenix* landed under the ownership of a couple of shady Dutch businessmen and was subsequently seized by the Dutch Revenue service. She was bought by tender in 1981 by an English sailmaker who took her to Littlehampton to be laid up for resale. She was bought in 1982 by an English businessman, Mr Barry Brenner, who had her refitted for passenger charter work. She sailed in late 1982 for Jamaica where she operated day trips out of Montego Bay in 1983–84. In 1984 she was repositioned in Bermuda but by then the *Phoenix* was suffering from absentee ownership and a succession of indifferent skippers; the owner ordered her delivered to Miami to be laid up for sale.

She remained in Miama for nearly four years without maintenance and was in a very sorry state when purchased in 1988 by her current owner. Fortunately he was a professional who had a wooden ship repair yard in Bristol, England, and who already owned or operated a number of tall ships, including the *Kaskelot* (p. 120), the *Søren Larsen* (p. 182) and the gaff schooner *Carrie*. He sent his own shipwrights, riggers and engineer to Miami to give the *Phoenix* a first-aid overhaul enabling her to sail back to England where she was given a proper rebuild. She was put back in service in 1990, for film work, promotions and corporate charters. At the time of writing, early 1992, she is in Costa Rica, rigged and mocked up as the *Santa Maria*, along with the *Carrie* rigged up as a caravel, for a film production about Christopher Columbus. Both the *Phoenix* and *Carrie* are due back in England in the summer of 1992 and will be restored to their normal appearances.

Name of vessel	Phoenix, *ex*-Gabriel, *ex*-Adella, *ex*-Skibladner, *ex*-Karma, *ex*-Jørgen Peter, *ex*-Palmeto, *ex*-Anna
Year built	1929
Designer	Hjørne & Jacobsen
Builder	Hjørne & Jacobsen, Frederikshavn, Denmark
Current Owner	Square Sail (Mr Robin Davies), Colchester, England
Current flag	United Kingdom
Rig	Brigantine
Construction	Wood
Length extreme	112.0 feet (34.14 m)
Length of hull	78.2 feet (23.84 m)
Length waterline	72.8 feet (22.18 m)
Beam	21.8 feet (6.64 m)
Draught	8.0 feet (2.44 m)
Tonnage	79.17 grt; 57.64 nrt; 151 t TM; 116 td
Sail area	4,000 sq. feet (370 m^2) (approx.)
Engine	240 hp Volvo
Complement	6 crew + 18 guests
Photograph date	1976
Photograph location	Plymouth, England

POGORIA

The *Pogoria* was built in 1979–80 at Gdansk, in the then Lenin shipyard, for the Polish Yachting Association in conjunction with the Iron Shackle Fraternity (hence the logos on the square sails), an association linked with Polish Television. She was launched by crane on 23 January 1980 and made her international debut, barely a few weeks after completion, in the 1980 Tall Ships Race Kiel-Karlskrona-Frederikshavn-Amsterdam and the windjammer gathering at Bremerhaven that followed.

The *Pogoria* has steel pole-masts (without doublings) and all the yards are standing. She originally had a gaff mizzen but it was found to give her too much weather helm and it was subsequently replaced by a Bermudan sail. She was built with an eye to performance in the Tall Ships Races and she is a fast sailing ship with a good windward performance. The *Pogoria* was conceived as a youth and adventure training ship and from the start she welcomed foreign Western trainees on most of her cruises, the first East European training ship to do so.

In the southern summer of 1980–81 she was chartered by the Polish Academy of Sciences as a relief vessel for a Polish scientific station on King George Island in the South Shetlands (Antarctica). On that voyage she called also at Stanley in the Falklands and in South Georgia.

The *Pogoria* took part in the 1982 Tall Ships Race Falmouth-Cadiz-Lisbon-Southampton. That winter she sailed in the Canaries and the following summer in the Baltic. From September 1983 to May 1984 she sailed for the 'Class Afloat' project with young Poles and some young (and a few 'adult') Westerners on a clockwise circumnavigation of Africa, with a loop to Bombay and Colombo.

From 1985 until the end of 1991 the *Pogoria* was under virtual full-time charter to the Canadian Educational Alternative of Ottawa and Montreal, working as a school afloat (with breaks only for maintenance and school holidays). She had a Polish crew of 9 and 20 to 40 Canadian students and their teachers. In 1985–86 she made another circumnavigation of Africa. That voyage ended in Montreal and the *Pogoria* sailed back to Poland, by way of the New York OpSail '86, for a refit. In 1987–88 she sailed around the world westabout and since then she has been operating in the Atlantic between Europe, the West Indies, the USA and Canada. The charter ended at Capetown just before Christmas 1991 and then the *Pogoria* ran a series of day cruises out of Capetown prior to setting sail for home, for another refit. In 1992 the Canadian Educational Alternative will no longer be needing her as they will be taking delivery of their own, larger, barquentine, the *Concordia*, which is being built at Szczecin, Poland. The *Pogoria* is looking for new partners and projects.

The *Pogoria* is the first of a class of near sisterships. Her construction was followed by that of the Polish Navy's *Iskra* (1982), of Bulgaria's *Kaliakra* (1984; p. 118) and of the Polish Academy of Sciences' *Oceania* (1985) which are between 2 and 3 feet (70–80 cm) longer on the hull. The *Oceania* does not however have a barquentine rig but a three-masted semi-automated experimental rig with a single, very tall, roller-furling square sail on each mast.

Name of vessel	Pogoria
Year built	1980
Designer	Zygmunt Choreń
Builder	Stocznia Gdanska, Gdansk, Poland
Current Owner	Polish Yachting Association
Current flag	Poland
Rig	Barquentine
Construction	Steel; steel deck
Length extreme	153.5 feet (46.80 m)
Length of hull	137.8 feet (42.00 m)
Length between perpendiculars	113.2 feet (34.50 m)
Beam	26.2 feet (8.00 m)
Draught	12.1 feet (3.70 m)
Tonnage	289 grt; 41 nrt; 314 t TM; 342 td
Sail area	11,302 sq. feet (1,050 m^2)
Engine	310 hp Wola Warszawa
Complement	6 permanent crew + 4 temporary officers + 44 trainees
Photograph date	1982
Photograph location	Falmouth, England

POLYNESIA II

The *Polynesia II*, or rather the *Argus* as she was originally called, was one of the last Portuguese Grand Bank fishing schooners to be built and one of the very last to fish under sail, right up to the dawn of the 1970s. Every year she would set out on a six-month campaign to the waters around Newfoundland to long-line for cod from dories. The fish was gutted and salted aboard and landed in Portugal at the end of the voyage. That life is well described by the Australian seafarer and writer Alan Villiers who sailed on her to make a documentary film and to write articles (notably in the *National Geographic*) and the book *The Quest of Schooner Argus*.

Although most of the Portuguese fishing schooners of that type and period were built in Portugal, the *Argus* was built on order in the Netherlands. She had a four-masted gaff rig with fidded topmasts and she crossed a single yard on her foremast. She had a powerful 475 hp auxiliary engine from the start. She had a crew of 72 and carried 53 dories on deck.

When her fishing days under sail were finally over the *Argus* was bought by a Canadian syndicate who resold her in 1974 to 'Cap'n' Mike Burke. He wanted her for his Windjammer fleet in replacement of the 1928-built staysail schooner yacht *Polynesia* which had been seized in 1971 by Fidel Castro after accidentally running aground on the Cuban coast.

Mike Burke had operated charter boats since 1947. He was the first to run 'mass market' holiday cruises in the Caribbean in 1956 with that first *Polynesia* which was soon complemented by other boats. To date his Windjammer Barefoot Cruises have carried more than 1,000,000 passengers, 40% of whom have sailed more than once on his ships. The formula is simple but it had to be thought of and implemented: convert large yachts, ex-windjammers or other suitable hulls, with as many cabins as possible to offer affordable carefree and informal sunshine cruises in one or two week packages.

In all Mike Burke has owned 22 ships, nearly all sailers. The fleet currently consists of six vessels: *Polynesia II, Fantome III* (see p. 96), the three-masted staysail schooners *Flying Cloud, Mandalay* and *Yankee Clipper* and the M/V *Amazing Grace*. A newly converted four-masted staysail schooner yet to be named will be entering service in 1992.

The *Argus* was renamed *Polynesia II*. She was built up one deck to increase the accommodation space and she was rigged with pole masts setting staysails, trysails, a Bermudan mizzen and a square foresail. Accommodation was built for 126 passengers: 12 deck cabins, 40 regular cabins and two 'admiral suites', all with private heads and shower, and 3 six-berth cabins for bachelor, bachelorettes or families.

The 'Poly' has been working different routes according to demand and requirements within the fleet (see also p. 96). At present in 1991 and 1992, she is operating six-day cruises out of St Martin, calling at St Barts, St Kitts, Saba, Statia, Prickly Pear and Anguilla during the first and third weeks of each month, and at St Barts, Nevis, Monserrat, St Kitts and Anguilla during the second and fourth weeks. Some cruises are for singles only — and the company offers also a 'follow up' service with the *Flying Cloud*: marriages at sea and honeymoon cruises!

Name of vessel	Polynesia II, *ex-*Argus
Year built	1938
Builder	De Haan & Oerlmans, Heusden, The Netherlands
Current Owner	Polynesia S.A.
Current flag	Honduras
Operator	Windjammer Inc., Miami Beach, Florida, USA
Rig	Four-masted foreyard staysail schooner
Construction	Steel; teak weather deck
Length extreme	248 feet (75.6 m)
Length of hull	210 feet (64.0 m)
Length between perpendiculars	173.5 feet (52.9 m)
Beam	32 feet (9.8 m)
Draught	19.5 feet (5.9 m)
Tonnage	430.85 grt; 306 nrt
Sail area	22,000 sq. feet (2,044 m^2)
Engine	700 hp MAN
Complement	45 crew + 126 passengers
Photograph date	1982
Photograph location	Antigua

QUEEN GALADRIEL

The *Queen Galadriel* was designed and built as a trading ketch by J. Ring Andersen's yard at Svendborg, the best-known Danish yard for the construction of 'Baltic traders'. As the *Queen Galadriel* is restored today she is a typical example of a Baltic trading ketch.

She began life as the *Else*, named after the daughter of her first skipper-owner. She was used to carry coal, grain and other commodities in the Baltic and up the Norwegian coast. In 1956 she was sold to a Norwegian, Bjørn Stensland, who cut down her mainmast to 15 feet (4.6 m) above the deck for use as a derrick, and who operated the *Else* as a motor coaster. In 1970 she was sold out of trade to Mr and Mrs Shattuck from the USA, and then to Don Knights, a Briton, who brought her to England and moored her in the River Crouch in Essex in 1971. She then became derelict and sank at her moorings in 1974. She was salvaged and sold for £500 in 1975. She was owned by Jean Thurston who, with a group of young people, tried to refit her, and then by Robert Norton who almost bankrupted himself trying to do the same. He changed the ship's name in 1978 to *Else of Thisted*, Thisted being the Danish port where she had been first registered. The ketch was acquired by the Cirdan Trust in 1983 and was renamed *Queen Galadriel*.

The Cirdan Trust, the driving force of which is the Rev. Bill Broad, was founded in 1982 as a non-profit making trust to enable youth organizations to allow their youngsters to experience the challenge and adventure of sail. It is a Christian Trust but does not restrict the use of its ships to Church or religious groups. It seldom runs scheduled 'open' cruises on which participants book directly with the Trust: it charters its vessels with a core crew, usually at below cost, to eligible groups which make up the trainee complement and decide the itineraries and 'style' of their cruises within the usual constraints. The Trust's first operational boat was a 33 ft (10 m) plastic Bermudan yacht; it also owns the Thames sailing barge *Xylonite* and the sea-going cruising yacht *Arwen of Burnham*. Cirdan, Arwen and Galadriel are names taken from J.R.R. Tolkien's *The Lord of the Rings* (but Galadriel was not a queen!)

The *Queen Galadriel* was rebuilt and commissioned as a training vessel in 1984. She has a permanent crew of 3 (quartered aft) and can carry up to 14 trainees (in tiered bunks along the sides of the saloon in the hold) and 4 adult leaders (in 2 two-berth cabins). The minimum and maximum age limits and whether or not the groups are boys, girls, or both, depends on the chartering organizations although they are normally youth organizations. Some 'special case' non-youth associations such as traditional sail clubs and the Tolkien Society are allowed to charter the *Queen Galadriel* subject to time availability. The Trust itself sometimes run head-berth scheduled cruises for 16 to 25 year olds (for instance for a Tall Ships Race) or for participants aged 18 or more, such as the passage to the Brest traditional sail festival in July 1992.

In 1987 the *Queen Galadriel* marked her 50th anniversary by sailing to Svendborg, Denmark, to the yard where she was built, but her normal sailing waters are the southern North Sea and the English Channel, including calls in Holland, France or Belgium.

Name of vessel	Queen Galadriel, *ex-Else of Thisted*, *ex-Else*
Year built	1937
Designer	J. Ring Andersen
Builder	J. Ring Andersen, Svendborg, Denmark
Current Owner	Cirdan Trust, Chelmsford, England
Current flag	United Kingdom
Rig	Ketch
Construction	Wood
Length extreme	104.0 feet (31.70 m)
Length of hull	75.0 feet (22.86 m)
Length waterline	70.0 feet (21.34 m)
Beam	22.35 feet (6.81 m)
Draught	6.8 feet (2.07 m)
Tonnage	85 grt; 75.24 nrt; 130 tdw
Sail area	2,500 sq. feet (230 m^2) approx.
Engine	200 hp Cummins
Complement	3 permanent crew + 4 adult group leaders + 14 trainees
Photograph date	1987
Photograph location	Cowes, England

RAPHAELO

The *Raphaelo* was built of oak at Viareggio by the reputed Benetti brothers' yard, as one of Italy's last trading schooners. She was launched in 1938 but further work was interrupted by the outbreak of war and she was not completed until 1941. She was an auxiliary three-masted gaff schooner and her original name was *Gerlando*. She was used for carrying marble from the quarries of Carrara, a trade going back to Antiquity from the place which gave its very name to the English word 'quarry'. The *Gerlando* carried the famed marble to consignees all over the Mediterranean. She traded until the late Fifties when she was 'discovered' and purchased in Egypt by Karma S.A (representing an Italian gentleman) for conversion to a luxury yacht.

The conversion was carried out in 1960–61 at the Valdettaro yard at Le Grazie near La Spezia. The conversion plans had been made by Anselmi Boretti and were carried out under his direction. It was the debut of this yacht designer who has since acquired a worldwide reputation. The rig and various details were however designed by Camper & Nicholson's of Southampton and the whole project was done under the surveillance of the American Bureau of Shipping.

The new yacht was named *Taitu* after an Ethiopian princess of Antiquity. Her head profile can be seen as a motif throughout the vessel and on some of the sails. The *Taitu* was commissioned in 1961 under the Panamanian flag but she later reverted to the Italian flag when she was registered at Messina under the ownership of Signor Matacena. The yacht's guest list included Princess Margaret and the Aga Khan.

In 1982 the *Taitu* was purchased by Almacoal Ltd and renamed *Raphaelo*; she was registered at Douglas, Isle of Man. Some time before then, the main mast installed during the 1961 conversion rotted at the base and was shortened. In 1983 a new mast to the original length was stepped and a sound length of the old mast was used to extend the bowsprit by a jibboom, increasing the length extreme from 143.5 ft (43.75 m) to 162.1 ft (49.40 m).

The *Raphaelo* has a raised fo'c's'le and poop and a spacious varnished mahogany midship deckhouse. This is a large deck saloon richly, but tastefully, appointed. It has varnished panellings and joinery, red carpetting, brass fittings and soft black leather settees including a circular settee around the foot of the mainmast. From this deck saloon a superb spiral staircase leads down to another saloon below deck and to the owner's and guests' accommodation which includes two master cabins and five two-bed cabins. These cabins are entirely finished in varnished panels and joinery but are well lit by opening skylights and portholes with brass frames.

The *Raphaelo* has a professional crew of 12 – British officers, European cook and Philippino deckhands. The *Raphaelo* is the private yacht of an Anglo-German gentleman. She is based at Cannes, France, and her usual cruising grounds are the French, Italian and Spanish Mediterranean; she has also sailed to the Canaries.

Name of vessel	Raphaelo, ex-Taitu, ex-Gerlando
Year built	1938–41
Designer	Anselmi Boretti (for conversion)
Builder	Cantieri Navali Fratelli Benetti, Viareggio, Italy
Current Owner	Raphaelo Marine Ltd., Isle of Man
Current flag	United Kingdom (Isle of Man)
Rig	Three-masted staysail schooner
Construction	Wood; teak deck
Length extreme	162.1 feet (49.40 m)
Length of hull	122.2 feet (37.25 m)
Length waterline	104.5 feet (31.85 m)
Beam	27.8 feet (8.47 m)
Draught	12.6 feet (3.85 m)
Tonnage	282.05 grt; 215.03 nrt; 390 td (light); 435 td (load)
Sail area	7,147 – 10,010 sq. feet (664–930 m²) (plain-total)
Engines	2 × 450 hp General Motors; twin propellers
Complement	12 crew + Owner + 10 guests
Photograph date	1990
Photograph location	St Tropez, France (during Nioulargue '90)

ROYALIST

The Sea Cadet Corps is a national organization that offers weekend and spare time nautical training to boys between the ages of 13 and 18. It is closely linked to the Royal Navy, its purpose being to encourage youngsters to follow naval careers — but there is no commitment on the boys' part to do so. The SCC consists of Units that are spread across the country. Many Units have their own inshore practice boats, but before the *Royalist* there was no national offshore training ship.

In 1966 the SCC chartered the 75 ft (23 m) brigantine *Centurion* (not the one on p. 60 but a previous yacht owned by the same gentleman) for that year's Tall Ships Race. The *Centurion* won in her class. The success of the operation led the SCC to think along lines that were to result in the *Royalist*.

The *Royalist* was designed by Colin Mudie who later went on to design the barque *Lord Nelson* (p. 132) and the brigantine *Young Endeavour* (p. 204). All three square riggers have a distinctive family likeness. The plans for the *Royalist* were also used for the building of a sistership in Bombay in 1980, the Bombay's Sea Cadet Corps' brig *Varuna*.

The *Royalist*'s hull is that of a large steel cruising yacht, with a long, external ballast keel. The deck is flush and abaft the sunk-in charthouse there is a deck cockpit. The masts are steel poles and the yards are aluminium; the standing rigging is stainless steel. The lower shrouds do not have ratlines but teak battens that make climbing much easier. The crosstrees separating the topmast section from the topgallant mast section of each mast are decked over like smaller replicas of the tops, a feature also found on modern Polish-built square riggers but which is not found on square riggers of the past.

The 24 cadets are berthed in the two forward compartments which are separated by a watertight door. The after one of these compartments is the largest and also serves as the cadets' mess. The permanent crew consists of the captain, sailing master and engineer, who each have a private cabin, and of the bo'sun and coxswain, who share a cabin. In addition there is a temporary cook. There are normally four other adults, the division officers, who sleep in the wardroom.

The *Royalist* is based at Gosport, Hampshire but during the sailing season she moves around the coasts of Britain to minimize travel expenses for the cadets who come from all over Britain. The *Royalist* is in commission from early March to late November and most of her cruises are one week long. Some cruises are reserved or block-booked by specific SCC Units; others have cadets who come from different Units. The division officers are either officers from the cadets' own units or qualified members of the *Royalist*'s supporters' organization, the Square Rigger Club. On normal cruises six berths are reserved for cadets from the Girls' Nautical Training Corps and some cruises are block-booked by the GNTC. The *Royalist* is a very regular participant in the European Tall Ships Races in which she has won many prizes. In addition to her cadet cruises she also runs a couple of weekend adult cruises every year, for members of the Square Rigger Club, and the occasional fund-raising day trips.

Name of vessel	Royalist
Year built	1971
Designer	Colin Mudie
Builder	Groves & Guttridge, Cowes, England
Current Owner	Sea Cadet Corps, Gosport, England
Current flag	United Kingdom
Rig	Brig
Construction	Steel; teak-clad deck
Length extreme	97.0 feet (29.57 m)
Length of hull	76.5 feet (23.32 m)
Length waterline	63.0 feet (19.20 m)
Beam	19.5 feet (5.94 m)
Draught	9.3 feet (2.84 m)
Tonnage	83.09 grt; 67.24 nrt; 110 t TM; 103 td
Sail area	4,660 sq. feet (433 m²)
Engines	2 × 230 hp Perkins; twin propellers
Complement	5 permanent crew + cook + 4 division officers + 24 cadets
Photograph date	1971
Photograph location	Cowes, England

R. TUCKER THOMPSON

In 1982 R. Tucker Thompson, an American tall ship skipper, began building a steel schooner of his own design at Mangawhai, a small town about half way between Auckland and Whangarei. Helping him were his son Tod Thompson and Russel Harris, a New Zealander — and local people gladly assisted also. Sadly R. Tucker Thompson died well before the schooner was completed but his son and his son's friend carried on the project to completion. The schooner was launched on 12 October 1985 and named after her late designer and builder. She crossed the shallow Mangawhai bar on the 15th and berthed on the 16th at her home port-to be, Whangarei, for inspection.

The *R. Tucker Thompson* is a very handsome, lofty, topsail schooner and she sails very nicely. Her fine-lined but sturdy steel hull is enhanced by beautiful woodwork. In fact, when aboard, there are very few clues to her steel construction as her deck, bulwarks, masts and spars are wood. The accommodation has very nice joinery and is cosy.

The *R. Tucker Thompson* began running day trips in the magnificent Bay of Islands, out of Opua and Russell. Her two owners, Tod and Russell, took turns at skippering her. Homemade scones and coffee would be served during the morning sail and the schooner would anchor in a secluded bay or another. A glass of wine would accompany lunch. Then the passengers were rowed ashore, and they sailed back again after swimming time.

In 1986 the *R. Tucker Thompson* was chartered for a Children's New Zealand television serial called *Adventurer*, in which she played a leading role under the stage name of *Sea Wolf*.

All along there had been the prospect of a charter by the Australian First Fleet Re-enactment. The charter was finally confirmed just in time for the longest possible delivery: New Zealand to London. The schooner sailed east-about, calling at Easter Island, and via Panama. She arrived at St Katharine's Dock, London, in April 1987, where most of the Re-enactment's charter fleet was assembling for a couple of weeks prior to sailing to Portsmouth. The voyage to Australia started on 13 May 1987 from the Solent, 200 hundred years to the day after, and from the same place from where the First Fleet of 11 ships loaded with stores and convicts had set sail for Botany Bay.

The voyage was by way of Tenerife, the Cape Verde Islands, São Salvador, Rio, Capetown, Mauritius, Fremantle and a number of ports along the Australian south and west coasts. The *R. Tucker Thompson* was partly sponsored by the Chase Corporation (Hanimex and Fuji) which shot a promotional video between Fremantle and Sydney and took some stills for a Hanimex exhibition.

The parade of sail in Sydney on 26 January 1988, Bicentennial Day, was followed by four months of fleet cruising along the East and South Coasts. After that, the *R. Tucker Thompson* returned to New Zealand and sailed cruises, in tandem with her former First Fleet 'mates' the *Søren Larsen*, *Tradewind* and *Anna Kristina*, to Polynesia, and short cruises and day cruises in New Zealand. She has been back operating short cruises and day trips in the Bay of Islands since 1989.

Name of vessel	R. Tucker Thompson
Year built	1982−85
Designer	R. Tucker Thompson
Builders	R. Tucker Thompson, Tod Thompson and Russel Harris, Mangawhai, New Zealand
Current Owner	Tod Thompson and Russel Harris, Opua, New Zealand
Current flag	New Zealand
Rig	Topsail schooner
Construction	Steel; wood deck
Length extreme	85 feet (25.9 m)
Length of hull	60 feet (18.3 m)
Length waterline	55 feet (16.8 m)
Beam	15 feet (4.6 m)
Draught	8 feet (2.4 m)
Tonnage	45 grt; 33 nrt; 55 td
Sail area	2,800 sq. feet (260 m^2)
Engine	120 hp Ford
Complement	4−6 crew + 10−12 cruise participants (total: 16); 41 day trip passengers
Photograph date	1987
Photograph location	Solent (First Fleet Re-enactment departure)

SAGRES

This barque's keel was laid down in June 1937 and she was launched on 30 October the same year under the name of *Albert Leo Schlageter*, after a Nazi party hero. She was the third schoolship of the German Reich's Navy. (See p. 106, for details of the Blohm & Voss barques of this series which were six in all).

The *Albert Leo Schlageter* had a complement of 298 crew and cadets. She had not been in service for two full seasons when war broke out. During the war she operated short training cruises in the Baltic. She struck a mine that caused extensive damage to the engine room.

She was seized by the United States at the end of the war. The Americans had however no use for her and, in 1948, they passed her on to Brazil which recommissioned her as a naval schoolship under the name of *Guanabara* (the name of the bay of Rio de Janeiro).

Meanwhile, since 1924, the Portuguese Navy operated a schoolship, the barque *Sagres*, a former German Cape Horn full-rigged ship. She had been launched at Bremerhaven in 1896 under the name of *Rickmer Rickmers*. The Portuguese had named her after the port of Sagres in southern Portugal where Prince Henry the Navigator (1394–1460) had founded Europe's first navigation school and from where many of the Portuguese voyages of discovery had sailed. By the late 1950s the Portuguese were seeking a replacement ship and they bought the *Guanabara* in October 1961 and the name of *Sagres* was transferred to her. The old *Sagres* was renamed *Santo André* and was laid up as a depot ship at the naval school at Alfeite, Lisbon. In 1983 she was sold and towed to Hamburg where she has been restored as a museum ship under her original name of *Rickmer Rickmers*.

The new *Sagres* sailed from Rio on 24 April 1962, bound for Lisbon. Like the old *Sagres*, she has a figurehead which is a bust of Prince Henry, and she displays red Lusitanian crosses on her sails. The quick way to identify which barque is seen on pictures is that the *Sagres* (I) has a single spanker whereas the *Sagres* (II) has a double spanker and the sheerline is virtually unbroken on (I) whereas that of (II) has conspicuous breaks at the poop and fo'c's'le.

The *Sagres* (II) is a very active schoolship, frequently sailing on long voyages. She carries on the 'tradition' of the *Sagres* (I) of being a frequent participant in the Tall Ships Races and she also takes part in other windjammer gatherings. As an example of a particularly active period, the *Sagres* sailed from Lisbon in June 1983 for the Osaka World Sail Festival in October, via Tenerife, La Guaira (Venezuela), Panama, San Diego, San Francisco and Honolulu. She sailed back via Pusan (Korea), Shanghai, Macao, Singapore, Malacca, Bombay, Jeddah, Suez and Tunis. She arrived home in March 1984 and after a quick turnover she sailed to Bermuda to join the Tall Ships Race to Halifax, Quebec, Sydney (Nova Scotia) and Liverpool.

She is undergoing a major refit in 1991–92 and will be ready to take part in the 1992 Columbus Regatta, Cadiz – Puerto Rico – New York – Boston – Liverpool.

Name of vessel	Sagres, *ex*-Guanabara, *ex*-Albert Leo Schlageter
Year built	1937
Designer	Blohm & Voss
Builder	Blohm & Voss, Hamburg
Current Owner	Portuguese Navy
Current flag	Portugal
Rig	Barque
Construction	Steel; teak-clad deck
Length extreme	293.6 feet (89.48 m)
Length of hull	266.5 feet (81.22 m)
Length between perpendiculars	230.0 feet (70.10 m)
Beam	39.4 feet (12.02 m)
Draught	18.0 feet (5.50 m)
Tonnage	1,784 t TM; 1,725 td (standard); 1869 td (load)
Sail area	20,828 sq. feet (1,935 m^2)
Engine	750 hp MAN
Complement	163 crew + 80 cadets
Photograph date	1982
Photograph location	Newport, Rhode Island, USA

SEA CLOUD

The *Sea Cloud* was built as the biggest and most luxurious private sailing yacht ever. She was the wedding gift of the American millionaire Edward Hutton to his wife Marjorie M. Post. Hutton had owned another big yacht, the 'black' *Hussar*, and the new yacht was called *Hussar II* and was also painted black. From 1932 until 1935 the Huttons made many long and happy voyages on the *Hussar II* and their guests included royalty, film stars and other celebrities. However the Huttons divorced and Marjorie went her own way with the yacht. Edward got to keep the name *Hussar* for his next yacht and the barque was re-named *Sea Cloud* and was painted white.

Marjorie re-married in 1935. Her new husband was the American diplomat Joseph Davies. When he was appointed US Ambassador to Moscow they took the *Sea Cloud* with them and berthed her in Leningrad. Joseph Stalin strictly forbade any Soviet person to go aboard that arch-cathedral of capitalism. Amusingly the writer has in his ship-memorabilia collection an invitation carton from the captain of the *Kruzenshtern* (p. 124) to the captain of the *Sea Cloud* when both four-masted barques were berthed near each other in Karlskrona, Sweden, during the 1980 Tall Ships Race. Both ships, similar in rig and size, could not have been more different in background: one had been the world's most luxurious yacht and was then an exclusive passenger sailing vessel running very expensive luxury cruises; the other, a former nitrate carrying Cape-Horner, then a schoolship training Soviet fishermen. After Leningrad the *Sea Cloud* moved to Antwerp when Davies was posted Ambassador to Belgium.

In 1942 the *Sea Cloud* was requisitioned by the US Navy, painted naval grey and unrigged for use as a weather ship and anti-submarine patrol boat off the US East Coast, with a complement of 300 sailors. She was returned to Marjorie Davies in 1944 and was fully restored in 1947. In 1952 she was sold to the Dominican dictator Rafael Trujillo and renamed *Angelita* after his daughter. After Trujillo's assassination in 1961, the yacht was sold by his exiled family to Mr John Blue of Florida who registered her in Panama under the name of *Patria* and the ownership of Corporation Sea Cruise Inc. She was overhauled and restored to sailing condition at Naples in 1967—8 and in 1969 she was sold to another American concern, Antarna Inc., and she was renamed *Antarna*, still Panamanian-flagged. She was refitted for charter work but was laid up and 'forgotten' in Panama in 1974.

She was sold in 1978, in a rather sorry state, to a German syndicate of Hamburg businessmen and shipowners. They re-named her *Sea Cloud* and, after a first-aid refit in Panama, took her, under the German flag, to the Scheel & Jönhk yard in Hamburg for a major overhaul which included adding an after deckhouse with 14 passenger cabins and an upper deckhouse over the midship deckhouse, with a further 8 cabins. The original 13 cabins below deck had amazingly survived with their original fittings (including marble bath tubs and solid gold taps). Reflagged under Cayman registry and, more recently, under Maltese registry, the *Sea Cloud* began passenger-cruising in 1978. She usually cruises in the West Indies in winter and in the Mediterranean in summer, although sometimes elsewhere, for instance in the Pacific in 1987 and since 1989 she also visits Black Sea harbours of the former Eastern Bloc such as Varna, Constanţa, Odessa and Yalta.

Name of vessel	Sea Cloud, ex-Antarna, ex-Patria, ex-Angelita, ex-Sea Cloud, ex-Hussar II
Year built	1931
Builder	Friedrich Krupp Germaniawerft, Kiel, Germany
Current Owner	Sea Cloud Ltd., Valletta, Malta
Operator	Sea Cloud Kreuzfahrten GmbH, Hamburg, Germany
Current flag	Malta
Rig	Four-masted barque
Construction	Steel; teak-clad deck
Length extreme	359.3 feet (109.50 m)
Length of hull	315.9 feet (96.29 m)
Length waterline	253.3 feet (77.21 m)
Beam	49.0 feet (14.94 m)
Draught	16.8 feet (5.13 m)
Tonnage	2,323 grt; 1,147 nrt; 3,075 td
Sail area	34,014 sq. feet (3,160 m²)
Engines	4 × 1,500 hp Enterprise; twin propellers
Complement	58 crew + 67 passengers
Photograph date	1980
Photograph location	Kiel, Germany

SEDOV

The *Sedov* is the world's largest sailing ship (excluding the *Wind Star* series which are quite a different type of ship). She was built for the Bremen shipowning firm F.A Vinnen under the name of *Magadelene Vinnen*. She was a Cape Horn nitrate clipper but from the start she had an auxiliary propulsion engine and carried 60 merchant navy cadets. In 1936 she was sold to the Norddeutscher Lloyd, also of Bremerhaven, and renamed *Kommodore Johnsen*. The trainee accommodation was expanded to receive 100 cadets by building a spardeck between the poop and the midship 'island'. The barque remained a cargo-carrier and was put into the South Australian grain trade. During the war the barque became purely a schoolship, operating only in the Baltic, in the summer months, and laying up at Flensburg in winter.

After the war the barque was handed over to the Soviet authorities who towed her to Swinemünde in January 1946. On the 11th she was officially incorporated in the Soviet Baltic Fleet under the name of *Sedov*, after the Russian polar explorer Georgij J. Sedov (1877–1917).

It was not until 1952 that the *Sedov* was fully refitted and put back into service as a naval schoolship. In 1957 she took part in the International Geophysical Year as a research vessel under the aegis of the Soviet Academy of Sciences, and sailed to Africa, the West Indies, in the North Atlantic and the Mediterranean. In 1958 she crossed the equator for the first time under the Soviet flag. In 1962–65 she sailed in company with the *Kruzenshtern*, both working as schoolships, and hydrographic and oceanographic vessels.

In 1965 the ownership of both barques was transferred to the Soviet Ministry of Fisheries for use as training ships for the future officers and men of the Soviet fishing fleets.

In 1972 the *Sedov* was laid up pending an overhaul. This was carried out at Kronstadt and involved the replacement of her old 500 hp engine by the present 1,180 hp one.

On 21 June 1981 the *Sedov* left her home port of Riga for a visit to Denmark: she made calls at Copenhagen, Horsens, Aarhus, Esbjerg, and Thorshavn in the Faeroes. In October 1981 she sailed round Europe to Sebastopol and the following year she called at Hamburg. She took part in the 1983 windjammer gathering at Bremerhaven, her former home port, and many of her former German officers and men were invited aboard.

The *Sedov* entered the Tall Ships Races for the first time in 1986, a North Sea Race. She took part in the 1989 race from London to Hamburg and that year, for the first time, she took some Western 'adventure' trainees – by the end of 1991 more than 800 Westerners, mainly Germans, had sailed on her.

In April 1991, in anticipation of the Latvian independence, the *Sedov's* registry was transferred from Riga to Murmansk. At the time of writing she is without legal owner as the Soviet ministry that owned her was abolished in November 1991, but she is expected to be taken over by the new Russian Ministry of Fisheries. In 1992 the *Sedov* will be taking part in the trans-Atlantic Columbus Regatta with a large proportion of Western trainees who are bringing in much needed hard currency.

Name of vessel	Sedov, ex-Kommodore Johnsen, ex-Magdalene Vinnen
Year built	1921
Builder	Germania Werft (F. Krupp), Kiel, Germany
Prospective owner	Russian Ministry of Fisheries (see text)
Operator	Higher Engineering Marine College, Murmansk, Russia
Current flag	Russia
Rig	Four-masted barque
Construction	Steel; wood-clad deck
Length extreme	385.5 feet (117.50 m)
Length of hull	357.6 feet (109.00 m)
Length between perpendiculars	321.2 feet (97.90 m)
Beam	48.1 feet (14.66 m)
Draught	24.7 feet (7.52 m)
Tonnage	3,709 grt; 2,972 nrt (before rebuild); 1,980 td (light), 7,320 td (load); 5,340 tdw (in trading days)
Sail area	45,122 sq. feet (4,192 m^2)
Engine	1,180 hp VEB SKL Magdeburg
Complement	64 crew + 180 cadets
Photograph date	1982
Photograph location	Southampton, England

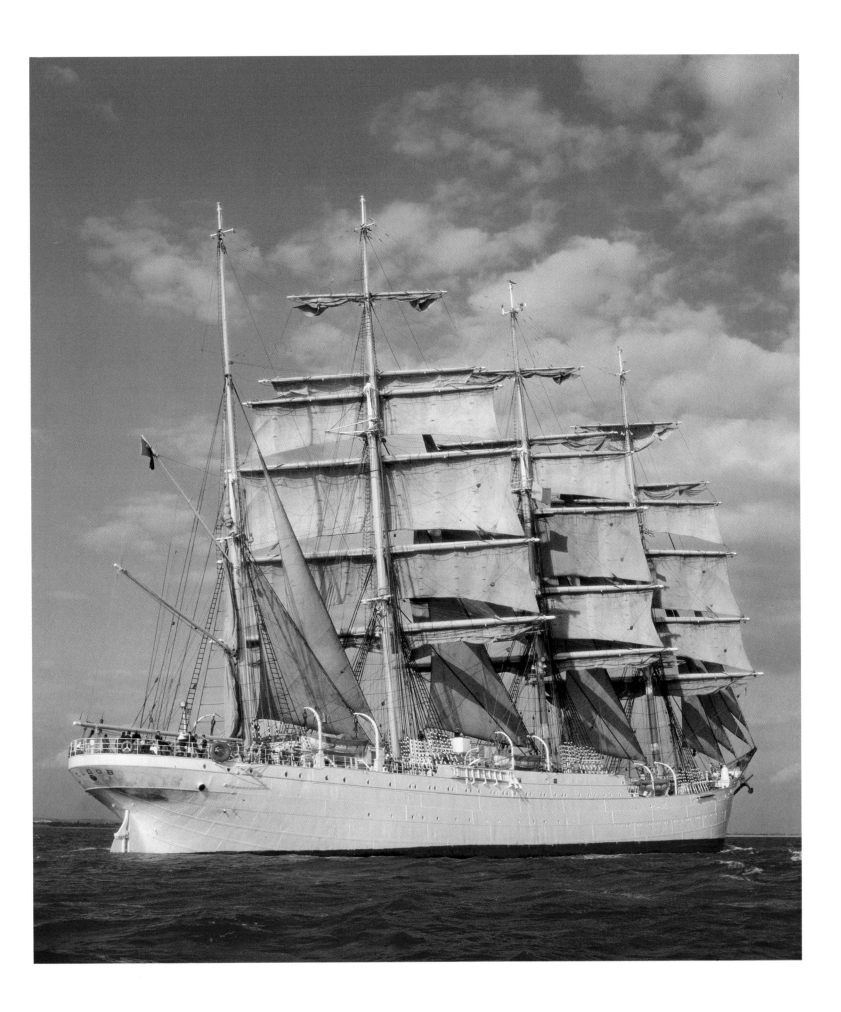

SHABAB OMAN

This impressive schooner-barquentine was built in 1971 for the Dulverton Trust as a three-masted topgallant schooner, the *Captain Scott*. She is the world's largest wooden sailing vessel in service. She was used for youth character training on 26-day cruises with 36 boys aged 16–21 and a crew of 8 permanent plus three volunteer watch officers. She was based at Loch Eil and sailed in the Hebrides. Her training programme included shore treks, camping and mountain climbing. The programme, with emphasis on real character building, physical challenge and toughness, was excellent in concept but flawed in its application. To cut a long story short, the *Captain Scott* was not a happy ship and soon ran out of support. She was laid up at the end of 1975 and put up for sale.

She was bought in 1977 by Sultan Qaboos bin Said of Oman and re-named *Youth of Oman*. Her livery changed from black to white, a necessity under the Arabian Sea sun. At first the *Youth of Oman* was operated by the *Ministry of Youth Affairs* which however was not well equipped to handle such a project, and there were problems of management, discipline and maintenance. The Project and the schooner were transferred in 1979 to the Omani Navy which re-named her *Shabab Oman* ('Youth of Oman' in Arabic) and put things right. The captain and mates were British or German with tall ship experience (ex-*Royalist*, ex-*Gorch Fock*, etc.) and they were backed by Omani naval officers.

For the normal three-week cruises in Omani waters the ship operates with the Captain and four officers, nine Omani crew, two technicians and three young officers under training and 24 cadets aged 17 to 25 and chosen from the Oman Navy, Army, Air Force, the Royal Guard Brigade and the Police. Several places are available on each course to Omani civilians, who are sponsored by the Ministry of Youth Affairs.

The schooner's range was vastly increased when she was fitted with a watermaker. A six-week cruise was undertaken for the first time in 1983, visiting the six Gulf States and taking on trainees from each country visited.

The sail plan was modified in 1984. A square fore-course was bent to the lower yard and the gaff foresail was replaced by two main staysails. The foremast and its standing rigging were not altered, so the *Shabab Oman*'s rig is not quite that of a 'true' barquentine but that of a schooner-barquentine.

In 1984 the *Shabab Oman* sailed on a two month Indian Ocean tour. In 1986 she made a seven month voyage, with three cadet crew changeovers, the high point of which was the New York Opsail. Her complement on that voyage was 5 officers, 20 crew and 24 cadets. In 1987–88 the *Shabab Oman* sailed to Australia, for that country's Bicentenary celebrations, and her complement on that voyage was 52, including 20 cadets. She sailed to western Europe in 1989 with, in addition to her own cadets, a number of foreign trainees from other Gulf States, Pakistan and Sri Lanka. She was at London for the start of the Tall Ships Race and then attended the tall ship gathering at Rouen that marked the bicentennial of the French Revolution.

Wherever she goes, the *Shabab Oman* cuts an impressive figure with her immaculate white hull and sails enlivened with red coats of arms of the Sultanate.

Name of vessel	Shabab Oman, *ex-*Youth of Oman, *ex-*Captain Scott
Year built	1971
Designers	Robert Clark, Cmdr. Victor Clark and Capt. Mike Willoughby
Builder	Herd & Mackenzie, Buckie, Scotland
Current Owner	Sultan Qaboos bin Said of Oman
Current flag	Oman
Rig	Schooner-barquentine
Construction	Wood
Length extreme	177.0 feet (53.95 m)
Length of hull	144.3 feet (43.97 m)
Length between perpendiculars	120.0 feet (36.58 m)
Beam	28.0 feet (8.53 m)
Draught	15.5 feet (4.72 m)
Tonnage	264.35 grt; 54.97 nrt; 380 t TM; 484 td
Sail area	8,750 sq. feet (813 m^2)
Engines	2 × 250 hp Caterpillar; twin propellers
Complement	16–23 permanent crew + 20–31 cadets and trainees (total complement from 43 to 54)
Photograph date	1989
Photograph location	Cowes

SHENANDOAH

The beautiful *Shenandoah* is one of a very few surviving big yachts from the golden age of yachting. She was designed by leading yacht designer T.E. Ferris for Wall Street financier Gibson Fahnestock, and she was built by Townsend & Downey. She was in fact very similar to the slightly bigger *Meteor III* of Kaiser Wilhelm II which was built at the same yard at the same time. The *Shenandoah*'s original rig was that of a three-masted double-topsail schooner which also set from her lower yard an inverted triangular fore-course. Her original bowsprit was a bit longer and her mizzen boom overhung the stern by a quarter of its length.

Fahnestock first sailed the *Shenandoah* from Newport, Rhode Island; then in 1905 he sailed her to the Mediterranean and based her in the French Riviera where she was host to many international personalities of the time. In 1912 she was sold to a German nobleman, Landrat von Bruining, who changed her name to *Lasca II*. He stationed her at Kiel, Germany, in the winter, and at Cowes in the summer. The outbreak of the First World War put an end to the golden age of yachting — and to von Bruining's ownership of *Lasca II*. She happened to be at Cowes at that time and was promptly confiscated by the British government as enemy property.

In 1919 the schooner became the property of Sir John Esplen, of London, who reinstated her original name. She was in turn bought by Godfrey H. Williams, of Southampton, in 1921, who sailed her in British waters. From 1924 until the late Twenties she was owned by Captain F.L. De Sales and then passed on to Prince Spado Veralli, the Governor of Rome, who renamed her *Atlantide*. In 1930 the *Atlantide* was bought by Count Viggo of Copenhagen who brought her to Denmark where she was refitted and modernized. She remained under his ownership until 1952 when she was acquired by the Compania de Navigacion San Augustin of Honduras and she disappeared from the yachting scene and apparently also kept a very low profile in respect to Central American Customs authorities.

She reappeared in the Mediterranean in the early Sixties and was confiscated by French Customs. She lay neglected in the South of France for about ten years, until bought in 1972 by Baron Bich, the French ballpoint pen magnate. He had her completely renovated at the Voisin yard at Villefranche and he restored her to her original name. Bich used her for personal cruising with family and friends and also chartered her to hand-picked clients. She was sailed in the Mediterranean and the West Indies.

In 1986 the *Shenandoah* was sold to Phillipe Bommer, a Swiss businessman with a passion for owning and restoring vintage yachts. The last major refit had been in 1973 and the *Shenandoah* was once more in need of a major overhaul. Her accommodation was splendid but the masts, sails, rigging, tanks and some engineering installations were in need of attention. The *Shenandoah* was refitted, and sailed by Mr Bommer with his family and friends, in the Mediterranean in summer and the West Indies in winter. In late 1990 he sold her to a Japanese buyer and shortly afterwards she set sail for Japan under Bermudan registry. In 1991 Mr Bommer bought the J-class yacht *Velsheda* which he is now having restored.

Name of vessel	Shenandoah, *ex-Atlantide, ex-Shenandoah, ex-Lasca II, ex-Shenandoah*
Year built	1902
Designer	Theodore E. Ferris
Builder	Townsend & Downey, Shooters Island, NY, USA
Current Owner	a Japanese businessman
Current flag	Bermuda
Rig	Three-masted foreyard schooner
Construction	Iron; teak deck
Length extreme	145.0 feet (44.20 m)
Length of hull	124.5 feet (37.95 m)
Length waterline	100.0 feet (30.48 m)
Beam	26.8 feet (8.17 m)
Draught	13.5 feet (4.11 m)
Tonnage	280 grt; 225 nrt
Engines	2 × 350 Volvo Penta
Complement	14 crew + 10 guests
Photograph date	1990
Photograph location	St Tropez, France (during Nioulargue)

SIMON BOLIVAR

The *Simon Bolivar*, built to order for the Venezuelan Navy, is the third of the four Senermar-designed and ASTACE-built barques that were built between 1967 and 1982. The first was the *Gloria*, for the Colombian Navy (p. 102), and the second was the *Guayas*, for the Ecuadorian Navy (p. 110). The *Simon Bolivar* was in turn followed by the *Cuauhtémoc* built in 1982 for the Mexican Navy. Each successive barque was a bit bigger than her predecessor.

The *Simon Bolivar*'s keel was laid down on 6 June 1979. She was launched five months later, on 21 November, and, after engine and sailing trials, she was delivered at Bilbao to the Venezuelan Navy on 12 August 1980. Without a midships deckhouse surmounted by a bridge, she is better looking than her predecessors; her wheelhouse and chartroom are on the poop deck, abaft the mizzen mast. Like her predecessors, her hull is white, but with a broad black band at main deck bulwark level and a black stripe lower down, the two bands being separated by a row of painted gunports. This colour scheme helps to reduce the apparent height of the topsides. The stem is decorated with a figurehead representing the effigy of Liberty wearing a Phrygian cap. This was made by the Venezuelan sculptor Manuel Felipe Rincon. The barque is named after Simon Bolivar (1783–1830), the *Libertador* who won by arms the independence from Spain of his native Venezuela and of most of Spain's South American colonies.

The *Simon Bolivar* has a permanent crew of 92 consisting of 17 officers, 24 warrant officers and 51 enlisted men. Her cadet complement is 102 which includes 18 young women.

After delivery in August 1980 the *Simon Bolivar* made a 'shakedown' cruise combined with courtesy visits to Spain and Portugal, including calls at El Ferrol, Cadiz, Barcelona and Palma de Mallorca, before crossing the Atlantic to her home base at La Guaira near Caracas.

The *Simon Bolivar* makes one long training voyage a year. In 1981 she sailed to the East Coast of the United States, calling at a number of ports including Bath, Maine, and Portsmouth, New Hampshire, then to Europe and back home via Santa Cruz de Tenerife. In 1982 she was at Philadelphia for that city's 300th anniversary celebrations and then went on to Newport, Rhode Island, to join the trans-Atlantic Tall Ships Race to Lisbon. She did not take part in the following race ending at Southampton, England, as relations between a number of South American countries, including Venezuela, and Britain were still strained in the aftermath of the Falklands War. In 1984 the *Simon Bolivar* took part in the Tall Ships Race Puerto Rico — Bermuda — Halifax — Quebec and in 1985 she sailed to Lisbon at the start of a European tour that included the Sail Amsterdam '85 tall ships gathering. The barque is a regular participant in the Tall Ships Races and other windjammer events in the Western Hemisphere, such as the 1986 New York OpSail where all four ASTACE barques were berthed next to one another at the South Street Seaport. The *Simon Bolivar* is also a frequent visitor to Europe and she sailed round the world in 1987–88, taking in the Australian Bicentenary tall ships parade at Sydney on 26 January 1988. In 1992 the *Simon Bolivar* will be taking part in the Columbus Regatta, the Tall Ships Race marking the 500th anniversary of Columbus' First Voyage.

The *Simon Bolivar* is seen here at the start of the 1984 Bermuda to Halifax Tall Ships Race. The vessel in the background is the Canadian brigantine *Belle Blonde* (p. 48).

Name of vessel	Simon Bolivar
Year built	1979–80
Designer	Sener Sistemas Marinos S.A. (Senermar), Madrid, Spain
Builder	Astilleros y Talleres Celaya (ASTACE), Bilbao, Spain
Current Owner	Venezuelan Navy
Current flag	Venezuela
Rig	Barque
Construction	Steel; teak-clad deck
Length extreme	270.3 feet (82.40 m)
Length of hull	229.7 feet (70.00 m)
Length between perpendiculars	191.9 feet (58.50 m)
Beam	34.8 feet (10.60 m)
Draught	14.3 feet (4.35 m)
Tonnage	934 grt; 1,260 td
Sail area	17,760 sq. feet (1,650 m^2)
Engine	750 hp General Motors
Complement	92 crew + 102 cadets
Photograph date	1984
Photograph location	Bermuda

SIR WINSTON CHURCHILL

The first Tall Ships Race, held in 1956 from Torbay, England, to Lisbon, had been conceived as a one-off event by Bernard Morgan, a London solicitor, to bring together the world's sail training ships, the last of the 'tall ships'. It was such a success that, even before it was over, it was decided to run further races on a regular basis. The committee that had organized the first TSR was re-organized under the name of Sail Training Association (STA) for the planning of future races.

Although the International Sail Training Races, or 'Tall Ships Races' as they came to be known, were a British initiative, Britain was at first very poorly represented in them, having no tall ship of her own. It was thus that the STA decided to endow the nation with a brand new three-masted topsail schooner to serve as a youth training vessel and which could represent Britain in the Tall Ships Races.

The STA had raised about half the money required for the building of the schooner when it signed the building contract. The keel was laid down on 21 November 1964. News that the schooner was no longer a mere paper project but was a-building encouraged further donations. The schooner was entirely paid by public subscriptions.

On 31 October 1965, nine days before the scheduled launching, a gale somehow triggered the launching mechanism; the schooner shifted on her stocks and fell sideways, breaking her masts. Repairs were made and she was finally launched on 5 February 1966. She was named after Sir Winston Churchill who had died the previous year. The *Sir Winston Churchill*

was commissioned, as originally scheduled, on 3 March 1966.

The schooner's rig was deliberately designed to incorporate all the main types of sail: square sails, gaff sails, staysails and a Bermudan mizzen. The masts are made of anodized aluminium to save weight aloft, but all the other spars are wood.

The hull has four watertight bulkheads and the lower deck is also watertight, with tanks and store rooms below. There is a large deckhouse which includes the galley, and a raised cockpit abaft it. The 36 trainees (later increased to 39), the three watch leaders and the bosun's mate, are berthed in the open-plan half-deck forward of the engine room. The cook's and purser's assistants have cabins in the deckhouse by the galley, and the permanent crew and senior afterguard are quartered below deck, abaft the engine room.

The *Sir Winston Churchill* was to operate fourteen-day cruises for nine months a year, for young men aged 16 to 24 inclusive — that girls could be interested in a sail training experience and, even more, that they could be quite capable of handling a big sailing ship, were concepts that were still unheard of in the sail training world in the mid-Sixties. But so many boys wanted to join, and the berths were so oversubscribed, that it became immediately apparent that there was a demand for a second schooner, and that economies of scale could be made by the operation of two sisterships. The second schooner was to be the *Malcolm Miller*, p. 134, to which the reader is referred for more information concerning both vessels.

Name of vessel	Sir Winston Churchill
Year built	1966
Designer	Camper & Nicholson's, Southampton, England
Builder	Richard Dunston, Hessle near Hull, England
Current Owner	Sail Training Association Schooners, Portsmouth, England
Current flag	United Kingdom
Rig	Three-masted topsail schooner
Construction	Steel; teak deck
Length extreme	150.3 feet (45.82 m)
Length of hull	136.0 feet (41.15 m)
Length waterline	105.0 feet (32.00 m)
Beam	26.7 feet (8.13 m)
Draught	15.9 feet (4.85 m)
Tonnage	218.46 grt; 31.75 nrt; 299 t TM; 281 td
Sail area	8,805 sq. feet (818 m²)
Engines	2 × 135 hp Perkins; twin propellers
Complement	5 permanent crew + 11 volunteer afterguard + 39 trainees
Photograph date	1976
Photograph location	Plymouth, England

SØREN LARSEN

The *Søren Larsen* was built in 1949 as an auxiliary three-masted trading schooner for ownership by the same family that owned the reputed shipyard where she was built. She was engaged in the Baltic and North Sea trades, carrying timber, wheat, beans and other commodities, until 1972.

After a laid-up period the *Søren Larsen* was bought in Denmark, in 1978, by her present owner, Anthony Davies, and his brother Robin Davies. They were the ship's third owners. They brought her to their home port of Colchester, Essex, where they rebuilt and converted her to a superb brigantine of late 19th century appearance. They had experience in such work, having previously rebuilt, converted and operated the Baltic trader *Clausens Minde* and the three-masted topsail schooner *Esther Lohse*. Nowadays, their cimbined present fleet consists of the barque *Kaskelot* (p. 120), the brigantines *Phoenix* (p. 154) and *Søren Larsen*, the wooden schooner *Carrie*, and a large former three-masted trading schooner under conversion to a ship of late 18th c. appearance. The *Søren Larsen's* deck was renewed in iroko and the masts were made from Douglas firs from the New Forest. By the spring of 1979 the brigantine was ready to sail for film charters, starting with the BBC Television drama series *The Onedin Line*. Since then she has been chartered for a number of feature and television productions. Her credits include the *Count of Monte Cristo*, *In Search of Marie Celeste*, *Dick Turpin*, *The French Lieutenant's Woman*, *Shackleton* and *Rights of Passage*.

In 1982 the *Søren Larsen* sailed to Greenland, for the *Shackleton* dramatized TV documentary, mocked up with an additional mizzen mast and a funnel to look like Shackleton's *Endurance*. From 1983 to 1985 the brigantine was chartered to the Jubilee Sailing Trust for sail training cruises aimed at able-bodied and disabled people of all ages. Methods and ideas developed during those cruises were incorporated into the barque *Lord Nelson* which was being built at the time for the JST (p. 132).

In April 1987 the brigantine began a charter as the flagship of the First Fleet Re-enactment. This event took her to Australia via Tenerife, Rio, Capetown and Mauritius and culminated in the parade of sail at Sydney on Bicentennial Day, 26 January 1988. The 'First' Fleet remained together for a further 4 months, crusing along the East Coast of Australia.

Then, from 1989 to 1991, the *Søren Larsen* operated passenger and adventure cruises around New Zealand, to Tahiti, the Cook Islands, Samoa, Tonga and Fiji, and she took part in New Zealand's Sesqui celebrations.

On 5 October 1991 she sailed from Sydney, in company with the brigantine *Eye of the Wind* (p. 92), on a homeward bound voyage round Cape Horn. The brigantines made a call at Auckland later the same month, then sailed non-stop to Stanley in the Falklands. The *Søren Larsen* rounded the Horn on 9 December and some of the participants were disappointed by the lack of snorters and greybeards. New participants joined at Montevideo on 2 January 1992 for the last leg to Europe, to Lisbon via St Helena, Tristan d'Acunha and the Azores. After a refit in Lisbon the brigantines will be taking part in the Columbus Regatta, Cadiz – Puerto Rico – New York – Boston, and ending at Liverpool in August 1992.

The *Søren Larsen* will then pay a visit to Nykøbing, her port of origin, prior to a total accommodation refurbishment in England. In April 1993 she will set sail once again for the South Pacific.

Name of vessel	Søren Larsen
Year built	1949
Designer	Søren Larsen
Builder	Søren Larsen yard, Nykøbing Mors, Denmark
Current Owner	Square Sail Pacific (Mr Anthony Davies), Gloucester, England
Current flag	United Kingdom
Rig	Brigantine
Construction	Oak on oak; iroko deck
Length extreme	138.8 feet (42.30 m)
Length of hull	105.3 feet (32.10 m)
Length waterline	92 feet (28.1 m) (approx.)
Beam	25.2 feet (7.67 m)
Draught	11.7 feet (3.58 m)
Tonnage	149 grt; 100 nrt; 350 td
Sail area	6,750 sq. feet (627 m²)
Engine	240 hp Burmeister & Wain Alpha
Complement	10 crew + 30 passage crew
Photograph date	1983
Photograph location	Cowes, England

SØRLANDET

The *Sørlandet* was built as a schoolship, for Kristiansand's nautical college, with money donated by shipowner A.O.T. Skjelbred. His one condition was that she was to be a real sailing ship, without auxiliary power. She was the last of the big square riggers to sail without an engine until, finally, an engine was installed during the winter 1959–60 refit. She represented Norway at the Chicago World Fair in 1933 and sailed until the outbreak of war. During the war she was commandeered in Norway by the German forces which used her as a prison hulk in Kirkenes where she sank at her moorings after being holed near the waterline during an Allied bombing raid. She was raised and then used as a submarine depot ship at Kristiansand. After the war she was repaired and put back into service in 1947. She took part in the first Tall Ships Race in 1956 and also in the 1960, 62, 64, 66 and 68 Tall Ships Races in which she was consistently in the top places. She was made redundant in 1973 when her school decided to replace her by a motorvessel. The following year she was bought by the Norwegian shipowner Jan Staubo only for the purpose of preventing her sale abroad.

In 1977 Jan Staubo sold her to another Norwegian shipowner Kristian Skjelbred-Knudsen, the son of her original benefactor. Skjelbred-Knudsen gave the ship to the town of Kristiansand which transferred her ownership to a purpose-created Foundation, the Stiftelsen Fullriggeren Sørlandet. By that time the ship needed a major overhaul: new decks, new engine, new generators, new sails, a complete overhaul of the rigging, etc. Kristiansand is only a small town of about 50,000 inhabitants, and to its great credit the Stiftelsen and its citizenry decided to restore the ship to full sailing condition and to keep her so in a way that had never been done before with a ship of that size and complexity, by operating adventure training cruises open to anyone above the age of 15 who wanted to experience crewing on a real tall ship. Her refit was financed partly by the town's Council and partly by private citizens and local businesses, and many Kristiansanders volunteered their time and labour.

The *Sørlandet's* inaugural cruise as an adventure training ship was in the 1980 Tall Ships Race. Her trainees came from a dozen different countries; their ages varied from 15 to 74; few had ever sailed before, let alone in square rig; and there was a high proportion of female trainees. They had set sail within hours of boarding. The other ships in her class were all professional schoolships manned exclusively by boy trainees who had trained for weeks in harbour before setting out to sea weeks or months before the race. The *Sørlandet* did not win either of the two racing legs, but neither was she last in her class. The ship has not taken part in other STA Tall Ships Races since then because of a disagreement on how those Races are organized.

The *Sørlandet* normally operates 12-day open (public) cruises out of Kristiansand during the Norwegian summer holidays. Before and after this three-month period she is usually chartered or employed for other purposes. For several years she was chartered after her summer season by the Royal Norwegian Navy, for the sea-training of midshipmen, but with her merchant navy crew still in command. In the early season of 1991 she ran a long square-rig seamanship course for master mariners from several different countries. During that course she sailed to Iceland and back. She made two open trans-Atlantic voyages in 1981 and another in 1986.

Nowadays several other big square riggers offer mixed and mixed-ages adventure training cruises but the *Sørlandet*, which was the first to do so, is still in the lead for the professionalism and smoothness of her operation.

Name of vessel	Sørlandet
Year built	1927
Builder	Høivolds Mek. Verksted, Kristiansand, Norway
Current Owner	Stiftelsen Fullriggeren Sørlandet, Kristiansand, Norway
Current flag	Norway
Rig	Full-rigged ship
Construction	Steel; teak deck
Length extreme	216.0 feet (65.84 m)
Length of hull	186.0 feet (56.70 m)
Length between perpendiculars	158.0 feet (48.16 m)
Beam	29.1 feet (8.87 m)
Draught	14.5 feet (4.42 m)
Tonnage	559 grt; 153 nrt; 644 t TM
Sail area	12,550 sq. feet (1,166 m²)
Engine	564 bhp Deutz
Complement	18 crew + 70 trainees
Photograph date	1956
Photograph location	Torbay, England (First Tall Ships Race)

STAR FLYER

The *Star Flyer*, the first of the new breed of 'sailiners' to be a real sailing ship rather than a sail-assisted power-driven vessel, is the brainchild of Swedish-born Mikael Krafft, of Brussels, who combined his merchant-shipowning experience with his love of old clipper ships to produce this barquentine and her sisters to come.

The rig was designed by Olivier Van Meer of Enkhuizen, Holland. The yards are all standing and the square sails hydraulically roller-furl inside them. There is a manual override in the event of hydraulic failure but, to date, in the first nine months of sailing the system has worked without a hitch. The braces lead to hydraulic brace winches and the square sails are controlled by joystick command and only need three men to operate them. The main topmast staysail is hydraulically roller-furled with manual override. There are no ratlines or footropes as there is no need to go aloft, but the masts are fitted with rungs in case of emergency. The other sails are hoisted and stowed in the old-fashioned way but the halyards can be led to electric winches, as can the sheets. The ship only requires ten deckhands. The speed under sail can reach 17 knots.

Under power the *Star Flyer* can cruise at 12 knots. The four-bladed variable-pitch propeller is fully feathering to reduce drag when under sail. There is a bow thruster and there are anti-roll tanks that are effective even at anchor.

There are four full-length decks: the tank top, with the engine room, tanks, storerooms, galley and crew's quarters; the 'Commodore' deck with 44 passenger cabins; the 'Clipper' deck with the dining room, purser's office, gift shop and 37 cabins, and the Main deck with a piano bar, a library, an outdoor Tropical Bar and 6 deck staterooms. The sun deck, above the Piano Bar and main deck cabins, has a swimming pool with a transparent bottom that forms a skylight to the Piano Bar. The 'aft deck' (poop deck) has another pool and two passenger staterooms. The interior design was done by Studio Acht of Moordrecht (Netherlands).

The accommodation is airconditioned throughout. Most cabins are fitted with twin lower beds that readily convert to double beds. The cabins have en-suite shower and toilet and are equipped with video, radio and international telephone. Some cabins have a third berth, for families, etc. The dining room, which seats 210 (meals are served in single sittings) can be quickly converted to a meeting or a conference room with screen, projectors, video monitors, podium and microphone. The Tropical Bar, on deck and under an awning, doubles up as dance floor and as an alternative venue for breakfasts and buffet lunches.

The *Star Flyer* was launched on 14 January 1991 and was delivered at Antwerp on 15 May. Her homeport is Antwerp but she is registered in Luxembourg and flies the European Community ensign. She is based at St Martin in the Caribbean and operates seven-day cruises that alternate between the Virgin and the Leeward Islands. Her first sistership, the *Star Clipper*, was launched on 3 October 1991 and will be delivered in March 1992; she will operate in the Mediterranean. Both barquentines will be at Barcelona for the 1992 Olympics, chartered as 'floatels' by the Belgian and Dutch Olympic Committees.

Name of vessel	Star Flyer
Year built	1991
Designer	Robert MacFarlane (UK)
Builder	Langerbrugge Shipyards, Langerbrugge, Ghent, Belgium
Current Owner	White Star Clippers NV, Brussels, Belgium
Current flag	Luxembourg/EEC (port of registry: Antwerp, Belgium)
Rig	Four-masted staysail barquentine
Construction	Steel; teak-clad weather decks
Length extreme	357.0 feet (108.80 m)
Length of hull	300.0 feet (91.40 m)
Length between perpendiculars	230.0 feet (70.20 m)
Beam	48.0 feet (14.60 m)
Draught	18.5 feet (5.60m)
Tonnage	2,298 grt, 869 nrt; 2,018 td (light), 2,556 td (load)
Sail area	36,000 sq. feet (3,340 m²)
Engine	1,500 hp Caterpillar
Complement	58 crew; 180–196 passengers
Photograph date	1991
Photograph location	Off Isle of Wight, England

THOR HEYERDAHL

The *Thor Heyerdahl* was built in 1930 as a motor-freighter. For nearly fifty years she carried cargoes between Europe, South Africa and the West Indies. She was bought in 1979 for conversion by two German captains, Gunther Hoffmann and Detlef Soitzek, who had experience in sail, social work and youth training. Captain Detlef Soitzek had been the navigator on Thor Heyerdahl's *Tigris* reed boat expedition in the Persian Gulf, Indian Ocean and Red Sea, in 1977–78, and as a devoted admirer of this Norwegian navigator and ethnologist, he decided that the schooner should be named after him.

The conversion work was done in Kiel in 1979–83. The hull being that of a motor-freighter, has a quasi-rectangular section, with an almost flat bottom, so a long external keel, made of welded steel plates and containing some ballast, had to be added to prevent excessive leeway when sailing to windward. The rig, with wooden masts and spars, is that of a conventional three-masted topsail schooner with a square, double fore-topsail. Since 1990 there is also a square fore-course that can be set below the lower yard, adding 1,076 sq. ft. (100 m²) of driving power when running free in moderate or light winds. The vessel has a short, slightly raised fo'c's'le deck below which there are traditional quarters for the deckhands. A watertight bulkhead separates them from the fore hold which has store rooms, a generator and a workshop. Another bulkhead with a watertight door leads from this hold to the next compartment aft which has 2 six-berth trainee cabins. Yet another watertight door aft of these leads to the main trainee accommodation which consists of 2 four-berth, 6 two-berth cabins and a large mess room

at the after end (beyond which is the engine room). The galley, trainee showers and toilets are in the deckhouse. The poop is raised and has sunk-in accommodation below for the officers. The engine room is below this poop accommodation. A new, more powerful engine was installed in 1990.

The *Thor Heyerdahl* has been sailing since 1983. In summer – May to September – she sails 3 to 14 day cruises and day trips in the Baltic and North Sea, occasionally engaging in longer voyages to northern Norway. The cruises are mostly block-booked by youth organizations, although some are open, and a few periods are booked by corporate charters. Since 1989 the *Thor Heyerdahl* has received a number of Polish trainees (mixed with the usual German trainees) with the help of German sponsorship. The scheme is likely to be extended soon to youngsters from other eastern Baltic States. The *Thor Heyerdahl* usually takes part in windjammer gatherings in that part of the world, and sometimes enters Tall Ships Races.

In winter – December to March – the *Thor Heyerdahl* operates one or two-week cruises in the Canaries or two or three-week cruises in the West Indies. These cruises are sometimes block-booked by groups but are mostly open to individual bookers who are (or become) members of the ship's supporters' club. Because of transport costs and the season, most participants in these winter cruises are adults. The delivery passages, which are split into legs with optional crew changes, are also marketed. In the winter of 1990–91 the Thor Heyerdahl operated in the Canaries; in that of 1991–92 she was in the Caribbean, her third winter in those parts.

Name of vessel	Thor Heyerdahl, ex-Minnow, ex-Silke, ex-Marga Henning, ex-Tinka
Year built	1930. Converted 1979–83
Builder	E.J. Smit & Zoon, Westbrock, The Netherlands
Current Owner	Segelschiff 'Thor Heyerdahl' e.V., Kiel, Germany
Current flag	Germany
Rig	Three-masted topsail schooner
Construction	Steel; steel deck
Length extreme	163.5 feet (49.83 m)
Length of hull	137.8 feet (42.00 m)
Length between perpendiculars	127.8 feet (38.96 m)
Beam	21.5 feet (6.56 m)
Draught	7.9 feet (2.40 m)
Tonnage	211.21 grt; 118 nrt; 315 tdw; 370 td
Sail area	7,858 sq. feet (730 m²)
Engine	400 hp Deutz
Complement	12 crew + 32 trainees
Photograph date	1988
Photograph location	Cowes, England

TOVARISHCH

The German Navy had this barque built as a replacement for its former schoolship, the barque *Niobe*, that had capsized and sunk with the loss of 69 lives in a squall in the Fehrman Belt of 26 July 1932. The new barque was launched and named *Gorch Fock* on 3 May 1933, and was commissioned on 27 June that same year. She had a steel deck clad with teak (re-clad in another timber in the 1980s) and, as today, a long fo'c's'le joined to the fore deckhouse, and a long poop. Her first spanker was a single sail (not the later and current double spanker). She was the first of a series of six barques built by Blohm & Voss (see p. 106).

Each year before the war the *Gorch Fock* made several short cruises in the Baltic and North Sea, and one long cruise which was usually trans-Atlantic. Her training role was intensified in home waters, during the war. She was given a more powerful auxiliary in 1942, a 220 hp MAN, to increase her manoeuvrability among the minefields. She was scuttled by her crew at Stralsund on 1 May 1945, to prevent her capture.

The *Gorch Fock* was nonetheless raised by a Soviet salvage team in 1948 and was taken for repairs to the Neptun yard in Rostock (East Germany). On 15 June 1950 the Soviet flag was hoisted on her and she was renamed *Tovarishch* ('Comrade'). She was the second Soviet schoolship to bear that name. The first had been the former British four-masted barque *Lauriston*, built in Belfast in 1892 and purchased by Russia in 1914 for the transport of war supplies from the UK to Murmansk. She was turned into a schoolship in 1921, under the name of *Tovarishch*; she was sunk by enemy action in 1941.

When the refit was completed, in 1951, the *Tovarishch* (II) sailed to her new home port of Kherson, in Crimea. She was affected to the Kherson Nautical Preparatory College 'Lieutenant Schmid' which trains young people for merchant and naval careers.

She sailed in the Black Sea until 1957–58 when she made a seven-month voyage from Odessa to Port Said, Bombay, Colombo, Singapore, Jakarta, Capetown, St Helena, Dakar, Gibraltar and back to Odessa. In 1967–68 she underwent a major refit in which her 1942 MAN was replaced by the current Škoda. Her sail area was also slightly increased from 18,837 sq. feet (1,750 m²) to 19,989 sq. ft. (1,857 m²).

In 1972 she sailed to Baltimore, Maryland. In 1974 she and the *Kruzenshtern* (p. 124) were the first Soviet vessels to enter a Tall Ships Race. Again with the *Kruzenshtern* she entered the 1976 American Bicentennial trans-Atlantic Tall Ships race, and, like the *Kruzenshtern*, she was under orders from 'up above' to win at all cost, and thus 'won' the nickname of 'Motorich'. After that the authorities back home got the message that the spirit of the Tall Ships Races is not about winning and is not that of the Olympics.

From 1977 to 1989 the *Tovarishch* was restricted to summer sailing in the Black Sea on account of her condition but she was given a refit and appeared at Tall ships gatherings at Bordeaux in 1990 and at Delfzijl in 1991. There are, or were, plans for her participation in the 1992 Columbus Regatta but, with the changes sweeping the former Soviet Union, at the time of writing her legal owner has ceased to exist and her nationality is uncertain.

Name of vessel	Tovarishch, ex-Gorch Fock
Year built	1933
Designer	Blohm & Voss
Builder	Blohm & Voss, Hamburg, Germany
Past Owner	USSR Ministry of Merchant Marine, Moscow
Operator	Nautical Preparatory College 'Lieutenant Schmid', Kherson, Ukraine
Past flag	USSR
Rig	Barque
Construction	Steel; wood-clad deck
Length extreme	269.4 feet (82.10 m)
Length of hull	241.6 feet (73.64 m)
Length between perpendiculars	205.1 feet (62.51 m)
Beam	39.4 feet (12.02 m)
Draught	17.2 feet (5.23 m)
Tonnage	1,392 grt; 230 nrt; 1,505 t TM; 1,350 td (standard); 1,760 td (load); 292 tdw
Sail area	19,989 sq. feet (1,857 m²)
Engine	550 hp Škoda
Complement	51 crew + 134 cadets
Photograph date	1976
Photograph location	Plymouth, England

UNICORN

The *Unicorn* is a former Finnish trading schooner. Like hundreds of others she was skipper-owner-built on improvised ways on a beach near to where grew the trees used in her construction. They were built for carrying sand and building materials to rebuild war-ravaged Finnish towns. The *Unicorn*'s owner, builder and skipper was Helge Johansson, and he named that schooner *Lyra*. He was to operate her for 23 years, first as a schooner and later as an unrigged motorized sand carrier.

Jacques Thiry, a French-American and a former Air Force and UNICEF photographer, bought her from Johansson in 1971 and renamed her *Unicorn*. He motored her to southern Sweden for rebuilding and conversion. His project was to rig her as a trading brig and to seek cargoes. The rigging plan was derived from that of the 1876 French brig *Adolphe et Laure* and Underhill's *Masting and Rigging*. Thiry and his helpers cut trees in the forest for the masts and yards and hand-made themselves the blocks, deadeyes and belaying pins, and forged many of the metal fittings. In 1972, after 14 months, the *Unicorn* headed south under reduced sail while the upper yards were still being finished on deck — but she was fully rigged by the time she reached the Canaries.

She sailed across to Barbados in the spring of 1973, then sailed to the US East Coast before returning to the British West Indies in search of cargo. She finally found a regular freight between Honduras and the Cayman Islands, carrying fresh produce — but this was short-lived as it came to an end when hurricane Fifi devastated Honduran crops.

The *Unicorn* then sailed to Fort Lauderdale where she was bought in late 1974 by Unicorn Inc., a company formed by Mr William Wycoff Smith, a businessman from Philadelphia who was also the Chairman of the Philadelphia Maritime Museum. He wanted to enter the *Unicorn* in the American Bicentennial Tall Ships Race from Bermuda to Boston via Newport and New York, and to operate her as a sail training vessel thereafter. First she had to be upgraded, and that represented more than a 50% rebuild. A fair amount of timber was replaced around the ship and the bottom was copper sheathed. Two watertight bulkheads were built in; five passenger double cabins and accommodation for 12 crew were built. The masting and rigging were overhauled and new sails were made (flax), including stun'sails. A new engine was installed. Tragically Bill Smith died of a heart attack in 1975, at the age of 55, but the project went ahead anyway, and Jacques Thiry, the former owner, was still the captain.

After the Tall Ships Race events the brig was chartered for the filming of the film *Roots*, and she was used in several productions, including *Ghosts of Cape Horn*. The *Unicorn* passed at that time through several successive underfinanced cultural or sail training organizations, including the Florida Ocean Sciences Institute and the Tampa Sea Scouts. She took part in the 1978 East Coast Tall Ships Race, Baltimore-Philadelphia-Newport-Boston, and in the 1980 Norfolk to Boston Race, but finally she was sold abroad later that year.

Her new owner was Mr Robert Elliot, an English hotel owner in St Lucia. He based the *Unicorn* at Castries, Santa Lucia, and he has been running very successful day trips since then, carrying up to 150 passengers five days a week, often with a steel band aboard, for short cruises to the magnificent Baie des Pitons or to Soufrière, and he has kept the *Unicorn* well maintained.

Name of vessel	Unicorn, *ex-Lyra*
Year built	1948. Converted 1971–72
Builder	Helge Johansson, Sibbo, Finland
Current Owner	Mr Robert Elliot, UK/Santa Lucia
Current flag	United Kingdom
Rig	Brig
Construction	Wood
Length extreme	148 feet (45.1 m)
Length of hull	94 feet (28.7 m)
Beam	22 feet (6.7 m)
Draught	9 feet (2.7 m)
Tonnage	190 t TM
Sail area	7,362 sq. feet (684 m²) (incl. stun'sails)
Engine	335 hp Caterpillar
Complement	8 crew + up to 150 day passengers
Photograph date	1976
Photograph location	New York, USA

UNICORN

The *Unicorn* was built in 1947 as a Dutch motor fishing vessel for the North Atlantic (Icelandic) fishing grounds but her lines are those of the earlier generation of sail loggers. As she had a hull in sound condition, it was therefore not surprising that she was bought for conversion to sail when her fishing days were over.

The buyers were a Dutch skipper and his wife, Pieter and Agnes Kaptein of Hoorn, who had owned and operated large traditional sailing vessels before.

They removed the superstructure and sandblasted the hull. They added a false clipper bow plate to soften the straight and nearly plumb profile of the logger stem. They built two sunken deckhouses — one is a nice and airy saloon — and they laid 1½ inch (38 mm) iroko planks over the steel deck. The small turtle-backed wheelhouse-cum-chartroom may be a feature kept from the fishing days. In front of it there is a large deck wheel with hydraulic transmission to the tiller. Below deck there is another saloon abaft the collision bulkhead with a galley corner and bar. There are five guest cabins with a total of sixteen berths (12 singles and 2 doubles), and there is even a bath tub. The skipper-owner and crew quarters are aft, with their own galley.

The masts and spars were made of solid Oregon pine and are assembled in the traditional way with fidded topmasts and a separate jibbom over the bowsprit. At first there was a single topsail, the lower one. The upper topsail yard was added during a further phase of conversion. The sails are Duradon.

The Kapteins renamed this schooner *Eenhorn*, 'One horn', the Dutch for 'Unicorn', and they registered her in Amsterdam. Starting in 1981 they operated the *Eenhorn* as a charter vessel cruising in the North Sea and English Channel. They also took parties of youngsters on sail training cruises.

In 1986 they sold the *Eenhorn* to Mr Morris Henson, an American who had owned the three-masted Mallorcan schooner *Berta of Ibiza* (by then rotting away on a beach near Puntarenas, Costa Rica) and who owned the steel brigantine *Taiyo* (also based on the Pacific coast of Central America) and a Bermudan yacht in Spain. Henson registered the *Eenhorn* in Jersey under the anglicized name of *Unicorn*. He had her refitted to his requirements at Southampton in 1986–87, with improvements made to the accommodation and systems, and with enough duplicated electronics and other equipment to fit out a chandlery. The schooner was put back into Lloyds class. The hull was painted black, retaining the white rail and gunwale stripes.

The owner is often aboard and sometimes skippers her but usually the *Unicorn* has an employed skipper. The *Unicorn* operated day charter trips, with up to 60 deck passengers, out of St Martin in the West Indies, in 1988. The following year she cruised up the Amazon and then sailed to Gibraltar and Soto Grande in Spain where she operated charter trips. In 1991–92 she was operating out of Tortola in the British Virgin Islands.

Name of vessel	Unicorn, *ex*-Eenhorn
Year built	1947. Converted 1979–81
Builder	at Alphen, The Netherlands
Current Owner	Cocos Island Productions, St Helier, Jersey, Channel Islands
Current flag	British
Rig	Topsail schooner
Construction	Steel. Iroko-clad deck
Length extreme	115 feet (35.05 m)
Length on deck	87.6 feet (26.70 m)
Length waterline	78.0 feet (23.76 m)
Beam	19.7 feet (6.00 m)
Draught	8.5 feet (2.59 m)
Tonnage	95.26 grt; 56.53 nrt
Sail area	9,688 sq. feet (900 m²)
Engine	300 hp Henschel
Complement	18 berths
Photograph date	1983
Photograph location	Cowes, England

VANESSA ANN

The *Vanessa Ann* — which never changed name during her varied career — was built at Lowestoft in 1951 as a 188 grt Arctic trawler. She operated out of Fleetwood under the number FD 133 and was owned by the Dalby Steam Fishing Company. She was a typical deep-sea side trawler with a raised fo'c's'le and a wheelhouse above a long deckhouse. She fished in Icelandic waters and played an active role in the Cod War.

She was later bought and converted for use as a stand-by vessel for North Sea oil rigs. She was subsequently laid-up when her engine crankshaft broke. She was found by a Briton who was looking for a hull to convert to a sailing trader for work between Pacific islands. He had been recommended by surveyors and others to look for an Arctic trawler built in the 1950s and with a riveted hull as these vessels have excellent sailing lines (fine entrance, much deadrise and a clean run) and are of sturdier construction than later ones. When he found the *Vanessa Ann* and saw what beautiful lines she had, he bought her and towed her to Denmark to have a Hundested engine and variable pitch propeller fitted in her. He then motored her to London where he was going to convert her. Sadly he then fell seriously ill and had to sell the ship.

The *Vanessa Ann* was bought in 1984 by Mr Reg March and Mr Jack Scott. Reg March, a marine engineer and rigger, had recently been in charge of the rebuilding and rigging of the brig *Ciudad de Inca* (now the *Maria Asumpta*, p. 136) and he had always wanted to convert his own ship. The *Vanessa Ann* was motored to Padstow, Cornwall, for conversion. Her raised fo'c's'le and the bridge structure were razed off. The 'lower' deckhouse was retained, for conversion to a deck saloon and bar, with a new chartroom in its after part, and was decked over with a sun deck extending as an awning deck to the ship's sides. The *Vanessa Ann* being intended for day trips, her original crew accommodation forward (4-berth fo'c's'le) and aft (two single cabins plus a 7-berth after fo'c's'le) was retained, and the former fishroom was converted into a large air conditioned disco and bar. The vessel was rigged as a handsome three-masted topsail schooner with steel lower masts (the mizzen mast served also as engine exhaust), and wooden topmasts, yards gaffs and booms. She was equipped for 200 day passengers.

She made her sailing trials in May 1985 and proved a very good sailing ship. She set sail for Antigua in June and arrived in July. The project was to run day trips out of Antigua but things did not work out as expected as her arrival there ran up against vested local interests. In 1986, under new ownership, the vessel was stationed in Barbados, running day trips from that island. However, there also the day-cruise market was already exploited by another vessel and the combination of absentee owners living in England and a local crew was not one to ensure competitiveness, even though the *Vanessa Ann* was by far the best vessel in the field.

Eventually the *Vanessa Ann* was ordered home in March 1988, via St Thomas in the US Virgin Islands where she was given a refit for the passage. After a very long passage she arrived at Plymouth on 3 July, her nearly-new sails damaged, her nearly-new Hundested working on one piston and her accommodation in a state of filth. She was laid up for sale near Plymouth and at latest news is still on the market.

Name of vessel	Vanessa Ann
Year built	1951. Converted 1984–85
Designer	Reg March (conversion)
Builder	Richards Ironworks, Lowestoft, England
Current Owner	Charles W. Clowes and David Cox, England
Current flag	United Kingdom
Rig	Three-masted topgallant schooner
Construction	Steel. Steel deck plank-clad except fore-deck
Length extreme	145.0 feet (44.20 m)
Length of hull	112.0 feet (34.14 m)
Length between perpendiculars	103.0 feet (31.39 m)
Beam	23.0 feet (7.01 m)
Draught	12.0 feet (3.66 m)
Tonnage	153.57 grt; 80.16 nrt; 316 td
Sail area	5,800 sq. feet (539 m²)
Engine	250 hp Hundested
Complement	12 crew + up to 200 day passengers
Photograph date	1986
Photograph location	Antigua

HMS VICTORY

HMS *Victory* is the only surviving example of a ship-of-the-line, and of a first rate one at that — these were the capital ships that ruled the seas for two and a quarter centuries, from 1637 until 1860. In Nelson's days first rate ships carried 100 or more guns. Along with the three-decked second rates and two-decked third rates, they formed the line-of-battle fleets, hence the expression 'ships-of-the-line'.

First rate ships were always few in numbers: they were enormously expensive to build and to man. The *Victory*'s construction required 2,000 to 2,500 110-year old oak trees. Her keel was laid down on 23 July 1759, during the Seven Year War (1756–63) but the success of British arms removed the urgency from her construction and she was not completed and floated out of her dock until 1765 —— and then was immediately laid up in ordinary (in reserve). She had sufficiently aged and decayed to warrant a rebuild before her first commission in 1778, when the American War of Independence brought England in renewed conflict with France (soon joined by Spain). The *Victory* did not take part in any major battle in that war and she was laid up again at its conclusion, in 1783. She was briefly commissioned in 1790, and again in 1793 for the French Revolutionary and Napoleonic Wars.

HMS *Victory* was the flagship of Admiral Sir John Jervis (later Earl St Vincent) at the battle of Cape St Vincent (14 February 1797). This brilliant victory was largely due to the initiative and disobedience of orders of the captain of HMS *Captain*, 74 guns, one Commodore Horatio Nelson. After that action the ageing and battle-scarred *Victory* was demoted to a PoW

hospital hulk but timber shortages for new ships caused her to be rebuilt once more in 1800–03. She was modernized at that time and was given the aspect and armament she was to have at the battle of Trafalgar. Her lower gun deck battery consisted of thirty 32-pounder guns (firing 32 lb shot); the middle gun deck had twenty-eight 24-pounders and the upper gun deck carried thirty 12-pounders. The quarter deck was armed with twelve 12-pounders and the fo'c's'le with two 12-pdr bow chasers and two 68-pdr carronades.

The *Victory* was commissioned in 1803 as the flagship of Admiral Horatio Nelson. It was not until 21 October 1805 that Nelson's fleet finally engaged the combined French and Spanish fleet off Cape Trafalgar. Once again Nelson displayed his tactical genius in that decisive battle, but he lost his life in the action.

The *Victory* remained in active service until 1812, went in for a rebuild in 1814–16 and was then laid up. In 1824 she was commissioned in a harbour-bound capacity at Portsmouth, as the Port Admiral's flagship. She has remained in stationary commission ever since, except for the period 1869–1889; today she is the flagship of the Commander-of-Chief Naval Home Command. She is the world's oldest warship in commission.

She remained afloat until 12 January 1922 when she was permanently berthed in the No. 2 Dock in the Plymouth Dockyard. After approximate restoration to her 1805 appearance she was opened to the public in 1928. Today she is completely restored to that period's appearance and detail and she attracts around half a million visitors every year.

Name of vessel	Victory (*HMS*)
Year built	1759–65 (first commissioned: 1778)
Designer	Thomas Slade
Builder	Chatham Dockyard, Chatham, England
Current Owner	Royal Navy
Current flag	United Kingdom
Rig	Full-rigged ship
Construction	Wood
Length extreme	335.0 feet (102.11 m)
Length of hull	226.5 feet (69.03 m) (incl. figurehead)
Length waterline	152.5 feet (46.48 m)
Beam	51.8 feet (15.79 m)
Draught	23.5 feet (7.16 m)
Tonnage	3,500 td (approx.); 2,162 t burthen
Armament at Trafalgar	104 guns
Complement at Trafalgar	842 officers and men (nominal); 819 (actual)
Photograph date	1981 (21 October, Trafalgar Day)
Photograph location	Portsmouth, England

VROUWE GEERTRUIDA MAGDALENA

When Mr Berend Groen sold his shipyard in 1972 he wanted to buy a seagoing schooner. He remembered something a friend had told him years before. That friend had been involved in 1962 in the mass rebuilding of former wartime German Navy composite-built patrol boats (such as *Henryk Rutkowski*, p. 114) which had been seized as war prizes by the Netherlands for conversion to fishing boats. In 1962 that friend had replaced by steel plates the ageing planking on some 50 of these *vor Posten Kutter*, turning them into 'regular' steel boats, when two hulls turned up that would not quite fit the pre-cut plates. Some research uncovered the fact that the wartime *vor Posten Kutter* design was closely derived from Dutch pilot schooners built in 1910 – just the sort of boat that Mr Groen was seeking. The two odd boats also appeared to be much older than the others, so they had to be former Dutch pilot schooners of 1910 vintage.

So, in 1972, Mr Groen went on the trail of these two fishing boats. One he missed by a few days: all he found were some cut-up parts in a scrap yard in Belgium. The other he sought in vain as far afield as East Germany, Poland, Denmark, Poland, Morocco and Tunisia.

In 1975 Mr Groen found himself looking at trawlers on some other business when his eye caught one rusty stern among a row of 60 old trawlers laid up side by side: 'There she is!' He had found her – 50 km from his home town! She bore the name of *Flevo* and had been beam-trawling out of Wieringen until 1972. Her owner was only too pleased to sell her.

The schooner had first worked for the Texel & Ijmuiden pilot station, for a couple of years. Then she was sold to Germany and worked as a pilot schooner,

No. 3 or No. 6, for the Weser station, until a few years before the Second World War when she was laid up in reserve at Bremerhaven. During the war she was requisitioned by the German Admiralty; her false clipper bow was removed, her rig was taken out and an engine was fitted. She was commissioned in 1943 as a weather and airplane spotter ship stationed offshore.

In 1963 her transom stern was shortened and converted to a round stern.

Mr Groen restored the vessel to her original appearance (except for the stern) and fitted her out for charter with 14 guest berths in 4 cabins and with two small deckhouses. She went into her new service in 1976 under the name of *Vrouwe Geertruida Magdalena* (*Vrouwe* = Mrs) and the more convenient 'nickname' of *Geertruida M.* She operated charters from the North Cape to the Mediterranean, but mostly in the southern North Sea and the Channel, as part of the Zeilvaart Enkhuizen agency charter fleet. In 1990 she began a seven-year bareboat contract with the *Outlaw Verein* (p.150) but this was terminated at the end of 1991 as the owner was dissatisfied by the way she was being maintained.

From late 1991 until May 1992 she underwent a major rebuild and upgrading at Zaandam for the luxury charter market for 12 guests with en-suite heads and shower or 34 guests on day cruises. Her original transom stern was reconstructed, lengthening the hull to 94.8 ft (28.90 m) and the Length Extreme to 128.0 ft (39.00 m). The fore deckhouse, which was only a workshop, was removed and the after deckhouse was rebuilt further forward, with a deck lounge. A new deck of laid teak on plywood was laid and the hull is now painted white.

Name of vessel	Vrouwe Geertruida Magdalena, *ex-*Flevo, *ex-?, ex-*Weser No 3 or No 6, *ex-*Texel No 2
Year built	1910
Builder	Bodewes, Groningen, The Netherlands
Current Owner	Mr Berend P. Groen
Current flag	The Netherlands
Rig	Schooner
Construction	Steel (originally composite); teak deck
Length extreme	118.1 feet (36.00 m)*
Length of hull	86.0 feet (26.20 m)*
Length waterline	77.1 feet (23.50 m)
Beam	20.3 feet (6.20 m)
Draught	10.7 feet (3.25 m)
Tonnage	128 grt*, 63 nrt*, 220 td*
Sail area	5,920 sq. feet (550 m²)*
Engine	340 hp Caterpillar
Complement	4 crew + 14 cruise passengers* or 35 day passengers*
Photograph date	1988
Photograph location	Cowesm England
* At time of photograph, prior to 1992 rebuild	

HMS WARRIOR

Since the Napoleonic Wars the Royal Navy had become somewhat complacent and fossilized in the belief of its superiority. It was woken up with a jolt in 1859 when the French launched *La Gloire*, the world's first ironclad frigate and which was armed with rifled shell-firing guns that made wooden walls obsolete.

Alarmed, Britain put all her engineering and industrial might into producing a new class of ship that would in turn outclass *La Gloire*. The result was the *Warrior* and the *Black Prince* (which was launched one year later) which alone could destroy the complete French fleet. They were the first battleships and were quickly followed by a fleet of even mightier ships that reaffirmed Britain's uncontested naval superiority for another 50 years.

The *Warrior* was the first ocean-going iron fighting ship and her iron construction, with watertight bulkheads, was combined with an impenetrable 4½ in. (114 mm) armour plating, with the most powerful artillery yet to be fitted on any ship, and with the fastest speed of any fighting ship. Although she still had a full rig and broadside batteries, she was the direct ancestor of the battleships of the two World Wars.

Her keel was laid on 25 May 1859 and she was launched on 26 December 1860. She was commissioned on 1 August 1861. Her armour cladding, backed by 18 inches (46 cm) of teak separating it from the brittle iron hull, extended the length of the battery (213 ft−65 m), forming a citadel the ends of which were sealed off by armoured bulkheads. The side armour plating extended from the spar deck to 6 ft (1.8 m) below waterline. The single expansion steam engines were enormously powerful for the day and gave a top speed under power of 14.3 knots. The range under power at cruising speed was only 1,420 miles, so the ship had a full sailing rig under which she could reach 13 knots. Under sail and steam the *Warrior* could reach 17.5 knots.

The *Warrior* had an uneventful career. She ensured peace just by her existence. She went into refit in 1864−67 during which time her armament was modernized. Her new ideas were quickly developed and improved in the ships that followed and she had lost her prime strategic importance by 1872, when she was laid up. She was recommissioned in 1875 as a guardship at Portland and from 1881 to 1883 she was a Royal Naval Reserve drill ship. She went into the Fleet Reserve on 31 May 1883. She was hulked in 1900 and renamed *Vernon III*, used by HMS *Vernon* torpedo school as a workshop and floating classroom. In 1923, the year that the *Black Prince* was scrapped, she was deleted from the Navy List but regained the name of *Warrior*. She remained unused at Portsmouth until 1929 when she was towed to Pembroke Dock, Wales, for use as a fuelling jetty. She was re-named *C.77* when the name of *Warrior* was given to a new aircraft carrier in 1944.

In 1977 the Navy no longer wanted the *C.77* and gave it to the Maritime Trust. In 1978 the hulk was towed half way around Britain to Hartlepool where it was restored by the Ship Preservation Trust Ltd (a subsidiary of the Maritime Trust), with major financial help from the Manifold Trust. With most of the external restoration and significant parts of the internal reconstruction completed, the *Warrior* was towed in 1987 to her permanent berth afloat at Portsmouth, where she is open to the public a short walk away from HMS *Victory* and the *Mary Rose*.

Name of vessel	Warrior, *ex-*C.77, *ex-*Warrior, *ex-*Vernon III, *ex-*Warrior
Year built	1859−60
Designer	Isaac Watts and John Scott Russell
Builder	Thames Ironwork and Shipbuilding Company, Blackwall, London
Current Owner	The Warrior Trust, Portsmouth, England
Current flag	United Kingdom
Rig	Full-rigged ship
Construction	Iron; armour-clad
Length extreme	465 feet (141.7 m)
Length of hull	418 feet (127.4 m)
Length between perpendiculars	380 feet (115.8 m)
Beam	58 feet (17.7 m)
Draught	26 feet (7.9 m)
Tonnage	9,210 td
Sail area	30,000/48,400 sq. feet (2,787/4,497 m^2) (plain sail/all set)
Engines	1,250 hp John Penn & Sons (Greenwich) single expansion steam; one propeller
Complement (in 1861)	704 men (51 officers, 83 petty officers, 382 seamen, 63 boys and 125 marines)
Armament (in 1861)	40 guns: 10 × 110 pdr and 4 × 40 pdr breech-loading rifled guns + 26 × 68 pdr smooth bore muzzle loaders
Photograph date	1987
Photograph location	Portsmouth, England

YOUNG ENDEAVOUR

It was Arthur Weller, a retired British Master Mariner, who had the idea that Britain should offer the youth of Australia a sail training vessel to mark and remember Australia's 200th anniversary. Thus was formed the Britain-Australia Bicentennial Schooner Trust which raised the funds for the project (£1.7 million, half from private and corporate donations, half from the British Government) and managed it. Mr Colin Mudie, who had designed the brig *Royalist* (p. 164) and the barque *Lord Nelson* (p. 132) was commissioned to draw the plans which, in the event, were those of a brigantine, square rig having so much more to offer sail training than fore-and-aft rig.

Although (part) named after the *Endeavour* with which Captain Cook discovered the shores of New South Wales, this brigantine is no replica of an 18th century vessel. She is very modern, built of steel with 7 watertight compartments. Her aluminium masts and yards set terylene sails. The square sails are handed the old-fashioned way but the staysails (except the fisherman) are roller-furled and the mainsail brails to the mast. The bowsprit is a walk-on type, with pulpit. Under the waterline the hull is that of a modern yacht, with cutaway fore-foot, ballast keel and with the rudder hung from a separate skeg. The 24 trainees are berthed in 1 twelve-berth and 2 six-berth cabins; the nine crew have twin berth cabins except the master who has his own cabin. In addition there are 4 supernumerary berths. In 1989 Brooke Yachts built a sistership of *Young Endeavour* for Malaysia, the *Tunas Samudera*.

The *Young Endeavour* was launched by crane on 21 May 1987 and was named by the Duchess of Kent on 2 June. The brigantine sailed from Cowes on her delivery voyage on 3 August under British registry and with 12 British and 12 Australian trainees, half of whom were girls; she was given a royal send-off by Prince Philip. After calls in the Canaries and at Rio she arrived in Australia, at Fremantle, on 1 November. She then made a number of calls along the South Coast prior to joining the Hobart-Sydney Tall Ships Race in January 1988, in which she was First in her class and Third over all. On 25 January she was formally donated to the Australian Government and the Australian White Ensign replaced the British − white because the brigantine is maintained and crewed by the Royal Australian Navy and has the status of a RAN Tender − a non-commissioned naval vessel. She is however used purely for civilian youth training through the Young Endeavour Youth Scheme. The following day, 26 January 1988, Bicentenary Day, the *Young Endeavour* led the parade of tall ships into Sydney Harbour, an event watched by 2 million spectators − a very big crowd by Australian standards.

Normally the *Young Endeavour* operates about 20 ten-day training cruises a year, along the East Coast, with boys and girls aged 16 to 23. In addition she runs a number of day trips for people with disabilities. In 1989−90 she sailed to New Zealand for the New Zealand Tall Ships Race and the Commonwealth Games.

On 1 December 1991 she sailed from Sydney on a one-year round-the-world cruise. The first leg is to Athens via Suez, the second from Athens to Annapolis, USA, by way of Cadiz and the Columbus Regatta, and the third is from Annapolis to Sydney by way of the West Indies, Panama, the Galapagos, Polynesia and New Caledonia, with a homecoming scheduled for 19 December 1992.

Name of vessel	Young Endeavour
Year built	1987
Designer	Colin Mudie
Builder	Brooke Yachts International, Lowestoft, England
Current Owner	Australian Federal Government
Current flag	Australia
Rig	Brigantine
Construction	Steel; teak-clad ply deck
Length extreme	144.3 feet (44.00 m)
Length of hull	114.8 feet (35.00 m)
Length waterline	92.8 feet (28.30 m)
Beam	25.6 feet (7.80 m)
Draught	13.1 feet (4.00 m)
Tonnage	175 grt; 51 nrt; 239 td
Sail area	6,987 sq. feet (649 m²)
Engines	2 × 187 hp Perkins; twin propellers
Complement	9 crew + 24 trainees
Photograph date	1987
Photograph location	Cowes, England

ZEBU

The *Ziba*, as she was then called, was the 102nd vessel to be built at the yard of Holms in Råå, Sweden. She was a gaff-ketch-rigged trading vessel. She remained in trade for 34 years, carrying cargoes of timber, salt and grain in the Baltic. She traded under sail until 1950, when she was converted to a motorcoaster.

The *Ziba* was bought in 1972 by an Englishman who converted her in 1972–78 to a Bermudan-rigged charter ketch with a big motor-yacht-style plywood deckhouse. He sold her to a UK-based syndicate who wanted to sail her around the world. At that time the vessel was renamed *Zebu* and registered in Jersey. The new owners entered the yacht in the 1980 Tall Ships Race in the Baltic and to Amsterdam and, upon their return, they set out from England for the West Indies. They only got as far as the Channel Islands, owing to the failure of a skin fitting which caused extensive flooding. The owners gave up their project and put the *Zebu* up for sale.

She was bought in 1982 by Nick Broughton and his wife, of London. They planned to re-rig the *Zebu* as a brigantine and to sail her around the world with an expense-sharing crew. She needed an extensive rebuild which was begun at Southampton, where the *Zebu* was re-registered, and it was completed at Lowestoft. The ugly deckhouse was replaced by a more appropriate structure. A turned-stanchion rail was placed around the poop. The rig was designed by Wally Buchanan and completed by Captain Adrian Small. While the work was in progress, the Broughtons obtained a charter agreement with Operation Raleigh for a four-year voyage around the world, with young people. The *Zebu* was to obtain a Loadline Certification (which she did) and to be commanded by a master mariner, but the owners could be among the adult crew. There would be a crew of 7 (including the Broughtons) and 16 Young Venturers, aged 17 to 24. The latter would join for three-month legs.

The *Zebu* left from London on 11 October 1984 and returned at Southampton on 6 October 1988 after having sailed more than 60,000 miles, having visited 30 countries and having carried more than 300 Venturers of many different nationalities. During the voyage there had been wreck-diving and surveying in a number of locations, archaeological surveys in Honduras, filming in the Galapagos, community projects in the Solomon Islands, Japan and Kenya, scientific studies in Hawaii, on-going whale and dolphin recordings and meteorological measurements, etc.

The *Zebu*'s Loadline Certificate expired upon her return and she could not obtain its renewal without expensive alterations as new rules had come into force while she had been away. The owners did not feel like spending the money required and anyway felt like a long spell ashore after four years at sea, so they put the *Zebu* up for sale. She was bought in Southampton in December 1988 by her present owner who has based her in Liverpool. He is seldom in England and has no time to sail the brigantine, so he has lent her to the Merseyside Heritage Trust in exchange of her upkeep. The Trust uses her for day trips and short cruises with various groups, and for quayside functions.

Name of vessel	Zebu, ex-Ziba
Year built	1938. Converted 1982–84
Builder	Holms yard, Råå, Sweden
Current Owner	Mr Stephen Rodger
Operator	Merseyside Heritage Trust, Liverpool
Current flag	United Kingdom
Rig	Brigantine
Construction	Wood
Length extreme	106.0 feet (32.31 m)
Length on deck	72.0 feet (21.95 m)
Length waterline	67.0 feet (20.42 m)
Beam	20.2 feet (6.17 m)
Draught	6.8 feet (2.06 m)
Tonnage	61 grt; 47 nrt; 112 td
Sail area	4,250 sq. feet (395 m^2)
Engine	84 hp Gardner
Complement	6 crew + 12 guests
Photograph date	1988
Photograph location	Cowes, England

── FULL-RIGGED SHIP ──
Three or more masts, all square-rigged.

── BARQUE ──
Three or more masts, all square-rigged except the after mast which is
fore-and-aft rigged.

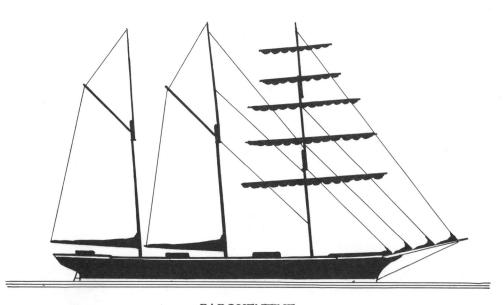

── BARQUENTINE ──
Three or more masts, all fore-and-aft rigged except the foremast which is fully
square-rigged.